EIGHTEENTH CENTURY SHAKESPEARE

No. 22

General Editor : Professor Arthur Freeman, Boston University

AN INQUIRY

INTO THE

AUTHENTICITY OF CERTAIN PAPERS AND INSTRUMENTS

Attributed to Shakspeare, &c.

An Inquiry

INTO

THE AUTHENTICITY OF CERTAIN MISCELLANEOUS PAPERS AND LEGAL INSTRUMENTS,

PUBLISHED DEC. 24, 1795

and Attributed to

SHAKSPEARE, QUEEN ELIZABETH,

and

HENRY, EARL OF SOUTHAMPTON:

ILLUSTRATED BY

Fac-Similes of the Genuine Hand-Writing of that
Nobleman, and of Her Majesty;
A new Fac-simile of the Hand-Writing of Shakspeare,
never before Exhibited;
And other Authentick Documents:

In a Letter Addressed to the

RIGHT HON. JAMES, EARL OF CHARLEMONT,

BY

Edward Malone

Reprints of Economic Classics

AUGUSTUS M. KELLEY PUBLISHERS
New York, 1970

Published by

FRANK CASS AND COMPANY LIMITED

67 Great Russell Street, London WC1

Published in the United States by
Augustus M. Kelley, Publishers
New York, New York 10010

New Preface Copyright © 1969 Arthur Freeman

First edition   1769
Reprint of First edition
with a new preface   1970

ISBN 0 678 05123 2

Library of Congress Catalog Card No. 73–96356

Printed in Great Britain

PREFACE

Edmond Malone's devastating and summary exposure of the Shakepeare forgeries by S. W. H. Ireland was restricted to those examples published, with elaborate facsimiles in magnificent format, by the precocious contriver's credulous father Samuel (*Miscellaneous Papers and Legal Instruments under the Hand and Seal of William Shakespeare, including the Tragedy of King Lear, and a Small Fragment of Hamlet, from the Original MSS. in the Possession of Samuel Ireland*). *Miscellaneous Papers* issued from the press in December, 1795, although dated 1796, and Malone tells us, in a note at the beginning of his own copy of *An Inquiry*, that the necessary reply was 'Begun to be written about the 10th of Jany Begun to be printed about the 20th of Jany—finished at the press Monday March 2d—published March 31. 1796'. The hiatus of nearly a month between being 'finished at the press' and being released to readers may have owed, as Malone claimed in a newspaper advertisement during the month, to difficulties with the engravings, but more likely publication date was linked up with that of the first—and last—performance of Ireland's ultimate imposture, *Vortigern*, at Drury Lane—originally scheduled for April Fools' Day by a whimsical J. P. Kemble, but held back, for obvious reasons, until the following evening.

Couched originally as 'A Letter addressed to the Right Hon. James, Earl of Charlemont [James Caulfield, 1728–1799, Irish statesman and literary patron]' (Malone wisely deleted 'A Letter' in his revision for a proposed second edition), *An Inquiry* swelled from the 'pamphlet' promised by its author to an unstinting critique of over 400 pages. Nevertheless, Malone tells us, 'five hundred copies sold on that day [31 March] and the next', a remarkable total for so deliberately unpopular and costly a volume. Critical reception was likewise enthusiastic: Burke applauds the revival of 'that sort of criticism by which false pretence and imposture are detected', and George Steevens, despite a current antagonism toward his own chosen successor, declared it 'one of the most decisive pieces of criticism that was ever produced'. Those who ventured to reply comprised mainly Samuel Ireland himself, his immediate friends, and George Chalmers, but their rebuttals are inevitably rather attacks on the methodology of Malone (and interesting as such) than defences of the tainted papers. Within weeks, at any rate, the young forger had publicly confessed to his misdeeds, and much of the later controversy concerns itself with the complicity or innocence of the elder Samuel—who swore to the latter on his deathbed, as ever before, although to the end he refused to admit himself duped and maintained a desperate faith in the genuineness of the manuscripts. It is unfortunate that the two fullest and only recent treatments of the entire affair (John Mair, *The Fourth Forger*, London, 1938, and Bernard Grebanier, *The Great Shakespeare Forgery*, New York, 1965) are both journalistic and slipshod. A good life of Ireland and a painstaking history of the forgeries are still to be desired; meanwhile, we must turn directly to the contemporary materials (Malone, the Irelands, Hardinge, Caldecott, and Chalmers, among others), rendered all the more indispensable for the poor use made of them in secondary accounts.

Perhaps because of the haste called for in compiling *An Inquiry*, Malone appears to have intended to reissue it in a corrected form. His own copy, extensively marked up '*For a second edition*' survives, lacking ten leaves, in the British Museum; the revisions consist entirely of deletions of redundant arguments, stylistic adjustments, and—primarily—added evidence from the vast arsenal of his own learning. Absolutely no attention is paid controversy or counterattack; *Vortigern* is nowhere mentioned; and there is no evidence of any withdrawal or bolstering up of arguments specifically assailed by the few hostile critics. Precisely when Malone revised his text is uncertain, but the issue had been virtually closed by his own first edition; no second edition seems to have been published at all.

Jaggard, probably following Lowndes, says that twenty-five large-paper copies were prepared, and locates two, at Warwick Castle [?Folger] and Boston Public Library. Malone's working copy mentioned above is on large (and thick) paper as well, likewise another Museum example, presented by Malone to Cracherode. These latter two have been collated with the copy-text employed, as have two other copies on regular paper also in the Museum, one of which (the Grenville) lacks terminal half-sheet 31^2. The present text is reprinted from an unsophisticated copy in the possession of the publishers; it collates [ ]^{4}B–Z^{4}AA–ZZ^{4}3A[sic]–3H^{4}31^2; there are no cancels, but the three plates, originally assembled at the end, have been replaced where the 'Directions to the Binder' instructs.

May 1969   A.F.

A N

INQUIRY

INTO THE

AUTHENTICITY

OF CERTAIN

PAPERS AND INSTRUMENTS

ATTRIBUTED TO

SHAKSPEARE, &c.

A N

INQUIRY

INTO THE

AUTHENTICITY

OF CERTAIN

MISCELLANEOUS PAPERS

AND

LEGAL INSTRUMENTS,

PUBLISHED DEC. 24, M DCC XCV.

AND ATTRIBUTED TO

SHAKSPEARE, QUEEN ELIZABETH,

AND

HENRY, EARL OF SOUTHAMPTON:

ILLUSTRATED BY

FAC-SIMILES OF THE GENUINE HAND-WRITING OF THAT
NOBLEMAN, AND OF HER MAJESTY;

A NEW FAC-SIMILE OF THE HAND-WRITING OF SHAKSPEARE,
NEVER BEFORE EXHIBITED;

AND OTHER AUTHENTICK DOCUMENTS:

IN A LETTER ADDRESSED TO THE

RIGHT HON. JAMES, EARL OF CHARLEMONT,

By EDMOND MALONE, Esq.

DEMENS! QUI NIMBOS ET NON IMITABILE FULMEN
AERE ET CORNIPEDUM PULSU SIMULARAT EQUORUM.
VIRG.

LONDON:
Printed by H. Baldwin:
FOR T. CADELL, JUN. AND W. DAVIES,
(SUCCESSORS TO MR. CADELL,) IN THE STRAND.
M DCC XCVI.

DIRECTIONS TO THE BINDER.

Stitch the Engravings at the lower part of the plate, and then fold them in.

Plate I. is to face p. 111.
Plate II. to face p. 137.
Plate III. to face p. 189.

PLATE I.

No. I. Part of Queen Elizabeth's *pretended* Letter to Shakspeare; copied from the *fac-simile* in MISCELLANEOUS PAPERS.

No. II. Conclusion of a Letter from Queen Elizabeth to James the Sixth of Scotland. MSS. Cotton. Caligula. C. ix. p. 307.

No. III. Conclusion of a Letter from the same Queen to a person unknown. MSS. Cotton. Vespasian. F. 3. p. 13. b.

PLATE II.

No. IV. Superscription of Lord Southampton's *pretended* Letter to Shakspeare. Copied from MISCELLANEOUS PAPERS.

No. V. A *pretended* Receipt given by John Heminges to Shakspeare. From the same Collection.

No. VI. A genuine Autograph of John Heminges; from a deed executed by him in 1617-18.

No. VII.

No. VII. Two lines of a theatrical Account, *pretended* to have been written by Shakspeare; copied from MISCELLANEOUS PAPERS.

No. VIII. A *pretended* autograph of Shakspeare; copied from the same Collection.

No. IX. Part of Shakspeare's *pretended* Letter to Lord Southampton.

No. X. A new Autograph of Shakspeare; from a Deed executed by him, March 10, 1612-13, in the possession of Albany Wallis, Esq.

No. XI. XII. XIII. Autographs of Shakspeare, copied from his Will.

No. XIV. Autograph of Richard Burbadge, from a deed executed by him, Dec. 22, 1593.

No. XV. Autograph of John Duke, the player; from Henslowe's MS.

No. XVI. Autograph of Joseph Taylor, the player; from a deed executed by him in 1612.

No. XVII. Autograph of Nat. Field, the player; from a Letter written by him.

No. XVIII. Autograph of Chapman, the poet, from Henslowe's MS.

No. XIX. Autograph of R. Hathwaye, the poet, from Henslowe's MS.

No. XX. Autograph of Massinger, the poet, from an original Letter.

No. XXI.

No. XXI. Autograph of Robert Dudley, Earl of Leycester; from an original in my possession.

PLATE III.

No. XXII. Part of Lord Southampton's *pretended* Letter to Shakspeare; copied from MISCELLANEOUS PAPERS.

No. XXIII. Part of a genuine Letter from Lord Southampton to Lord Keeper Williams, in 1621. MSS. Harl. 7000. p. 46.

No. XXIV. Part of a genuine Letter from Lord Southampton to a person unknown. MSS. Cotton. Vespasian. F. 13. p. 311.

CORRECTIONS.

PAG. L.

26. 16. *For* Elizabethe, r. *Elyzabethe*.

78. 12. Add this other instance of the substantive *Complement* used by Shakspeare in the present sense: " Saving in dialogue of *complement*—"

K. JOHN, Act I.

88. ult. of note. *For* in Sept. r. *6th* Sept.

97. 4 from the bottom. *For* take such care, r. *have been so anxious*.

15. *For* Elizabeth, r. *Elyzabethe*.

101. 15. *For* MIDSUMMER's, r. MIDSUMMER-

113. n. 56. l. 2. *For* vol. i. r. vol. F.

211. 2 of Note. *For* set down in, r. " *sette onne*."

243. 10. In part of the impression, *for* original, r. *originals*.

IT IS PLAIN, THAT IN THIS SLIPPERY AGE WE
LIVE IN, IT IS VERY EASY TO MAKE A BOOK LOOK
AS OLD AS YOU WOULD HAVE IT.
LORD CH. JUSTICE, in Lady Ivy's Case;
STATE TRIALS, Vol. VII. p. 572.

But hear ME further: Japhet, 'tis agreed,
Writ not, and Chartres scarce could write or read,—
In all the Courts of Pindus guiltless quite;
But pens can forge, my friend, that cannot write.
POPE.

A

LETTER

TO THE

EARL OF CHARLEMONT.[1]

MY DEAR LORD,

THOUGH I have had the honour and
pleasure of your lordſhip's friendship
and correspondence for twenty years, during
which time I have been in the habit of occasionally furnishing you with an account of
what was doing here in the literary world, I

[1] As my noble friend's name appears in the List of
Subscribers prefixed to the MISCELLANEOUS PAPERS, &c.
here examined, I am authorized by him to say, that he subscribed to that work at the request of a gentleman who furnished him with a splendid PROSPECTUS of it, which he
carried from hence to Ireland ; and that if Lord C. had
known as much of it as he now does, he would not have
given either his name or his money to the publication.

do not recollect ever to have employed my pen
on any topick more interesting than that which
I mean to make the subject of this letter. In
mentioning your long-continued kindness to
me, I trust I shall not be charged with any
idle vanity; a weakness, if I at all know
myself, most foreign from my nature and
disposition. If the desire *laudari a laudato
viro* be natural and excusable, I surely may
be allowed to feel some degree of pride in
the consciousness of having so long enjoyed
the friendship of him, whom all who know
him personally love and esteem, and whose
virtues and attainments are admired and
venerated wherever the name of Englishman
is known.

IT has been said, and I believe truly, that
every individual of this country, whose mind
has been at all cultivated, feels a pride in
being able to boast of our great dramatick
poet, Shakspeare, as his countryman : and
proportionate to our respect and veneration
for that extraordinary man ought to be our
care of his fame, and of those valuable writings that he has left us; and our solicitude
to preserve them pure and unpolluted by any
modern sophistication or foreign admixture
                                        what-

whatsoever. Strongly as I am impressed with this sentiment, I hasten to discuss a question in which the reputation and character and history of my great MASTER are necessarily and immediately involved ; and I am the more anxious to seize the present moment, because, in this interval of the political warfare, the cause of Shakspeare and the Muses has a chance to be heard.

PREVIOUS to the publication of my edition of this great poet's works in 1790, I had collected some curious circumstances relative either to himself, his family, or estate, which I appended by way of notes to Mr. Rowe's very meagre Life of him; and which, according to the modern mode of *making* books, after having been properly sliced and hashed and stewed, have been ferved up in a late work, without any acknowledgment where the ingredients of the literary mess were found. Since that time I have pursued my inquiries on the same subject with unremitting ardour ; and have amassed such an accumulation of materials for a more regular Life of our poet, as have exceeded my most sanguine expectations, and are now swelled to such a size as to

B 2   form

form a considerable volume. In my researches
into the early history of the Stage [2], I have
been equally successful, and have obtained
such curious and valuable accessions to what
I formerly published on that subject, as to
ascertain, with a degree of precision beyond
my hopes, the actual state of our theatres
and the performances they exhibited, almost
up to the time when Shakspeare appears to
have commenced his dramatick career.——
With all this ardour of inquiry, and all this
mass of information, your lordship will easily
judge how much I must have been surprized
in the beginning of the last year, when I was
informed that many original pieces were discovered, in the hand-writing of this poet,
which had never before been heard of; and
how much that surprize was increased, when
I found from the information of various

[2] When the Books of the late Mr. Topham Beauclerk
were sold by auction in April 1781, I neglected (I know
not by what accident) to purchase or even to examine
the lot numbered 4137, which was sold for 3l. 6s. and
contained seven small tracts; among which was one relative
to our ancient stage, that I have never met with. If these
sheets should fall into the hands of the purchaser, (with
whose name I am unacquainted, the Sale-Catalogue having
been mislaid,) he will oblige me by favouring me with his
address.

intelligent

intelligent persons who had viewed and examined the supposed originals, that every date affixed to these papers, and almost every fact mentioned in them, were alike inconsistent with the history of the time and with all the ancient documents of which I was possessed. These extraordinary manuscripts are at length given to the publick, by whose judgment their authenticity or spuriousness will, if I mistake not, be very speedily ascertained.

It is not at all to be wondered at, that the possessor and discoverer of these curiosities should set a very high value upon them, and thinking them to be genuine ancient manuscripts, should publish them in a splendid form : those persons also who are convinced of their authenticity, have a perfect right to adorn the shelves of their libraries with what they think a valuable treasure : but in this free country every intelligent reader claims a right to judge for himself, uninfluenced by any authority but that of right reason, and the best information he can procure ; and by the judgment of the intelligent part of the publick must the fate of these papers be finally decided. To aid those in

the

the course of their investigation, who, though they may fall within this description, may not be endowed with your lordship's fagacity, or may not have devoted so many years as you have done to the most curious literary researches, as well as to all the liberal arts, is the object of the present inquiry ; which, with your permission, I mean to lay before that tribunal by which the adjudication on one of the most important questions that has for many years been agitated in the literary world must now be given.

In his Preface the Editor informs us, that all the scholars, all the men of taste, antiquaries, and heralds, who viewed them previous to their publication, have " unanimously testified in favour of their authenticity ; and declared, that where there was such a mass of evidence internal and *external*, it was impossible, amidst such various sources of detection, for THE ART OF IMITATION to have hazarded so much without betraying itself, and consequently, that *these papers can be no other than the production of* Shakspeare *himself.*"

WHAT is meant here by *external* evidence,

dence, it is not easy to conjecture. The writer should seem to have supposed that the labels and seals appendant to the deeds, because *exterior*, were *external evidence:* but neither these, nor the faded ink and discoloured paper or parchment, in my apprehension, come within that description. The only external evidence, strictly speaking, that has been produced, is the narrative, which I shall presently transcribe, stating that these treasures were found in a nameless place, in the custody of a nameless person. If these profound Scholars, Antiquaries, and Heralds are satisfied with that account, I can only say that they are very easily satisfied; and that, if the hand-writing is also to be considered as external evidence, their credulity on that head is perfectly consistent with the satisfaction which they feel in the manner in which these papers have been ushered to the publick.—In the position that " it was impossible so much could be hazarded without betraying itself," I entirely agree with these gentlemen: the fabrication of these manuscripts, by whomsoever made, *has* accordingly betrayed itself almost in every line; so as to shew, beyond a possibility of doubt, that not a single piece in this collection was the pro-

duction

duction of Shakspeare, or of the other persons to whom they are ascribed.

THE manner in which these curiosities are said to have been found being extremely material to the present question, that I may proceed in due form, and do no injustice to the editor, I shall give his account of the discovery in his own words:

" IT may be expected (says he) that something should be said by the editor, of the manner in which these papers came into his hands. He received them from his son, Samuel WILLIAM HENRY Ireland, a young man then under 19 years of age, by whom the discovery was accidentally made at the house of a gentleman of considerable property.

" AMONGST a mass of family papers, the Contracts between Shakspeare, Lowine, and Condelle, and the lease granted by him and Hemynge to Michael Fraser, which was first found, were discovered ; and *soon afterwards* the deed of gift to WILLIAM HENRY Ireland, (described as the friend of Shakspeare, in consequence of his having saved his life

on the river Thames, when in extreme
danger of being drowned) and also the Deed
of Trust to John Hemynge, were discovered.
In pursuing this search he was so fortunate
as to meet with some deeds very material to
the interest of this gentleman, and such as
established, beyond all doubt, his title to a
considerable property : deeds of which this
gentleman was as ignorant, as he was of
his having in possession any of the MSS. of
Shakspeare. In return for this service, added
to the consideration that the young man bore
the same name and arms with the person
who saved the life of Shakspeare, this gentleman promised him every thing relative to
the present subject, that had been, or should
be found either in town, or at his house in
the country. At this house the principal
part of the papers, together with a great
variety of books, containing his MS. notes,
and three MS. plays, with part of another,
were discovered.

" FORTIFIED as he is with the opinion of
the unprejudiced and intelligent, the editor
will not allow that it can be presumption in
him to say, that he has no doubt of the truth
and authenticity of that which he lays before
c   the

the publick. Of this fact he is as fully satisfied, as he is with the honour that has been
observed towards him, throughout the whole
communication made to him upon this
subject. So circumstanced, he should not feel
justified in importuning or any way request-
ing a gentleman, to whom he is known only
by obligation, and not personally, to subject
himself to the impertinence and licentious-
ness of literary curiosity and cavil, unless he
should himself voluntarily come forward.
But this is not all. It was not till after the
mass of papers received became voluminous,
that Mr. Ireland had any idea of printing
them : he then applied to the original possessor for his permission so to do ; and this
was not obtained but under the strongest
injunction that his name should not appear.
This injunction has, throughout all the stages
of this business, been uniformly declared :
and, as this gentleman has dealt most liberally
with the editor, he can confidently say, that
in his turn he has with equal openness and
candour conducted himself towards the
publick ; to whom, immediately upon every
communication made, every thing has been
submitted without reserve.

" BUT

" BUT, it is said, that the disclosure of the name of the gentleman, from whom these papers came, would remove all doubts, and settle men's minds upon the subject. He believes, and is confident, that with some it would. But who is it that says this? It cannot be the real Critic or Antiquarian. He will not say that his art or science amounts to nothing, and that his lucubrations are idle and useless. But if the point cannot finally or satisfactorily be decided either by the thing written, its paper or parchment vehicle, or seals appendant, or the other circumstances under which it was introduced, and must depend *wholly* upon the place and person from whom they came, what becomes of the acumen of the Critic, or the skill and labour of the Antiquarian? By this rule it is a question for another jurisdiction; and the occupation of the Critic and Antiquarian is gone."

AFTER perusing this account, we are naturally led to ask one or two questions. It is observable that we are not here told *where* the three deeds which are said to have been first discovered, were found. The *principal part* of the whole mass, indeed, is said to

have

have been found in a mansion-house in the
country ; but whether the first discovery was
made in town or country, we are not told.
Neither are we informed what led the
discoverer to examine the deeds and papers
of the unknown gentleman. They, however,
who recollect the first production of these
curiosities, may remember that it was then
said by those who gave credit to their authenticity, that the discoverer met the possessor, to whom he was wholly unknown,
at a coffee-house, or some other publick
place : that the possessor was a gentleman
of large fortune, who lived chiefly in the
country, and was devoted to rural amusements, but had chambers in the Temple, to
which he occasionally resorted : that the
conversation turning on old papers, and
autographs, of which the discoverer said
he was a collector, the country-gentleman
exclaimed, " If you are for *autographs*, I am
your man ; come to my chambers any morning, and rummage among my old deeds ;
you will there find enough of them :" that
accordingly the discoverer went there, and
on taking down a parcel of old deeds from
a shelf, in a very few minutes lighted on
the

the name of Shakspeare, or some of his
fellows of the theatre, which induced him to
proceed further.—Such was the account then
circulated by the persons who were the most
strenuous partisans for the authenticity of
these papers ; but whether this relation may
not have gained additional circumstances as
it rolled along, I am unable to ascertain. I
merely state what was then the report of the
day. I am sensible I am *travelling*, as the
lawyers call it, *out of the record* ; and therefore shall only advert to one other matter
which the statement above-quoted suggests.
The discovery of a title to a considerable
estate must be acknowledged to be so fortunate and beneficial, that one cannot at all
wonder at the great liberality of the unknown
gentleman on the present occasion, in giving
up to the discoverer all his right to these
valuable MSS. ; but one naturally wishes
to know in what county this estate lies,
and whether any suit has been instituted
within this last year, in consequence of
this discovery ; as, on the trial of an Eject-
ment, the learned Counsel employed by
the defendants (who, by themselves, or
those under whom they derive their title,
must have been in possession for near two
centuries,)

centuries,) would, I apprehend, require a more explicit account of the manner and place in which these deeds were found, than that which has so completely satisfied the profound Scholars, Antiquaries, and Heralds, already mentioned.

LEAVING, however, these considerations, let us advert to the editor's statement above given in his own words; the sum and substance of which is, That the unknown gentleman has behaved most liberally and honourably to him; that he has desired his name to be concealed, lest he should be exposed to the impertinence and cavils of criticism; (in which he seems to be over-scrupulous, for what imputation could fall on him, if it should be proved that all these controverted papers, which by some accident have found their way among his family-deeds, were forged by some undiscovered person;) that therefore the Editor thinks himself bound to act with equal honour to the unknown, and not to divulge his name.

THE subsequent position, that the disclosure of the name of this gentleman would remove all doubts, is one, I conceive, to which

which no person who knows any thing of the rules of evidence will subscribe. It would not substantiate the most insignificant paper that has been exhibited; though it is justly required, and ought to be made, before any one of these pretended ancient MSS. can be entitled even to an examination.

In the Prerogative Court, if any Will or testamentary writing is exhibited at a time when, or from a quarter where, it might not reasonably be expected, the party producing it is always asked, in the first place, in what cabinet or coffer belonging to the deceased, or where else, it was found; how long it has been in his possession; when, and to whom he first mentioned the discovery, &c. The ground of these questions is obvious. In such a case a suspicion concerning the genuineness of the instrument or paper produced naturally arises; and therefore to repel that suspicion, and to set the claimant right in the opinion of the Court, he is called upon to account for its not having been produced sooner, and to state where it was found. This is the first thing required to be done; without which the claimant is not allowed to advance a single step. His

account, however satisfactory, will not substantiate or establish the paper or instrument
produced ; it merely entitles it to be read
and examined : and then it is to be tried by
all those tests by which falsehood is distinguished from truth. But suppose a person
should come into that court, and, after
refusing to give any answer whatsoever to
the inquiries which on such an occasion
are always made, should throw his paper on
the table, and address the very learned and
respectable Judge who presides there in these
words ; —" Wherefore, Sir, are you placed on
that bench, unless you are able to ascertain
whether the testamentary writing under
which I claim, be genuine or not ? you have
the aid of his Majesty's Advocate General,
a man of as much ability and integrity as
any person who ever filled that high office ;
you are surrounded by many other Doctors
learned in the law; what avails all your
reading, to what end have you expended so
many years in perusing your INSTITUTES,
your PANDECTS, and your CODES, if all
your lucubrations, and all your sagacity will
not enable you to discern whether this little
paper be authentick or not : I will give you
no account of it ; but I call upon you to do

me

me justice, and either to allow my claim, or to assign some satisfactory reasons why it should not be established." What, I say, would be the answer to this fine harangue? the claimant would be turned out of court, and his paper immediately flung after him.

In that court, as in all other courts, it is an established rule that the best evidence the nature of the case will admit of, shall always be required, if possible to be had; but, if not possible, then the best evidence that can be had shall be allowed: " for, if it be found (says Sir William Blackstone) that there is any better evidence existing than is produced, the very not producing it is a

---

[3] " The design of the law is to come to rigid demonstration in matters of right; and there can be no demonstration of a fact without the best evidence that the nature of the thing is capable of: lefs evidence doth but create suspicion and surmise, and does not leave a man the entire satisfaction that arises from demonstration; for if it be plainly seen in the nature of the transaction that there is some more evidence that doth not appear, the very not producing it is a presumption that it would have detected something more than appears already, and therefore the mind does not acquiesce in any thing lower than the utmost evidence the fact is capable of."

Gilbert's LAW OF EVIDENCE, p. 5.

presumption

presumption that it would have detected
some falsehood that at present is con-
cealed⁴."

BUT in requiring similar evidence in the
present case, it is said, we transfer the matter from a literary tribunal to another jurisdiction: we are not now in a court of law.—
It is true, we are not; but all the principal
rules of evidence, as Blackstone's great pro-
totype, Lord Chief Baron Gilbert, has clearly
shewn in his admirable treatise, are founded
on right reason, on which ground alone they
are adopted; and this first and most general
rule is just as applicable to the papers in
question, as to any deed or other instrument
produced in a court of law.—The great object, however, of this requisition does not
seem to be well understood. It is not from
any idle curiosity to learn the name of the
original owner of these treasures, that the
inquiry is made; for it is of very little importance to the world whether he is called
Smith, or Johnson; whether he lives in
London or Middlesex; whether he is a
fair or a black man; a dwarf or six feet
high:

Blackſt. COM. iii. 368.

Nil

Nil nimium studeo, Cæsar, tibi velle placere,
Nec scire, utrum sis albus, an ater homo :

It is not, I say, from any idle curiosity of
this kind, that the cautious examiner makes
this demand; but because every new circumstance stated, every new fact adduced,
furnish additional materials to work with, and
supply means either to corroborate or disprove
the point contested. Thus, for example, if
it should be said in the present instance, that
this gentleman's name is Johnson,—that he
lives in the county of Derby,—that he has
been possessed of these papers for several
years, that his great grand-father derived
them from Sempronius, from whom he purchased an estate in the year ———, and
Sempronius from Titius, who was an Attorney that had been employed by Shakspeare,
or Heminge, or Condell, in law-business,
and on the death of some one of these
persons without a will, got possession of
them; if this or any other similar narrative
should be given, then every one of these
facts might be controverted, and eventually
either strengthen or diminish the credit of
the MSS. in question.

PERSONS who are not conversant with
legal

legal subjects, or the true object of lawyers
in their examination of evidence, are frequently surprised at minute questions put to
witnesses, which they think either vexatious
or impertinent; and on such occasions the
well-known question which a late admirable comick actor introduced into one of his
pieces, and which he rendered ſtill more
ridiculous by imitating the thin and stridu-
lous voice of an emiꞏꞏent barrister who was
afterwards raised to the Bench,—" Pray,
now let me ask you, was—the—toast buttered
on *both* sides ?" is often mentioned with
much satisfaction and applause by those who
have attended more to the humour of the
theatre, than the investigation of truth. But
the judicious lawyer, when he asks, not
precisely such questions as the English
Aristophanes has invented for him, but, in
the case (we will suppose) of a disputed
Will,—whether the testator, when he made
and published it, was sitting up in his bed
or in an arm-chair;—what was the size
or form of the room,—how many persons
were present,—who lighted the candle, or
furnished the wax with which it was sealed,
&c. perfectly understands what he is about;
and in cases of fiction and fraud the event
often

often proves the propriety of such an examination; for by the answers given to
these questions, compared with the testimony of others and the real fact, the
instrument set up is quickly overthrown.

" BUT if the point cannot finally or
satisfactorily be decided either by the thing
written, its paper or parchment vehicle, or
seals appendant, or the other circumstances
under which it was introduced, and must
depend WHOLLY upon the place and person
from whom they came, what becomes (we
are asked) of the acumen of the Critick, or
the skill and labour of the Antiquarian?"—
To this question it is only necessary to
answer, that, it is believed, no person of
common sense was ever so absurd as to say
that the authenticity of these papers depend-
ed WHOLLY on the place from whence, or
the perſon from whom, they came; though
the inquirer ought, in the firſt instance, to
have been informed on these points. This
information, as I have already shewn, merely
entitles them to be read. I concur, however, with the editor, that if these MSS.
be spurious, the Critick and Antiquary will
be able to detect them. Relinquishing
therefore

therefore every claim to that information
which I have shewn would be required
in the ecclesiastical and common-law
Courts, and which in the present case the
Literary World has an equal right to demand ; and judging of these papers merely
as they appear in the printed copy and in the
fac-similes, which I make no doubt faithfully represent their originals,⁵ I undertake
to

⁵ You may perhaps wonder that curiosity did not lead
me to view and examine these pretended originals. I very
early resolved *not* to inspect them at the house of the possessor, and I was glad to find that my friend Dr. Farmer,
and Mr. Steevens, had made the same determination ; from
an apprehension that the names of persons who might
be supposed more than ordinarily conversant with the subject of these MSS. might give a countenance to them, to
which, from the secrecy that was observed relative to their
discovery, they were not entitled. I had, however, no objection to view them elsewhere ; and therefore very early
after their first production, when a gentleman invited me to
see these inestimable treasures, as he considered them, at
his house, where, as I understood him, he frequently had
them in his hands, (in which I afterwards found I had
misapprehended him,) I readily accepted the invitation, and
waited on him on a subsequent day by his appointment :
but these rarities were not then visible. A few days afterwards, having obtained a *fac-simile* of the hand-writing of
the earl of Southampton, I informed him by a line, that if
he could procure the letter said to be written by that nobleman to Shakspeare, I could furnish a *fac-simile* of his undoubted

to prove, from 1. the Orthography, 2. the Phraseology, 3. the Dates given or deducible by inference, and 4. the Dissimilitude of the Hand-writing, that not a single paper or deed in this extraordinary volume was written or executed by the person to whom it is ascribed.

THAT your lordship may see at one view the extent and quantity of these inventions, I shall, in the first place, lay before you a List of them. In the newly published volume they appear in the following order :

doubted hand-writing, which would at once ascertain the truth or falsehood of the supposed original : I added, that I wished my name not to be mentioned ; and my reafon for doing so was, that I was unwilling it should directly or indirectly give the fmallest sanction to these papers. He did not, however, procure the Letter in question, and I gave myself no further trouble about the matter.

This transaction, as I have been informed by several of my friends, having been related, *devested of the circumstances which led to it*, and decorated, as is often the case where tales are transmitted from ear to ear, with circumstances that did not belong to it, I have thought it proper to state the plain and simple fact.—If there was any breach of the strictest propriety and decorum in accepting the invitation thus made, or afterwards, in consequence of that invitation, in proposing to the inviter a test from which no genuine paper ever shrunk, I confess I am not clear-sighted enough to discover it.

1. *Queen*

1. *Queen* Elizabeth's *Letter to* Shakspeare.

2. *Extracts from Miscellaneous Papers.*

3. *A Note of Hand, and a Receipt.*

4. *A Letter from* Shakspeare *to* Anna Hather-rewaye.

5. *Verses by* Shakspeare, *addressed to the same lady.*

6. *A Letter from* Shakspeare *to the* Earl of Southampton.

7. *The* Earl of Southampton's *Answer.*

8. Shakspeare's *Profession of Faith.*

9. *A Letter from* Shakspeare *to* Richard Cowley, *the player.*

10. *A Portrait, enclosed in the same.*

11. *Reverse of ditto.*

12. *A Deed of Gift from* Shakspeare *to* William Henry Ireland.

13. *Tributary Lines to the same.*

14. *View of* William Henry Ireland's *House and Coat of Arms.*

15. *Engraved Portraits of* Bassanio *and* Shylock.

16. *An Agreement between* Shakspeare *and* John Lowin, *the player.*

17. *An Agreement between* Shakspeare *and* Henry Condell, *the player.*

18. *A Lease from* Shakspeare *and* John Heminge

Heminge *to* Michael Fraser *and his wife.*
19. *Deed of Trust to* John Heminge.

SUBJOINED to these Miscellaneous Papers, &c. are the tragedy of KING LEAR,
and a fragment of HAMLET, both alleged
to be in the hand-writing of Shakspeare;
but these I shall reserve for a distinct consideration.

1. QUEEN ELIZABETH'S LETTER.

THE first piece which we are to examine
is, the pretended Letter from Queen Elizabeth to Shakspeare. As this and a few
other pieces in this volume are very short,
and cannot be well understood by partial
extracts, I shall transcribe them, as by this
means my objections will appear in a clearer
light.

HER Majesty, if we are to credit these
MSS., writes as follows: She no more "stands
upon points" than BOTTOM, the Weaver;
her Letter is " like a tangled chain, nothing
impair'd, but all disorder'd :"

" WEE didde receive youre prettye
Verses goode Masterre William through
the hands off oure Lorde Chambelayne
E   ande

ande wee doe Complemente thee onne theyre
great excellence Wee shalle departe
fromme Londonne toe Hamptowne forre
the holydayes where wee Shalle expecte
thee withe thye beste Actorres thatte thou
mayste playe before oureselfe toe amuse usse
bee notte slowe butte comme toe usse bye
Tuesdaye nexte asse the lord Leycesterre *
wille bee withe usse.

Elizabeth. R.

[*Superscribed*]

" For Master William Shakspeare atte
the Globe bye Thames.

[*On a small paper stuck on.*]

" Thys Letterre I dydde receyve
fromme mye moste gracyouse Ladye Elizabethe ande I doe requeste itte maye bee
kepte withe alle care possyble.
" W^m· Shakspeare."

Before I enter on the examination of
this curious paper, permit me to make a few

* I have here followed the *fac-simile* of the pretended
original. In the printed copy, I suppose by an error of the
press, we have *Leiscesterre.*

preliminary

preliminary remarks. Your lordship will at once perceive, that it has not been dipped in that stream in which Achilles is said to have been plunged by his mother. It is indeed so far from being vulnerable only in one place, that there is scarcely a single spot in this and all the other papers, in which they are not assailable. The badges of fiction are so numerous, that the only apprehension I entertain is, that you may be fatigued before I have done, for I can with perfect truth say with the Orator,—" *non mihi tàm copia quàm modus in dicendo quærendus est* ;" and the topicks of detection are so obvious that they must immediately strike every reader who has been at all conversant with these studies ; consequently many of the observations I shall make, before these papers shall have passed through the press, may be anticipated by others. However, I shall proceed in my own way ; and if any such coincidence should be found, it will only serve to corroborate my arguments.

THE next observation I beg leave to make is, that this and some other of these papers have, each of them, an archetype, after which it has been formed ; a model, either now existing or which once existed, on which it has been constructed.—In the year 1710, Bernard Lintott, the bookseller, published our author's Poems, from copies (as I have lately discovered) furnished by Mr. Congreve, which, though not the original editions, were then considered as great curiosities ; so little at that time were the shops of booksellers, or the libraries of the learned, furnished with the early impressions of the works of the English Poets. In the preface to that publication, he for the first time mentioned that King James the First honoured Shakspeare " with an amicable Letter written with his own hand," (probably, as Dr. Farmer has conjectured, in consequence of the production of MACBETH,) " and that this Letter remained long in the hands of Sir William D'Avenant, as a credible person then living could testify." This person, as appears from a MS. note written by Mr. Oldys, who probably derived his information from Lord Oxford, was Sheffield, Duke of Buckinghamshire. Sir William D'Avenant having died intestate and insolvent, and his goods having been seized by his creditors, this Letter was unfortunately lost, and I fear will never be recovered.

recovered.—Here we have the germ and
first principle of the Letter from Elizabeth
to Shakspeare, now before us.

OUR late excellent and ever-lamented
friend, Sir Joshua Reynolds, used to maintain, that even in fancy-pieces no painter
should attempt to delineate the human figure
without a model before him, however he
might deviate from it; for by this means he
would always be preserved from running
into wildness and extravagance. Though
the fabricator of several of these papers (as I
have already observed) had in his thoughts, an
imaginary archetype which gave birth to his
performance, and after which he wrought,
yet when he came to the execution, and was
obliged actually to exhibit the hand-writing
of Queen Elizabeth, Southampton, Heminge,
Condell and Lowin, he had no archetype
whatsoever: that is, he had never seen any
of the hand-writing of Elizabeth, but her
sign-manual, (which he has imitated most
miserably,) nor the hand-writing of Southampton and the rest at all. Hence in
every part of their Letters, &c. (excepting
only the Queen's autograph,) you may
observe the wild flutter of fiction; or in
other

other words that unnatural and licentious extravagance and irregularity, which would not have been found, had any model whatever been followed, however clumsily it might have been imitated.

But it is now time to examine more particularly this gracious and condescending epistle of our virgin Queen. According therefore to the method I have laid down. I proceed to prove from the orthography, the phraseology, the date, and the total dissimilitude of the hand-writing, that it is a forgery. You will perhaps smile at my reserving the hand-writing for my last topick; as, if I am able to shew that it has not the smallest resemblance to the Queen's hand-writing, the question is at an end.—When a certain Potentate of Spain happened to pass through a town in his dominions which he had not visited for a long time, it was thought proper by the magistracy of the place to congratulate him on his arrival into that part of his kingdom. The deputy-bailiff, as I remember, being introduced, began an harangue, which he had conned with much care, lamenting in the first place his own insufficiency, which he trusted his Majesty
would

would have the goodness to pardon, his principal being unable to attend. For his absence, he added, he should presume to state several substantial reasons, the first of which was, that he was *dead*. It is almost needless to say, that the simple deputy was told, he might " spare his arithmetick," and that it was unnecessary to give himself any further trouble on that head. By following the example of this provincial orator, and producing at once a genuine specimen of her Majesty's hand-writing, I might certainly save myself some trouble ; but I choose rather to follow the course I have chalked out, and to take a wider range ; because, though I am perfectly aware that the disquisition is supererogatory, it may tend to produce a more full and complete conviction in the minds of many of my readers.

1. THE first topick I am to consider is, the ORTHOGRAPHY.—In the Chattertonian Controversy, in order to ascertain the spuriousness of the poems attributed by the youth, Chatterton, to Thomas Rowley, the author of one of the earliest pamphlets [6]

[6] CURSORY OBSERVATIONS on the Poems attributed to Thomas Rowley, 8vo. 1782.

that

that appeared on that subject, produced
numerous specimens of really ancient poetry,
which when contrasted with the verses of
the pseudo-bard of the fifteenth century
proved, with irresistible force, that the
authors of those specimens, and of the pretended ancient reliques, could not have lived
within the same period. By what he called
a DOUBLE TRANSFORMATION, that is, by
devesting several of Rowley's verses of the
disguise of ancient spelling, and cloathing
some of Chatterton's undoubted poetry in
old language, he also shewed that they
might change places very commodiously,
and that the one was just as ancient or just
as modern as the other.[7] And though the
author of the Strictures alluded to, and the
late Mr. Warton, who a few months afterwards followed him with more ability
in the same inquiry, and Mr. Tyrwhitt
in his admirable VINDICATION OF HIS
APPENDIX, produced many additional and

[7] The former of thefe methods obtained the approbation of Mr. Tyrwhitt ; (VINDICATION of the APPENDIX
to the Poems called Rowley's, &c. p. 82.) and to the
propriety of the latter teft Mr. Warton bore testimony.
AN ENQUIRY into the authenticity of the Poems attributed
to Thomas Rowley, &c. p. 93.

incon-

incontrovertible proofs of that forgery, they were all given *ex abundanti*, and the cause, in my apprehension, might have been rested on those specimens alone. In like manner, in the present case, it might be sufficient merely to contrast the orthography of this and the other papers with that of Elizabeth herself, or any of the writers of her age.

In the controversy above-mentioned, it was justly observed that the orthography and language of the poems called Rowley's, were not the language or orthography of any particular period, but of various and different ages. In the papers before us, the orthography is infinitely more objectionable; for I will venture to assert, without the smallest apprehension of being refuted, that the spelling in this letter, as well as in all the other papers, is not only not the ortho-graphy of Elizabeth, or of her time, but is for the most part the orthography of no age whatsoever. From the time of Henry the Fourth, I have perused, I will not say several hundred, but some thousand deeds and other MSS., and I never once found the copulative *and* spelt as it is here, with a final *e*. The same observation may be made on the

word

word *for*, here and almoſt uniformly afterwards exhibited *forre :* a mode of orthography, I believe, unprecedented. The
clumsy fabricator had seen *far* written in
old books *farre*, and took it for granted, that
a word so nearly similar as *for* had anciently
the same terminating letters.

THE absurd manner in which almost
every word is over-laden with both consonants and vowels will at once strike every
reader, who has any knowledge of the state
of our language at the period referred to :
but instead of wearying you with minute
remarks, the most satisfactory mode, I conceive, will be to produce a few specimens
of orthography from the time of Chaucer to
near the end of the sixteenth century, a
period of above two hundred years. Out
of some hundred books of that period,
with which I am surrounded, I shall quote
a few which happen to be near at hand, and
which will shew the progressive changes
in the mode of orthography during that
time.

To begin with Chaucer, who, we know,
died in the year 1400 ;—I quote from the
excellent

excellent edition of the CANTERBURY
TALES, by Mr. Tyrwhitt, who adhered to
his author's orthography with the most
scrupulous fidelity.

IN his PROLOGUE, the old Bard, after
describing the Knight, who was " besmotred
with his habergeon,—

> " *For* he was late ycome fro his viage,
> " *And* wente *for* to don his pilgrimage,—"

thus graphically introduces the young gallant
of those days :

> " With him ther was his sone, a young SQUIER,
> " A lover, and a lusty bacheler,
> " With lockes crull 8 as they were laide in presse ;
> " Of twenty yere of age he was, I gesse.
> " Of his stature he was of even lengthe,
> " And wonderly deliver 9, and grete of strengthe.
> " And he hadde be 10 somtime in chevachie 11,
> " In Flaundres, in Artois, and in Picardie,
> " And borne him wel, as of so litel space,
> " In hope to stonden in his ladies grace.
>
> " Embrouded 12 was he, as it were a mede 13
> " Alle ful of freshe floures, white and rede.

---

8 Curled.   9 Nimble.   10 been.   11 A military
Expedition.   12 Embroidered.   13 A Meadow.

" Singing

" Singing he was, or floyting [14] all the day,

" He was as freshe, as is the moneth of May.

" Short was his goune, with sleves long and wide ;

" Wel coude he sitte on hors, and fayre ride.

" He coude songes make, and wel endite,

" Juste [15] and eke dance, and wel pourtraie and write.

" So hote he loved, that by nightertale [16]

" He slep no more than doth the nightingale.

" Curteis [17] he was, lowly, and servisable,

" And carf [18] before his fader at the table."

My next specimen shall be taken from Sir John Fortescue's Treatise on *The Difference between an absolute and limited Monarchy*.* He was probably born about the year that Chaucer died, and in the twentieth year of King Henry the Sixth (1441–2) was made Lord Chief Justice of England. Whether he composed this curious work before or after he retired into France with Prince Edward and his mother, after the battle of Tewksbury in 1471, has not been ascertained.

---

[14] Playing on the Flute.   [15] Tilt.   [16] Night-time.
[17] Courteous.   [18] pa. t. of carve, v. Sax.

 * Published from a MS. Copy in the Bodleian Library, by John Fortescue Aland, Esq. 8vo. 1714.

" *Here-*

" *Hereafter be schewyd, the Frutes of* Jus Regale, *and the Frutes of* Jus Politicum & Regale.

" AND hou so be it, that the French Kyng reynith upon his people *Dominio Regali*, yet Saynt Lewes sumtyme Kyng ther, ne any of his progenytors set never talys or other impositions upon the people of that lond, without the assent of the three astatts, which, whan thay be assemblid, ar like to the court of parlement in England. And this order kept many of his successours until late days, that Englishmen made such a war in Fraunce, that the three estats durst not come to geders. And than for that cause and for grete necessite which the French Kyng had of goods, for the defence of that lond, he took upon hym to set talys and other impositions upon the commons, without the assent of the three estats; but yet he would not set any such chargs, nor hath set upon the Nobles, for feare of rebellion. And because the Commons, though they have grutchid, have not rebellid or be hardy to rebell, the French Kyngs have yearly sythen sett such chargs upon them, and so augmented the same chargis, as the same Commons be so

impoverishid

impoverishid and distroyyd, that they may unneth [19] lyve. Thay drynke water, thay eate apples, with bred right brown made of rye. Thay eate no flesche, but if it be selden [20], a litill larde, or of the entrails or heds of bests sclayne for the nobles and merchaunts of the lond. They weryn no wollyn, but if it be a pore cote under their uttermost garment, made of grete canvas, and cal it a frok. Their hosyn be of like canvas, and passen not their knee; wherfor they be gartrid, and their thyghs bare. Their wifs and children gone bare fote; they may in non otherwyse lyve. For sum of them, that was wonte to pay to his lord for his tenement, which he hyrith by the yere, a scute [21], payyth now to the Kynge, over that scute, fyve skuts. Wher thrugh they be artyd [22] by necessite, so to watch, labour, and grub in the ground, for their sustenaunce, that their nature is much wastid, and the kynd of them brought to nowght. Thay gone crokyd, and ar feble, not able to fyght, nor to defend the realme; nor they have wepon, nor monye to buy

---

[19] Scarce.   [20] Except or unlefs it be seldom.

[21] *Escus*, or *ecus d'or*, a gold crown-piece of the value of 3s. 4d.   [22] Coarcted, compelled.

them

them wepon withal; but verely thay lyvyn in the most extreme povertie and myserye, and yet thay dwellyn in one the most fertile realme of the world: wher thrugh the French Kyng hath not men of his owne realme, able to defend it, except his Nobles, which beryn non such imposisions, and therfor thay ar ryght likely of their bodys; by which cause the said Kyng is compellid to make his armys and retennys for the defence of his land, of straungers, as Scotts, Spaniards, Arragonars, men of Almayn, and of other nacions; els al his ennymys might overrenne hym; for he hath no diffence of his own, excepte his castells, and fortrasis. Loo this the frute of hys *Jus Regale*. Yf the realme of England, which is an ile, and therfor may not lightly get socoures of other londs, were rulid under such a lawe, and under such a prince, it would conquere, robbe, and devouer yt; which was well prouvyd in the tyme of the Brytons, whan the Scotts and the Pyctes so bette and oppressyd this lond, that the people therof soughte helpe of the Rŏmayns, to whom they had byn tributorye. And whan thay could not be defendyd by them, they sought helpe of the Duke of Brytayne, than

than callid Litil Brytayne; and grauntyd
therfor to make his brother Constantine their
Kyng. And so he was made Kyng heere,
and raynyd many yers, and his children
after hym, off which grete Arthure was
one of their yssue. But blessid be God,
this lond ys ruled under a better lawe, and
therfor the people therof be not in such
penurye, nor therby hurt in their persons,
but thay be wealthye and have al thyngs
necessarye to the sustenaunce of nature.
Wherfor thay be myghty, and able to re-
syste the adversariis of the realme, and to
bett other realmes, that do or will do them
wrong. Loo this is the frute of *Jus Politicum & Regale*, under which we lyve.
Sumwhat now I have schewyd you of the
frutys of both lawys, *Ut ex fructibus eorum
cognoscatis eos*, &c[23]."

THE

[23] I have selected this chapter, as it exhibits a curious
picture of a country, which has lately been so much the
object of men's thoughts, and which every friend to the
welfare of mankind, and the peace and true interest and
happiness of England, must wish blotted from the map of
the world.

When we reflect on the pernicious principles which
have been made the basis of all their proceedings, and that
their successive blood-stained rulers, not contented with
desolating France by anarchy, depredation, and every species
of sanguinary cruelty, have for these five years past endeavoured

THE following Letter is selected from the
Paston Collection, as it exhibits the spelling
and

deavoured to light the fire-brands of sedition and misrule
in this and every other country which their arts, or arms,
or ill-gotten wealth could reach, it is impossible to contem-
plate without horrour the period when it may be found
convenient to enter into any kind of amity with such a
nation. The only safety for us, in my apprehension, will
be, to form a barrier to prevent any Frenchman ever enter-
ing into this country; which would naturally produce a
similar prohibition on their part. This, I acknowledge,
would only be a kind of smothered war : but unless some
such measure be adopted, on the day on which any treaty
of peace shall be signed with that nation, on that day will
be signed the death-warrant of the Constitution of England.
Its destruction indeed, will not be immediate : the man of
narrow income will be pleased with the prospect of a
diminution of taxes ; the merchant will look to his money-
bags, and anticipate in imagination the commerce of the
world ; the leveller and republican will clap his hands,
and rejoice ; and the gay and inconsiderate will not perceive the ruin impending over our heads : but, ere a very
few years shall have passed away,

" This royal throne of kings, this scepter'd isle,
" This earth of majesty, this seat of Mars,
" This other Eden, demi-paradise,
" This fortress, built by nature for herself,
" Against *infection*, and the hand of war, - - -
" This nurse, this teeming womb of royal kings,
" Fear'd by their breed, and famous by their birth, - - -
" This land of such dear souls, this dear dear land,
" Dear for her reputation through the world, - - -

G   " This

and phraseology of an English Princess. It was written, as Sir John Fenn conjectured, in the reign of Edward the Fourth, before 1479, by Elizabeth, sister to that monarch and Richard the Third. She married, as he observes, John de la Pole Duke of Suffolk, and her son the Earl of Lincoln was declared by Richard after the death of his own son, heir to the crown.

" On to [Unto] Jan Paston in hast.

MASTYR Paston I pray yow y^t it may plese yow to leve your logeyng for iii. or fore [24] days tyll I may be porved [25] of anodyr and I schal do as musche to yowr plesyr, for Godys sake say me not nay and I pray yow rekomaund me to my lord Chambyrleyn. [26]

𝔓our frend 𝔈lizabeth. [27]

" This England, that was wont to conquer others,
" Will make a shameful conquest of itself:"
and, if we ourselves do not live to the fatal period, our children will see the fairest structure ever formed by human ingenuity, devested of all its glories, and levelled with the dust.

[24] So the original, of which a *fac-simile* has been given. By some mistake in the printed letter we find *for*.

[25] Purveyed.   [26] William, Lord Hastings.

[27] Paston Letters, vol. ii. p. 292.

The

" *The Christening of Prince* ARTHUR."[28]

" ON St. Eustachius' day, which was in the year of our Lord M.CCCC.LXXXVI. the Dominical letter A, and the ijde yere of the reigne of our saide Souveraigne, [Henry VII.] the Prince Arture was born at Winchester, whiche was the firste begotten sone of our said Souveraigne Lorde King Henry the VIIth, and cristened in manner and forme as ensueth, but not untill the Soneday next folowing, bycause th Erle of Oxynforde was at that tyme at Lanam in Suffolke, which shulde have ben on of the Godfaders, at the font, and also that season was al rayny. Incontynent after the birth, *Te Deum* with procession was songe in the cathedrall chirche, and in all the chyrches of that citie ; great and many fiers made in the streets, and messengers sent to al the astats and cities of the realme with that comfortable and good tydynge, to whom were geven great giftes. Over al *Te Deum Laudamus* songen, with ringyng of belles, and in the moest parties, fiers made in the praysing of God, and the rejoysing of every true Englisseman."

[28] Leland's COLLECTANEA, iv. 204.

SIR

SIR Thomas More was born in the year
1480, and is supposed to have written his
History of Richard the Third about the year
1513, when King Henry the Eighth had sat
on the throne four years. The following
passage in that work, which relates to a
lady whom Shakspeare, and Rowe's tragedy,
have made well known to every class of
readers, may compensate for some of the
minute verbal disquisitions in which I shall
have occasion very soon to engage.

" Now then by and bi, as it wer for
anger, not for couetise, ye Protector sent into
ye house of Shores wife, (for her husband
dwelled not with her,) and spoiled her of al
y^t ever she had, above ye value of ii or iii
M. marks, and sent her body to prison.
And whan he had a while laide unto her,
for the maner sake, y^t she went about to
bewitch him, & y^t she was of counsel with
the lord Chāberlein to destroy him, in conclusion when y^t no colour could fasten upon
these matters, then he leyd heinously to her
charge ye thing y^t her self could not deny,
that al ye world wist was true, & that natheles every man laughed at to here it then so
sodainly so highly taken, y^t she was nought
[naught]

[naught] of her body. And for this cause as a goodly continent prince clene and fautles of him self, sent out of heaven into this vicious world for the amendment of mens maners, he caused the bishop of London to put her to open penance, going before the crosse in procession upon a sonday with a taper in her hand. In which she went in countenance & pace demure so womanly, & albeit she were out of al array, save her kyrtle only, yet went she so fair & lovely, namelye, while the wonderinge of the people caste a comly rud in her chekes, (of whiche she before had most misse,) that her great shame wan her much praise among those that were more amorous of her body then curious of her soule. And many good folke also y^t hated her living, & glad wer to se sin corrected, yet pitied thei more her penance then rejoyced therin, when thei considred that ye Protector procured it, more of a corrupt intent then ani vertuous affeccion.

" This woman was born in London, worshipfully frended, honestly brought up, and very wel maryed, saving somwhat to sone; her husbande an honest citezen, yong & goodly, & of good substance. But for-asmuche

asmuche as they were coupled ere she wer
wel ripe, she not very fervently loved for
whom she never longed. Which was
happely the thinge that the more easily made
her encline unto ye Kings appetite, when he
required her. Howbeit ye respect of his
royaltie, ye hope of gay apparel, ease, pleasure, and other wanton welth, was hable
soone to perse a softe tender hearte. But
when the King had abused her, anon her
husband, (as he was an honest man and one
that could his good) not presuming to touch
a Kinges concubine, left her up to him al
togither. When the King died, the Lord
Chāberlen toke her. Which in the Kinges
daies, albeit he was sore ennamored upon
her, yet he forbare her, either for reverence
or for a certain frendly faithfulnes. Proper
she was & faire : nothing in her body you
wold have changed, but if you would have
wished her somewhat higher. Thus say thei
y^t knew her in her youthe. Albeit some
that now se her (for yet she leveth) deme
her never to have ben wel visaged. Whose
jugement semeth me somwhat like, as
though men should gesse ye bewty of one
long before departed by her scalpe taken out
of the charnel-house : for now is she old,
lene,

lene, withered & dried up, nothing left
but ryvilde skin & hard bone. And yet
being even such, whoso wel advise her
visage, might gesse which partes, how filled,
wold make it a faire face. Yet delited not
men so much in her bewty, as in her ple-
sant behauiour. For a proper wit had
she, & could both rede wel & write;
mery in company, redy & quick of aunswer,
neither mute nor ful of bable, sometime
taunting without displeasure & not without disport. The King would say that he
had iii. concubines, which in three divers
properties diversly exceled : one the meriest,
an other the wiliest, the thirde the holiest
harlot in his realme, as one whom no man
could get out of yᵉ church lightly to any
place, but it wer to his bed. The other
two were somwhat greter parsonages, &
natheles of their humilitie content to be
nameles, and to forbere the praise of those
properties. But the meriest was this Shores
wife, in whom the King therfore toke
speciall pleasure. For many he had, but
her he loued; whose fauour, to sai the
trouth, (for sinne it wer to belie yᵉ deuil)
she neuer abused to any mans hurt, but to
many a mans comfort & relief: where
the

the King toke displeasure, she would miti-
gate and appease his mind; where men
were out of fauour, she wold bring them in
his grace. For many that had highly
offended, shee obtained pardon. Of great
forfetures she gate men remission. And
finally in many weighty sutes she stode
many men in grete sted, either for none or
very smal rewardes, & those rather gay
then rich: either for that she was content
with the dede selfe well done, or for that
she delited to be suid vnto, & to show
what she was able to do wyth the King, or
for that wanton women and welthy be not
alway covetouse.

"I DOUBT not some shal think this
woman to sleight a thing to be written of
& set amonge the remembraunces of great
matters: which thei shal specially think,
y^t happely shal esteme her only by y^t thei
now see her. But me semeth the chaunce
so much the more worthy to be remembred,
in how much she is now in the more
beggerly condicion, unfrended and worne
out of acquaintance, after good substance,
after as gret fauour with the prince, after
as grete sute & seking to with al those y^t
in

in those days had busynes to spede, as
many other men were in their times, which
be now famouse only by the infamy of their
il dedes. Her doinges were not much lesse,
albeit thei be muche lesse remembred, because thei were not so evil. For men vse,
if they have an euil turne, to write it in
marble ;´ & whoso doth vs a good tourne,
we write it in duste; which is not worst
proued by her, for at this daye shee beggeth
of many at this daye liuing, y^t at this day
had begged if she had not bene."[29]

" *The Christening of Prince* EDWARD,
the most dearest sonne of King Henry 8*th*,
of that Name.[30]

" BY the provision of the living God
on the 12th day of October the Feast of St.

---

[29] THE WORKES of Sir Thomas More, p. 56. Rastell's
edit. 1557. I have adhered faithfully to the original spelling,
but have in general supplied the *m's* and *n's*, which it was
the fashion of that time frequently to omit in writing,
(placing a mark of abbreviation over the word) and still
oftner in printed books, for the sake of getting a certain
number of words into a line. *Mē* for *men, sēt* for *sent,*
and *Lōdō* for *London,* would hardly have been intelligible
to a modern reader.

[30] Leland's COLLECTANEA, ii. 670.

H   Wilfride,

Wilfride, the vigil of St. Edward, which was on the Friday, about 2 of the clock in the morning was borne at HAMPTON COURT, Edward, sonne to King Henry the 8th, in the yeare of our Lord one M.V.XXXVII;* the Dominicall letter was G. in the XXIxth yeare of the reigne of our Souveraigne Lord; which was not christened till the Monday next following.

" INCONTINENT after the birth, *Te Deum* was song in the cathedrall church of Paules, right solempnly, and in all the other churches of LONDON; and many great fires in every streete, and so continued till night. And there was there goodly banqueting and triumphing, with shooting of gunns all day and night in the goodliest manner that might be devised. And messengers were sent to all the Estates and citties of the realme of that most joyfull and comfortable tydings, to whome were given great and large gifts. And over all *Te Deum* was sung with ringing of bells, and in the most part fiers made in praise of God, and rejoycing of all Englishmen.

* In the original there was probably a C. over the first V. which the editor of Leland's COLLECTANEA has omitted.

I

" *The*

" *The Preparations ordeined for the said Christening at* HAMPTON COURT.

" FIRST, The going to the church began at the presence lodging, convayed through the counsell chamber to the gallary leading through the Kings great chamber, and so through the hall and the second court to the gallary that goeth to the chappell, standing all that way torches borne by the Kings servants and other noblemens servants, and all that way barred where no walles be, and richly hung, and strawed with rushes.

" AT the chappell dore a large porch, and the same covered with rich cloth of gould or arras, and double hanged with arras rich, and the flore borded, and covered with carpetts. - - -

" THIS order was followed for going from the Princes lodging to the christening.

" FIRST certein Gentlemen, Esquires & Knights. – – –

" THEN the 3 Lords CHAMBERLEINS, and the Lord CHAMBERLEIN of England in the middest. – – –

" THEN the Chrysom richly garnished, borne by the Lady Elizabeth, the Kings daughter: the same lady, for her tender age,

H 2   was

was borne by the Viscount Beauchamp, with
the assistance of the Lord Morley," &c.

FROM the SONGES AND SONETTES of
Lord Surrey, I select the following short
poem written by an uncertain author, about
the year 1540.

*The Louer declareth his paines to excede far
the paines of hell.*

" THE soules that lacked grace,
  " Which lye in bitter paine,
" Are not in such a place,
  " As foolish folke do faine :

" Tormented all with fire,
  " And boile in leade againe,
" With serpents full of ire,
  " Stong oft with deadly paine ;,

" Then cast in frosen pittes,
  " To freze there certaine howers ;
" And for their painfull fittes,
  " Apointed tormentours.

" No, no, it is not so,
  " Their sorow is not such :
" And yet they haue of wo,
  " I dare say twise as much ;

" Which comes because they lack
  " The sight of the Godhed,
" And be from that kept back
  " Wherewith are aungels fed.

                              " This

" This thing know I by loue,
   " Through absence, crueltie,
" Which makes me for to proue
   " Hell pain before I dye.

" There is no tong can tell
   " My thousand part of care;
" Ther may no fire in hell
   " With my desire compare.

" No boyling leade can pas
   " My scalding sighes in hete;
" Nor snake that euer was,
   " With stinging can so frete

" A true and tender hert,
   " As my thoughtes dayly doe;
" So that I know but smart,
   " And that which longes thereto.

" O Cupid, Venus son,
   " As thou hast showed thy might
" And hast this conquest woon,
   " Now end the same aright:

" And as I am thy slaue,
   " Contented with all this,
" So helpe me soone to haue
   " My parfect earthly blisse." [51]

[51] SONGES AND SONETTES by Henry Hawarde, late earle
of Surrey, and other. Printed for Richard Tottel; 8vo.
1557.

In February 1548–9, the Protector and Council were apprehensive that too great familiarity subsisted between the Princess Elizabeth and Lord Seymour, brother to the Protector, and then Lord High Admiral of England, which might end in their marriage; Seymour having recently lost his wife, Queen Catharine Parr, the widow of Henry the Eighth, who died in childbed in Sept. 1548, at Sudley in Glocestershire. On that occasion the young Princess, in consequence of the Confessions of Thomas Parry her Cofferer, and Catharine Aschylye, (or Ashley) one of her female attendants, was herself personally examined at Hatfield; and her Confession (a very innocent one) is preserved among the Burghley Papers. It consists of eleven Articles, and the concluding paragraph; but this paragraph and the first article, alone, being in her own hand-writing, and printed from the original, I shall confine myself to those only : and in the present inquiry it may be curious to compare her orthography with that which has been attributed to her near forty years afterwards :

The

The Confession of the Lady Elezabeyths *Grace.*

1. " KAT. Aschylye tolde me, after that my Lord Admiralde was maried to the Quene, that if my Lorde migth haue had his owne wil, he wolde haue had me, afore the Quene. Than I asked her how she knewe that : than she sayd, she knewe it wel inougth, bothe by him selfe and by others. The place, wher she said this, I haue forgotten, for she hathe spoken to me of him manye times, and of the wiche I haue forgotten divers times.

[THE second and the nine following Articles are in the hand-writing of Mr. Tyrwhitt. Then the Princess added in her own hand-writing what follows.]

" MY Lorde, thes ar the Articles wiche I do remember ; that bothe she and the Coferar talked with me of ; and if ther be anye moe behind, wiche I have not declared as yet, I shall most hartely desire your Lordship and the rest of the Counsel, not to thinke that I do willingeli concille them, but that I have indide forgotten them. For
if

if I did knowe them, and did not declare
them, I wer wonderfullye and aboue al
the reste to be rebuked, consideringe how
frindely your Grace has bothe writen to me
in Letters, and conselled me by messages,
to declare what I knowe hirein. Also I
assure your Lordship that if ther be any
more wiche I haue not tolde (wiche I thinke
there be not) I wil send you worde of them,
as the come to my minde.

Your assured frende to my litel power,

ELIZABETH.[32]

THE Dedication of Sir Philip Sydney's
ARCADIA, written probably about the year
1580, will furnish us with the familiar
address and orthography of that time.

" *To My Deare Lady and Sister*, *the
Covntesse of* Pembroke.

" HERE now haue you (most deare, and
most worthye to bee most deare Lady,) this
idle worke of mine: which I feare (like
the spiders webbe) will be thought fitter

[32] BURGHLEY PAPERS, Vol. i. p. 102.

to

to be swept away, then worne to any other
purpose. For my part, in very trueth, (as
the cruell fathers among the Greekes were
woont to doe to the babes they would not
foster,) I could well find in my heart to cast
out in some desert of forgetfulnesse this
childe, which I am loath to father. But
you desired me to doe it, and your desire
to my heart is an absolute commaundement.
Now, it is done onely for you, only to yow :
if you keep it to your self, or to such
friends, who will weigh errors in the bal-
lance of good will, I hope, for the fathers
sake, it will be pardoned, perchaunce made
much of, though in it selfe it have deformities. For, indeed, for seuerer eies it is not,
being but a trifle, and that triflingly handled.
Your deare selfe can best witnes the manner,
being done in loose sheetes of paper, most
of it in your presence, the rest, by sheetes
sent vnto you, as fast as they were done.
In summe, a young head, not so wel staied
as I would it were, (and shall be when God
will,) hauing many many fancies begotten in
it, if it had not beene in some way deliuered,
woulde haue growen a monster; and more
sorie might I be that they came in, then that
they gat out. But his chiefe safetie shall be,

I   the

the not walking abroade, and his chief protection, the bearing the liuery of your name; which (if much much good will doe not deceiue me) is worthie to be a sanctuarie for a greater offender. This say I, because I know the vertue so; and this say I, because it may be euer so, or to say better, because it will be euer so. Reade it then at your idle times; and the follies your good iudgement will finde in it, blame not, but laugh at. And so looking for no better stuffe, then, as in a haberdashers shoppe, glasses, or feathers, you will continue to loue the writer, who doth exceedingly loue you, and moste moste heartilie praies you may long liue, to be a principall ornament to the family of the Sidneis.

Your louing brother,

Philip Sidney."[33]

FROM Puttenham's ARTE OF ENGLISH POESIE, published in 1589, I select the following passage, because it contains some of the poetry of our Virgin Queen, probably in her own orthography:

[33] Not having the original quarto edition of 1590, I quote from the folio, 1593.

ı " So

" So doth this figure, which therefore
I call the *Gorgious*, polish our speech, and as
it were attire it with copious and pleasant
amplifications, and much varietie of sentences all running vpon one point, & to one
intēt ; so as I doubt whether I may terme
it a figure, or rather a masse of many
figurative speaches, applied to the bewtify-
ing of our tale or argumēt. In a worke
of ours intituled PHILOCALIA, we have
strained to shew the vse & application of
this figure and all others mentioned in this
booke ; to which we referre you. I find
none example in Englishe meetre, so well
maintayning this figure as that dittie of her
Maiesties owne making, passing sweete
and harmonicall, which figure beyng, as his
very originall name purporteth, the most
bewtifull and gorgious of all others, it
asketh in reason to be reserued for a last
complement, and desciphred by the arte of a
Ladies penne, her selfe beyng the most
bewtifull, or rather bewtie of Queenes.
And this was the occasion : Our soueraigne
Lady perceiuing how by the Sc. Q. [Scottish
Queen's] residence within this realme at so
great libertie and ease, as were skarce meete
for so great and daungerous a prysoner, bred

secret factions among her people, and made many of the nobilitie incline to fauour her partie ; (some of them desirous of innouation in the state, others aspiring to greater fortunes by her libertie and life ;) the Queene, our soueraigne Lady, to declare that she was nothing ignorant of those secret practizes, though she had long with great wisdome and pacience dissembled it, writeth this Ditty, most sweet and sententious, not hiding from all such aspiring minds the daunger of their ambition and disloyaltie : which afterward fell out most truly by th' exemplary chastisement of sundry persons, who in favour of the said Sc. Q. declining from her Maiestie, sought to interrupt the quiet of the realme by many euill and vndutifull practizes. The ditty is as followeth :

" The doubt of future foes
  " Exiles my present joy,
" And wit me warns to shun such snares
  " As threaten mine annoy.

" For falshood now doth flow
  " And subject faith doth ebbe,
" Which would not be, if reason rul'd,
  " Or wisdom wev'd the webbe.

" But

" But clowdes of tois untried
 " Do cloake aspiring mindes,
" Which turne to raigne of late repent,
 " By course of changed windes.

" The toppe of hope supposed
 " The roote of ruth will be,
" And fruitlesse all their graffed guiles,
 " As shortly ye shall see.

" Then dazelld eyes with pride,
 " Which great ambition blinds,
" Shalbe unseeld by worthy wights,
 " Whose foresight falshood finds.

" The daughter of debate,
 " That eke discord doth sowe,
" Shal reap no gaine, where former rule
 " Hath taught still peace to growe.

" No forreine banisht wight
 " Shal ancre in this port;
" Our realme it brookes no strangers force,
 " Let them elsewhere resort.

" Our rusty sworde with rest
 " Shall first his edge employ,
" To poll their toppes that seeke such change,
 " And gape for [such like] joy."[34]

THE

[34] *Arte of Eng. Poesy*, 4to. 1589, p. 207. This sonnet,
Dr. Percy thinks [*Reliques of Anc. Eng. Poetry*, ii. 205.]
was composed in 1569, not long before the Duke of Norfolk
                                                        and

The Faery Queene of Spencer, whose orthography is at least as ancient as that of any of his contemporaries, opens thus :

" Lo I the man, whose Muse whylome did maske,
" As time her taught, in lowly shephards weeds,
" Am now enforst a farre vnfitter taske,
" For trumpets sterne to chaunge mine oaten
    reeds :
" And sing of Knights and Ladies gentle deeds,
" Whose praises hauing slept in silence long,
" Mee, all too meane, the sacred Muse areeds
" To blazon broade emongst her learned throng :
" Fierce warres and faithfull loues shall moralize
    my song."

and some other noblemen were taken into custody. In a late collection compiled from the papers of Sir John Harrington, [*Nugæ Antiquæ*, i. 58. first edit.] is a Letter written probably by Sir John, giving a curious account of the manner in which this ditty " of her highness own editing," got abroad : " My lady Wiloughby did covertly get it on her Majesties tablet, and had much hazard in so doing ; for the Queen did find out the thief, and chid for spreading evil bruit of her writing such toyes, when other matters did so occupy her employment at this time ; and was fearful of being thought too lightly of for so doing. But marvel not, good Madam ; her Highness doth frame her selfe to all occasions, to all times, and to all things both in business and pastime, as may witness this her Sonnet."

To

To this I shall subjoin one of the Dedicatory Epistles of the same author, which will furnish us with the mode of address at that period from a poet to a patron :

" *To the right Honourable, the* LADIE COMPTON *and* MOUNTEGLE.

" MOST faire and vertuous Ladie; hauing often sought opportunitie by some good meanes to make knowen to your Ladiship the humble affection and faithfull duetie, which I haue alwaies professed, and am bound to beare to that House [35] from whence yee spring, I haue at length found occasion to remēber the same, by making a simple

[35] Sir John Spencer of Althorpe, who died Nov. 8, 1580, leaving five sons and six daughters, one of whom was Anne, the lady here addressed ; married first to Sir William Stanley, Lord Mountegle ; afterwards to Henry Compton, Lord Compton ; and finally to Robert, Lord Buckhurst. She was now the widow of Lord Compton, who died in Dec. 1589.—In his Address to Lady Strange, one of Lady Compton's sisters, Spencer speaks of " the private bands of *affinitie,* which it had pleased her ladyship to acknowledge."

From Sir John Spencer, the noble lord who now presides with such distinguished reputation at the Board of Admiralty, is the tenth in lineal descent, and therefore is remotely related to the celebrated poet who bore his name.

present

present to you of these my idle labours;
which hauing long sithens composed in the
raw conceipt of my youth, I lately amongst
other papers lighted vpon, and was by others,
which liked the same, mooued to set them
foorth. Simple is the deuice, and the composition meane, yet carrieth some delight,
euen the rather because of the simplicitie &
meannesse thus personated. The same I
beseech your Ladiship take in good part, as
a pledge of that profession which I haue
made to you, and keepe with you vntill
with some other more worthie labour I do
redeeme it out of your hands,[36] and discharge
my vtmost dutie. Till then wishing your
Ladiship all increase of honour and happiness, I humblie take leaue.

Your La: euer

humbly;

ED. SP." [37]

---

[36] Shakspeare had perhaps this passage in his thoughts,
when he wrote his Dedication of the *Venus and Adonis*:
" —— and vow to take advantage of all idle hours, till I
have honoured you with some graver labour." See it in a
subsequent page.

[37] Epistle Dedicatory to MOTHER HUBBERD'S TALE,
4to. 1591.

IN

In 1593 John Norden prefixed to his
SPECULUM BRITANNIÆ the following
address to Lord Burghley :

" HAVING by your honourable meane,
(my good Lord) obteined, at the hands of my
sacred SOVEREIGNE, gratious passe & privi-
ledge for mine intended labours, the description of famous ENGLAND, I cannot but in
dutie render unto your Honor condigne
thanks, and with all diligence and dutifull
endeuour proceed therein : hoping that although (in regarde of my long sicknes &
other impediments) this beginning carrie
not so absolute perfection, as in your wise-
dom may be required, yet, may I enjoy
your patient directions, and gratious assistance, I shall effect the residue more fully to
answere honorable expectations.

Your Honors in all dutie,

Jo. NORDEN."

As we shall presently have occasion to
examine a pretended Letter of our poet to
Lord Southampton, I shall close these
specimens with his two undoubted epistles
to that nobleman; the only prose compo-

K   sitions

sitions of his writing, not in a dramatick
form, (if we except the argument prefixed
to his LUCRECE,) now known to be extant.
To his VENUS AND ADONIS the epistle
dedicatory is as follows:

" *To the Right Honorable* Henry Wriotheslie,
EARLE OF SOUTHAMPTON, *and* BARON
OF TICHFIELD.

" RIGHT Honorable, I know not how I
shall offend in dedicating my unpolisht lines
to your Lordship, nor how the world wil
censure mee for chusing so strong a proppe
to support so weake a burthen: onely if
your Honor seeme but pleased, I account my
selfe highly praised, and vow to take advantage of all idle houres, till I have honoured
you with some graver labour. But if the
first heire of my invention prove deformed,
I shall be sory it had so noble a god-father;
and neuer after eare [38] so barren a land, for
feare it yeeld me still so bad a haruest. I
leaue it to your Honourable survey, and your
Honour to your hearts content, which I

[38] Plow.

wish

wish may alwayes answer your owne wish, and the worlds hopefull expectation.

Your Honors in all dutie,

William Shakespeare." [39]

HIS LUCRECE he thus presented to the same nobleman, about a year afterwards:

" *To the Right Honourable* Henry Wriothesley, EARLE OF SOUTHAMPTON, *and* BARON OF TICHFIELD.

THE loue I dedicate to your Lordship is without end; whereof this pamphlet without beginning is but a superfluous moity.

[39] VENUS AND ADONIS, 16mo. 1596.—This poem was entered on the Stationers' Books, by Richard Field, April 18, 1593; and I long fince conjectured that it was printed in that year, though I have never seen an earlier edition than that above quoted, which is in my possession. Since I published that poem my conjecture has been confirmed, beyond a doubt; the following entry having been found in an ancient MS. Diary, which some time since was in the hands of an acquaintance of Mr. Steevens, by whom it was communicated to me: " 12th of June, 1593. For the Survay of Fraunce, with the Venus and Athonay p[r] Shakspere, xii.d."

The

The warrant I have of your Honourable disposition, not the worth of my untutord lines, makes it assured of acceptance. What I haue done is yours, what I haue to doe is yours, being part in all I haue deuoted yours. Were my worth greater, my duety would shew greater; meane time, as it is, it is bound to your Lordship, to whom I wish long life still lengthned with all hap-pinesse.

> Your Lordships in all duety,
>
> William Shakespeare."[40]

It is wholly unnecessary to make any observations on these genuine specimens of the orthography and language of Shakspeare's age, as well as of the preceding century. Without the aid of other specimens of Elizabeth's own orthography, almost at the very period to which her Letter must be referred, (which will be given hereafter,) they prove decisively and at the first view, that the paper before us, in which such laboured and capricious deformity of spelling

---

[40] Rape of Lucrece, 4to. 1594. This poem was entered on the Stationers' Books, May 9, 1594, by John Harrison, sen. by whom it was published.

is

is introduced, was not written by her Majesty, but is an entire forgery.

THE spelling, however, of two or three words in this royal epistle demands particular notice. *Masterre* was not the spelling of the word *Master* at this period, but *Maister*.⁴¹ The omission of the letter *r*

---

⁴¹ Out of an hundred instances that might be produced in proof of this assertion, I shall give only the following : *A Sighte of the Portugal Pearle*, that is, *the answere of D. Haddon*, Maister *of the Requests unto our souveraigne Lady Elizabeth, &c.* 16°. 1565. So, *The Secrets of* Maister *Alexis of Piemont*, &c. 4to. 1595. *Palladis Tamia, Wits Treasury*, &c. *by Francis Meres*, Maister *of Arts*, 8vo. 1598.—" Unto this *Maister* D. Gager replying, and desiring *Maister* Rainoldes to forbeare, *Maister* Rainoldes did rejoine as followeth." [30 May, 1593.] *Th' Overthrow of Stage-Playes*, 4to. 1599. So, in the *Returne from Parnassus*, 1606. " *Kempe*. It is good manners to follow us, *Maister* Philomusus, and *Maister* Otioso." So also in a Letter written by Queen Elizabeth to Sir Henry Sidney, in 1565, printed from the original at Penshurst, *Sydney Papers*, vol. i. p. 7. " Let this Memoriall be only committed to Vulcanes base keping, without any longer abode than the leasure of the reding therof, yea, and with no mention made therof to any other wight. I charge you, as I may comande you, seme not to have had but Secretaries letters from me.

Your lovinge *Maistres*,

ELIZABETH R."

The elder spelling of this word, *Mastyr*, may be found in the PASTON LETTERS, ii. 292.

in

in *Chamberlayne* is unprecedented. If the
Queen had chosen to omit any letter in that
word, it would have been the *m :* and *Chamberlain*, not *Chamberlayne*, was, I think, the
spelling of that period of her reign : but
this is of little consequence. LONDONNE is
more material, for no example of such
orthography can, I believe, be produced.
Even Robert of Gloucester, who flourished
in the time of Edward the First, might have
taught our forger that LONDON was " lighter
in the mouth."* In 1449, Margaret Paston
wrote LONDON. In Aggas's Map of that
city, which appears to have been executed in
1568, we find it written in the same way ;
and throughout the whole reign of Elizabeth,
the Burghley and Sydney Papers shew that
there was no variation in the orthography
of this word.—The next, and a still more
fatal objection lies to *Hamptowne*. Though
Hampton-Court, which was given to Henry
the Eighth by Cardinal Wolsey in 1526,
does not seem to have been so favourite a
residence with her Majesty, as Greenwich,
Nonesuch, and Richmond, she occasionally

---

* " *And* now me clepeþ it LONDON, þat ys lyȝter in
þe mouþ."

passed

passed some time there, and had probably
in the course of her reign signed several
hundred state-papers issued from thence,
and regularly dated *from the Honour of
Hampton-Court:* [42] yet this learned and
accomplished Queen, who was mistress of
eight languages, [43] is here exhibited as such
a dolt as not only not to know the true
orthography of a word thus familiar to her,
but not to be able to distinguish her palace
from the neighbouring town : and to mend
the matter, she is made to give to the *town* a
termination entirely repugnant to the genius
and analogy of the English language, in

---

[42] Such was the almost uniform spelling of the time, as far
as relates to the first part of this compounded word, which
never was separated till the publication of these Papers. See
BURGHLEY PAPERS, i. 4; *Hampton-Corte*; i. 6, & 574,
Hampton-Court. SYDNEY PAPERS, i. 86, 354; ii. 311, 312,
Hampton-Coorte: i. 233, 235; ii. 307, *Hampton-Courte.*
i. 272, *Hampton-Courght.* See also Norden's SPECULUM,
1593, p. 26: " *Hampton-Court*, an Honour of Queen
Elizabethes, a regall palace, statelie raysed of bricke. - - -
It is called Hampton-Court, of the parish of *Hampton*, which
standeth not farre thence," &c.

Since the above was written, I have met with one solitary
instance of *Hamptown*-Court, written by a clerk, Oct. 14,
1562, [Forbes's STATE PAPERS, ii. 109,] which probably gave rise to the spelling adopted in this forged letter.

[43] Florio's FIRST FRUTES, 4to. 1578. Hentzner.
ITIN. 4to. 1598.

I   which

which the Saxon *ton* is found to form the final syllable of many hundred names of places.

But all these MISNOMERS are trivial, compared with her not knowing the true orthography of the name of *Leycester*, for which we have here—*Leycesterre*. Her uniform attachment to that nobleman for the first thirty years of her reign, (excepting some little coldness while he was Governor of the Netherlands,) is so well known, that it makes a part of the scandalous chronicle of those times. Probably, scarce a day passed during that period without her seeing his name written, as he always wrote it, LEYCESTER; and how fairly and legibly he wrote, may be seen by looking on Plate II, where a *fac-simile* of his autograph will be found, from an original in my possession, written on the 30th of June, 1585. The old spelling of this title in the preceding century was not *Leycesterre*, but *Leycestre*; but the nobleman with whom we are concerned uniformly wrote it *Leycester*, as may be seen by looking into the Burghley and Sydney Papers, and other ancient documents. The Queen, it is well known, constantly attended

attended the sittings of her Privy Council, and took so active a part in what was doing, that we may be sure she perused the Register of each day's proceedings ; which she could not look at without the name of Leycester almost constantly presenting itself to her, while he was in England (a list of the Counsellors present each day being always set down) ; and in addition to all these circumstances, during the last three years of this nobleman's life, the greater part of which he passed in a high station abroad, she must have had innumerable Letters from him.

WITH respect to all the other minute deformities of spelling in this Letter, I shall content myself with merely referring to a curious comparison between her real and fictitious orthography, given below.[44]

I NOW

[44] In the BURGHLEY PAPERS, i. 102, are two paragraphs written by Elizabeth herself in 1548-9, (and printed from the original,) which have been given in a former page. In the SYDNEY PAPERS, i. 7, is an entire Letter written by her in 1569.—Other specimens will hereafter be given from the Cotton Library and the Heralds-Office. The gross variation in this pretended letter from the Queen's orthography, in several particulars beside those already noticed, will appear at one view from the following table, (for the scheme of which I am indebted to a friend,) which exhibits such words as occur both in these authentick papers,

L   and

2. I now come to the LANGUAGE and
PHRASEOLOGY.—The first word that occurs
worthy of notice is *pretty*,—" Wee did receive

and her spurious Letter. The figure annexed denotes how
often the word is repeated.

Spurious Letter.	Examin. Burghley Pap. i. 102.	Letter, Syd. Pap. i. 7.	Letters, Cotton MSS.	Letter to Shrews-bury, MS.
youre	your (4)	your (7)	your	your
goode	——	good (4)	good	——
off	of (3)	of (6)	of	of
ande	and (6)	and (8)	and	——
wee (3)	——	we (3)	——	——
doe	do (2)	do (2)	——	——
onne	——	on	——	——
theyre	——	ther *for* [their] (4)	——	——
shalle	shall	shall (3)	——	——
fromme	——	from (2)	——	——
toe (2)	to (6)	to (10)	to	——
forre	for	for (2)	——	for (2)
where	——	whare (1) wher (1)	——	——
beste	——	best	——	——
thatte	that (4)	that (8)	——	that
before	——	befor (1)	——	——
oure	——	our (3)	——	——
usse (3)	——	us (1)	——	——
bee	be (4)	be (13)	——	——
butte	but	but (2)	——	——
comme	come	come (3)	——	——
bye	by	by	——	——
asse	as (2)	as (6)	——	——
withe	with	with (4)	——	with
atte	——	at (1)		

your

your *pretty* verses ;" which was not, I think,
the language of the time. Shakspeare
indeed, and Ralegh, have—*pretty* TALES,
which approaches somewhat near to the
other; but both of them use *tale* in the
sense of a narrative or entertaining story
related: and I doubt much whether the
epithet *pretty* was then applied to *written*
compositions. On this objection, however,
I do not much rely; and here, once for all, I
enter my protest against the triumph of those
who may produce ancient examples of the
usage of certain words to which I object
only as *doubtful*. If indeed, where I make a
firm stand, and attempt to prove, as far as
a negative can be proved, that the word did
not exist at that time, I shall be found
mistaken, there may be some ground for
triumph : but even here, though my critical
sagacity or knowledge may be impeached,
nothing less than a complete refutation of
all the verbal objections will be sufficient to
establish the authenticity of this or any other
of the papers we are now considering : since
if out of four objections one only should be
found incontrovertible, it will establish the
spuriousness of the piece in question as well
as four hundred.—I need not employ many

words

words to shew, that no manuscript alleged to have been written in the age of Queen Elizabeth, can be genuine, in which a single word is found which was not in use till several years, or perhaps an age, after her death.

AFTER acknowledging the receipt of our poet's pretty verses, her Majesty proceeds to *complement* him on their great *excellence*. Now unfortunately no such verb active as to *complement*, in this sense, was known in that age, nor for some time afterwards : and when it did come into use, it was always coupled with a preposition not found here.

To begin with the substantive, *complemente*, for so it was then spelt. Barrett in his ALVEARIE or Quadruple Dictionary, 1580, has it not : but in 1589 we find it used by Puttenham, in a passage already quoted from his ARTE OF POESIE,[45] and in the sense which the word then universally bore, that of " *completing* or *filling up*." In Cawdrey's ALPHABETICAL TABLE of hard words, 8vo. 1604, it is defined " *a perfecting of any thing*." Bullokar in his ENGLISH EXPOSITOR, 8vo. 1616, brings it a little

[45] See p. 59.

nearer

nearer to its present acceptation, interpreting it—" Fulness; perfection; *fine behaviour.*" And so our poet himself in his LOVE'S LABOUR'S LOST:

" A man of *complements,* whom right and wrong
" Have chose as umpire of their mutiny."

i. e. a man adorned with all those *accomplishments,* which are " the varnish of a *complete* man."

AGAIN, in K. HENRY V. where the word has the same sense:

" Garnish'd and deck'd in modest *complement.*"

EVEN in 1611, the French word *compliment* does not seem to have been yet introduced into that language, for Cotgrave, whose dictionary was published in that year, has it not; and from Howel's republication of that work in 1650, compared with Sherwood's English and French Vocabulary subjoined to it, one might be led to suppose that our present word *compliment* was not borrowed from the French, as Dr. Johnson supposed, but their word from us: for Howel in the French part has it not; and Sherwood, in whose Vocabulary it appears,
(spelt—

(spelt—*complement*,) renders it not by the French word *compliment*, but by *entretien*; as he does *complements* by *fressurades*, *ceremonies*. However this may be, Shakspeare himself, after the death of Elizabeth, seems to have used the substantive in one of his late plays [TWELFTH-NIGHT] with the same signification as is now affixed to it; as Sydney had done before him :

" My servant, Sir ;—'twas never merry world,
" Since lowly feigning was call'd *complement*."

yet even here it may mean *accomplishment*.

IN Edward Philips's NEW WORLD OF WORDS, which, I think, first appeared in 1659, we have *complement* in its original and secondary sense : " A filling up ; also ceremony in speech and behaviour :" and in Cole's ENGLISH DICTIONARY, 1685, " *Complement*; a filling up : also a choice of the best words to express our minds by ; and (corruptly) too much ceremony in speech and behaviour." The same author in his LATIN DICTIONARY, (the early edition of which in 4to. 1679, throws much light on our old language,) has—" *Complement*, blandimentum, fucus." But all this
while

while we find no trace in any writer of the age of Elizabeth, of the *verb active*—" to complement," and therefore, till some instance shall be produced, I have a right to assume that it did not exist. Nor, if it had existed, would it exempt this letter from the charge of forgery; for when it was first used, it was always accompanied by the preposition *with*. Thus in Sherwood's Vocabulary, 1650, " To complement *with*; entretenir;" and in Cole's Latin Dict. 1679, " To complement *with*; *ablandire, blandis et benignis verbis et gestibus excipere*." Glanvill about this period used the verb without the adjunct *with*, if the quotation from that writer given by Dr. Johnson be correct; and probably he was the first who discarded that appendage. Thus therefore we see that the verb active *to compliment* was so far from being known in the age of Elizabeth, that it was not in use for half a century afterwards; and when it was introduced, it was not employed as it appears in this spurious epistle, but was always accompanied with the adjunct *with*, placed before the person addressed.

On the *excellence* of Shakspeare's verses, I have not much to say; but I call upon

those

those who may be inclined to maintain the authenticity of this Letter, to produce any example of that word being applied in his age to denote the purity or goodness of written compositions, whether in prose or verse : I know of no such example.

THE next word that demands our attention is *oureselfe*. Those who have the slightest knowledge of English grammar need not be told, that the capricious word *self* is sometimes considered as a substantive, and sometimes as an adjective; and that when used with the personal pronouns or pronominal adjectives, though joined in construction with them, it was formerly always written separately. In no instance have I ever found in any *manuscript* of the age of Elizabeth the words, *ourself*, *yourself*, &c. written as one word; though sometimes (but very rarely) such a combination may be found in printed books, either from the compositor's carelessness, or want of room. The uniform mode of writing at that time, and long afterwards, was, *our selfe*; *your selves*; &c. This observation alone, without any other aid, would be fatal to the letter before us.

WHEN

WHEN we next find that our poet is ordered by the Queen to attend with his best actors, in order to *amuze* her, what opinion can we entertain of the writer of this Letter, but that he knew no more of the language he endeavoured to imitate, than of the manners and history of the time. The word *amuze*, in its *present sense*, is perfectly modern.—As it certainly came to us from the French, let us first attend to Cotgrave's definition of it in 1611: " *Amuser*. To amuse, to make to *muse* or think of, wonder or gaze at; to put into a dumpe; to stay, hold or delay from going forward by discourse, questions, or any other amusements."—" *Amuse-fol*. One that with vaine pratling or toying holds fond people at gaze."—It is in this instance perfectly unnecessary to turn to Barrett, Cawdrey, Bullokar, Sherwood, Cockeram, or Philips. Coles is the first English Lexicographer, (that I have seen,) who has the word. In his English Dictionary, of which I know not the first edition, (mine is that of 1685,) we find—" To *amuse*, put in a dump ;" which in his Latin work, (1679) he renders—" *Detineo, animum in spectaculo occupare*." In that work he adds—" To

M   amuse

amuse (with words), *aliquem inanibus verbis ducere, trahere, morari, ludificari.*"

THE first writer (that I know of) who has the word even in a kindred sense to that in which it is now used, is the author of THE WHOLE DUTY OF MAN, who in that excellent work entitled THE DECAY OF PIETY, says, " — they think they see visions, and are arrived at extraordinary revelations, when indeed they do but dream dreams, and *amuse* themselves with the fantastical ideas of a busy imagination." I have not time to examine the original, though it is close at hand, but quote the passage as given by Dr. Johnson. Yet even here it may mean to *deceive.*—Of the word *amusement,* in its present sense, Rogers, the divine, has furnished that Lexicographer with the first example. Even so late a writer as Kersey, in 1708, gives no other definition of the verb *to amuse,* than—" to stop or stay one with a trifling story; to feed with vain expectation; to hold in play."

3. HAVING now done with the LANGUAGE of this letter, I proceed to consider
the

the other incongruous circumstances attending it ;—the superscription, the negative date, &c. Her Majesty, your lordship will observe, instead of sending this Letter to Master William Shakspeare, by one of her ordinary messengers or grooms of the chamber, or by the proper officer, the Master of the Revels, to honour the poet still more superscribes it herself, not indeed precisely in the fashion of a Letter sent by the modern penny-post, but with the formality of those epistles which in her time were conveyed by common carriers, or state-messengers, from one part of the kingdom to the other : " For Master William Shakspeare atte the Globe bye Thames." Had she added— " deliver these with speede,"—or " Hast, hast, post hast for thy lif," it would have been complete. To prevent a possibility of its miscarrying, in her superscription she writes the first letter of the word *For* in that print-like mode which she observed in her sign-manual : and the reason is obvious ; the true writer, as you will presently see, had no other archetype before him. But where is this Letter to find the poet ?—" at the Globe by Thames." So that we are to suppose there was no other house or tavern

in

in London or Southwark, to which the
Globe was a sign, but the theatre here intended to be described; and on which side
of the Thames it lay, whether north or
south, the messenger was to find out as he
could; if he did but perambulate *by Thames*
long enough, first on one side of the river,
and then on the other, he could not fail of
stumbling upon it. Unluckily, however,
the Globe theatre was not built at the time
to which this Letter must be referred; and
when it was built, it was not situated *by
Thames*, but in Maiden-lane, a street in
Southwark at some distance from the river,
as is proved by an authentick document in
my possession.

In Aggas's Map of London, which is
supposed to have been executed in 1568, and
had perhaps an earlier date, there are two
buildings in Southwark, one appropriated to
Bolle-baytinge, the other, which is more to
the east, to *Beare-baytinge*, but no theatre
is delineated or mentioned: nor is there any
found in Virtue's map of London in 1560, or
in that by Braun and Hogenbergius, in 1573.
The Itinerary of Chytræus, a German,
who visited London in 1579, shews that
no

no such building then existed in Southwark ;
for had it existed, he without doubt would
have alluded to it, as his countryman Hentzner did about twenty years afterwards :

" Opposita in Thamesis ripâ longa area parvis
" Distincta aspicitur tectis, ubi magna canum vis
" Ursorumque alitur, diversarumque ferarum,
" Quæ canibus commissæ Angliæ spectacula præ-
 bent
" Hospitibusque novis, vincti dum prælia mis-
 cent,
" Luctanctes aut ungue fero vel dentibus uncis.
" Totius ast urbis quam sit preciosa supellex,
" Parietibus quam sint storeæ, pictique tapetes
" Inducti egregie, ut juncis herbisque virescant
" Strata pavimenta, atque hominum quam mundus
 amictus,
" Omnia quid numerare refert ?" [45]

I DO not, however, mean to say that there
were no plays exhibited in Southwark at that
period, (for I have authentick proofs to the
contrary in my possession,) but that there was
no regular theatre on the Bankside expressly
built for scenick exhibitions. The drama-

[45] Nath. Chytræi POEMATA, 8vo. 1579. *Iter Angli-
cum*, p. 170.

tick

tick performances were at that time either in yards of inns, or in other buildings occasionally employed for that purpose.—— In Norden's Map of London in 1593, is found the first delineation of a playhouse in Southwark; but this was not the GLOBE, but the Rose Theatre, which was so denominated from Rose-Alley near which it stood, as the Globe probably derived its name from Globe-Alley. The Rose Theatre, of which the total cost was 103l. 2s. 7d., was built by Mr. Philip Henslowe in 1592, and opened by him in that year, as appears from his theatrical Register now before me. Norden in his Map only calls it *The Play-house*, its name probably not having then become familiarly known; but that this was the theatre there mentioned, may be deduced from other circumstances. A few weeks before I published the History of the English Stage, I discovered a Contract made the 8th of January 1599-1600, between Philip Henslowe and Edward Alleyn the player, on the one part, and Peter Streete, a carpenter, on the other, for building the Fortune Playhouse near Golding-Lane; which ascertained the dimensions and plan of the Globe theatre, there called " *the late-erected*

playhouse on the Bank," &c. [46] and I have
since discovered a Bond executed by Burbadge the player to this very Peter Streete,
on the 22d of Dec. 1593, (which has furnished me with the autograph from which
the *fac-simile* in Plate II. Nº. xiv. is taken,)
for the performance of all the covenants
contained " in a certaine paire of Indentures
of Articles of agreement, of the date above-
mentioned, made between the said Richard
Burbadge and Peter Streete." A similar
Bond was doubtless executed by this carpenter to Burbadge; and the Articles of
Agreement probably related to the building
of the Globe Theatre, and were similar
to those between Streete and Alleyn, which
have been already printed. [47] This may
fix the building of the Globe Theatre to
the year 1594, and probably it was opened
in that or the following year. Accordingly
in the Map of London as it appeared in
1599, we see this theatre. There also, is

---

[46] PLAYS and POEMS of WILLIAM SHAKSPEARE,
crown 8vo. 1790, Vol. I. P. II. p. 325.

A firm believer in the authenticity of these MSS. contends
that these words may very well allude to a playhouse erected
thirty years before ! COMPARATIVE REVIEW, &c. p. 53.

[47] PLAYS and POEMS of WILLIAM SHAKSPEARE,
ut supr.

delineated

delineated a small theatre near it, more to the west, to which the modern publisher has not affixed a name : it was the ROSE, which was much smaller than the GLOBE, and had already been noticed by Norden, though without a name, in the Map of 1593. The Rose theatre, which was thatched, and from the price it cost was probably very slight, fell into decay, I imagine about the middle of King James's reign, if not sooner; and there is no trace of it in the Map of London, &c. executed at Venice in 1629.

THUS we see the Globe theatre did not exist at the time to which this letter must be referred ; for though the writer cautiously avoided putting a date to it, he has furnished us with a negative date by mentioning Lord Leycester as then living. The Letter therefore must be referred to some period antecedent to Sept. 1588, in the early part of which month that nobleman died.[48] The

[48] Burghley's DIARY, in Murden's STATE PAPERS, p. 788.—The *Escaetria*, or Inquisition after the death of Lord Leycester, is not to be found in the Chapel of the Rolls ; but it appears from the SYDNEY PAPERS, i. 75, that his Will was proved in Sept. 1588.

I   greater

greater part of the last three years of his life
he spent abroad. On the 8th of December,
1585, with a view to assist the United
Provinces, he embarked with a considerable
force for Flushing, and on the 25th of the
following month he was sworn Governour
of the Netherlands. He was almost the
whole of the year 1586 abroad. In the
October of that year he fought the battle
of Zutphen, where unfortunately his nephew,
Sir Philip Sydney, loft his life. On the
23d of November following the earl returned
to London, at which time the Queen was
at Richmond; and he continued in England
till the 25th of June 1587, when he went
to the Hague, and remained abroad till the
latter end of that year. From the time of
his return to his death was a period of
about nine months, during the whole of
which, I believe, he remained at home.
This pretended Letter, therefore, if written
subsequently to the 8th of December 1585,
(and if, after what I have stated and have
yet to state, it should find any partisan,
I suppose he will not choose to refer it to
an earlier period,) muft have been written
either between the 23d of Nov. 1586, and
the 25th of June 1587, or between the

N   months

months of December 1587 and Sept. 1588.
Now it must also be shewn that the Queen
was at Hampton-Court during some part
of those two periods. The regular time
for the exhibition of plays at Court was
Christmas, Twelftide, (as it was called,)
Candlemas, and Shrovetide. Accordingly,
Shakspeare is very properly called upon to
play before the Queen in the *Holydayes*.
But I am able to shew, beyond a doubt,
that she was not at Hampton-Court during
the holydays in either of the periods above
mentioned.

FORMERLY, as is well known, the great
officers of state removed with the Sovereign
from palace to palace, and were accommo-
dated with no very convenient apartments
wherever the Court happened to reside.[49]

Hence

[49] The following Letter written by the eldest daughter
of John Duke of Northumberland, Lady Mary, the wife of
Sir Henry and mother of Sir Philip Sydney, furnishes us
with a curious view of the inconveniencies suffered on these
occasions. It also affords a specimen of the orthography of
a woman of high rank, at the period when it was written,
which, though inaccurate enough, (as the orthography of
ladies continued to be till the present century,) has no kind
of resemblance to the fantastical mis-spelling attributed to
Queen Elizabeth, Lord Southampton, &c. The words in
Italicks are particularly worthy of attention.

To

Hence it is that we find so many old Letters
dated *from the Court*; that is, from the
apartments

[To Edmund Mollineux, Esq.]

" Molenex,

" I thoght *good* to put you in remembance to moue my
Lord CHAMBERLEIN, [Thomas Ratcliffe, earl of Sussex,]
in my Lord's name,* to haue some other roome then my
chamber, *for* my *Lord* to haue his resort unto, *as* he was
woont to haue; or ells my *Lord* wilbe greatly trubled,
when he shall haue enny maters of dispache : my lodginge,
you see, beinge very lytle, *and* my sealfe continewaly syke,
and not able to be mouche out of my bed.   For the night
tyme, on [one] roofe, with Gods grace, shall serue *vs : for*
the day tyme the Quen will louke to haue my chamber
always in a redines for her Majesties cominge thether ; *and*
thoghe my *Lord* him sealfe cann be no impediment thearto
by his owen presens, yet his Lordshipe, trustinge to no
playce ells to be provyded *for* him, wilbe, as I sayd before,
trubled *for* want of a conuenient playce, *for* the dispache of
souche people *as* shall haue occasion to come to him.
Therefore I pray you, in my Lords owen name, moue
my Lord of Sussex for a room for that purpose, and I
will haue it hanged and lyned *for* him, with stoof from
hens.   I wish you not to be unmyndfull hearof ; and so for
this tyme I leue you to the Almyghty.   From Chiswicke,
this xi of october, 1578.

Your very assured louing

Mistris and Frend,

M. Sydney."

The officers to whom the arrangement of the apartments
belonged, were on these occasions often put to great diffi-

* Sir Henry Sydney was Lord President of Wales.

N 2   culties,

apartments of the Lord Treasurer or other
great officer of state, where the Court then
happened to be. The Privy Council in
the time of Elizabeth consisted of a very
small number, (not more than ten or twelve
persons,) and their meetings, which were,
I think, daily, were almost always held in
whatever palace the Queen then inhabited.
Hence the Registers of the Council ascertain the residence of the Queen. Now it
appears from the Council-books that her
Majesty spent the Christmas of the year
1586, at her favourite palace of Greenwich,
and continued there till May 1587, when
she went to Nonesuch; from which she
returned in June to Greenwich, where she
continued the whole of that month, on the
25th of which Leycester left England.—

culties. In 1574, when preparations were made at Archbishop Parker's palace at Croydon for the reception of the
Queen and her Court, Mr. Bowyer, Gentleman-Usher of
the black rod, writes,—" if my lady of Oxford should
come, I cannot then tell wher to place Mr. Hatton ; and
for my Lady Carewe, here is no place with a chimney
for her, but she must lay abrode by Mrs. Apparry and the
rest of the Privye Chamber : for Mrs. Skelton there is no
rome with chimneys. - Here is as mytche as I have any
wayes able to doo in this house."—From a MS. in the
Library at Lambeth. Lysons's ENVIRONS OF LONDON,
i. 174.

So

So much for the first of the two periods
which I have mentioned. Let us now see
whether the second period will be more
favourable to the *amusement* of her Majesty
and her favourite. From the beginning of
December 1587, to the 8th day of July
1588, she resided at Greenwich. On that
day she went to Richmond, where she remained to the end of July. She then removed
to St. James's, where she resided, making
the most vigorous preparations against a
second Spanish invasion, to the end of Sept.
1588; during which time the only excursion
she made was to the Camp at Tilbury,
(August 9th.)* when she pronounced that
celebrated harangue recorded by all our
historians. In neither of these periods does
her Majesty appear ever to have been at
Hampton-Court.

OUR great poet, your Lordship observes,
is here addressed not as a noviciate or pro-

---

* It has been suggested (COMPARATIVE REVIEW,
&c. p. 52,) that Shakspeare might have been summoned
to play before the Queen soon afterwards. The suggester,
I suppose, is possessed of an OXFORD Almanack for 1588,
from which it appears that at least *Shrove-Tuesday* in that
year, or perhaps the entire Christmas Holydays, were removed by authority to the month of *August*.

I   bationer

bationer on the stage, but an established actor; nay, as the manager and leader of a troop of actors. He was born, we all know, in April 1564. At what time precisely he came to London, though I have not been negligent in my inquiries, I have not been able to ascertain; but I have shewn in the Life of this poet, from an enumeration of various circumstances, that his first excursion to the metropolis could not well have been before the year 1586 or 1587; and that he had a natural and easy access to the theatre, without any introduction from either Hathwaye the poet, who was perhaps his wife's kinsman, or Thomas Greene the actor, who may have been his countryman; a conjecture which I found rather on his name, than the suspicious and insecure testimony of Chetwood. [50]—In the History of the Stage I have been more successful; and that History, when again presented to the publick, while it will exhibit its actual state and the dramatick perform-

[50] Chetwood, who had been prompter at Drury-Lane, quotes four lines from an old comedy in which Greene is spoken of as a native of Stratford; but no such lines are to be found in the piece. This man, as we shall see hereafter, was a very notable forger.

ances

ances from the year 1570 to about the year 1586, will prove from unquestionable documents, that it is in the highest degree improbable that Shakspeare should have produced a single drama till some time after that period.

IT is quite unnecessary here to enter into the particular circumstances on which this opinion is founded. Had he been at the head of a Company of Actors in 1587 or 1588, we cannot suppose him to have attained to so high a rank in less than five or six years; during which time he could not fail to have produced some of his incomparable pieces. But he is not mentioned by Nashe in his Epistle to the two Universities, prefixed to Greene's MENAPHON, 1589, (afterwards republished under the title of ARCADIA,) in which he reviews the celebrated poets of the time, and particularly praises George Peele, whom he calls the *Atlas* of Poetry, and *primus verborum artifex*, for his *drama* entitled THE ARRAIGNMENT OF PARIS; and Puttenham, whose ARTE OF POESY appeared in the same year, though one of the Gentlemen Pensioners, and therefore constantly near the Queen,

Queen, had never heard of this established and eminent *Coriphæus* of the Stage, though her Majesty's honouring him a year or two before with a Letter written by her own hand must necessarily have made some little noise at Court: for having occasion to speak of the dramatick poets of the time, he tells us—" that for tragedie, [under which was included any doleful poem,] the Lord of Buckhurst and Maister Edward Ferrys, for such doings as I haue sene of theirs, do deserue the hyest price; th' Earle of Oxford and Maister Edwardes of her Majesties chappell for comedy and enterlude."

SINCE these papers have been committed to the press, a pamphlet has been put into my hands, in which we are told that " within these few days a deed has been discovered that will put *this matter beyond all question*, [namely, that Shakspeare was at the head of a company of actors in or before 1588,] and which will in *due time* be laid before the publick at large."[51] Can your lordship help smiling at this second

---

[51] *Comparative Review of the Opinions of Mr. James Boaden,* &c. p. 51, 8vo. 1796.

part of the Chattertonian fiction? Whenever the supporters of that fiction found
themselves hard pressed, they appealed to
the *Green* or *Yellow Roll* given by that extraordinary youth to Mr. Barrett. I make
no doubt this new deed will settle this point
completely, and that it is just *as authentick*
as those which I shall presently have
occasion to examine.

BEFORE I come to that which I have
reserved for the last and fatal objection
to the spurious composition before us, I
must just notice the minute annexed to it:
" Thys Letterre I didde receyve fromme mye
moste gracyouse Ladye Elizabeth," &c.
Here we have the modest and careless Shakspeare, who flung his writings to the world
unconscious of their excellence, and negligent of their fate, sedulously docketing his
papers with the punctilious exactness of a
merchant or attorney.

I MAY also observe, that it is remarkable
the poet should here take such care that this
gracious Epistle should be " kepte with all
care possyble," and yet should not have preserved the *pretty verses* that gave occasion to

o it.

it. We shall presently be informed that he
kept a copy of his letter to Lord Southampton; and why he should not have been as
careful of his poetry as of his prose, it will
not, I conceive, be very easy to assign an
adequate reason.—If these " pretty verses"
had been presented to her Majesty, she
assuredly would not " commit to Vulcan's
base keeping" a poetical encomium which
was more likely to immortalize her charms,
and to make them for ever bloom in song,
than all the flattery of all her courtiers.
How then came it to pass that they never
got abroad? that no Lady Willoughby
stole them from among her papers? that
none of our poet's brethren of the stage
should have got a copy of lines which had
brought such honour to one of their fellows?—It is much to be lamented that
these questions were not put in time; as
without doubt they would have induced the
unknown gentleman in the county of ———,
who possesses all these treasures, to have
made a more diligent search than has yet
been made for these encomiastick verses,
and very probably they might have been
found either between the leaves of one of
the

the twenty thousand volumes[52] of Shakspeare's library, which he is said to possess,
or in one of the smaller pockets of that
greene sloppd suyte of velvette, which, as
your Lordship will presently find, this poet
intended for Master Rice, the actor; but
the person in whom Shakspeare confided
having basely broken his trust, poor Rice
was defrauded of it, and it is yet, I am
told, in fine preservation, and as fresh as
when it was first made, lying in the unknown repository, in that great chest with
six locks, which contains all the rest of the
wardrobe belonging to Shakspeare and the
Globe Theatre.[53]

I HAVE

[52] Some have gone so far as to say that this library vies
with that of the celebrated Mr. Lackington, and consists
of one hundred thousand volumes;—but this must be a
mistake.

[53] Since I wrote the above, on my mentioning this subject
to a friend, he told me he had the good fortune to obtain a
copy of Shakspeare's PRETTY VERSES to the Queen,
which were given to him by a Gentleman who was intimately acquainted with the possessor of these treasures,
and had no doubt of their authenticity: though he could
not pretend to say whether they were to appear in the
second or third folio volume of these reliques, which have
been promised to the publick.—As to many persons these
lines will undoubtedly appear a great curiosity, I shall give

them

I HAVE but one word more to add on
the subject of the facts mentioned in this
epistle.

them a place here. It would not become me to say whether
they are entitled to the character given of them by our
maiden Queen.—*Valeant quantum valere possunt.*

" To Her HIGHNESS the QUEENES MAJESTIE, from the
lowest of her Servants, WILLIAM SHAKSPERE.

" QUEENE of my thoughts by daye, my dreame by
  night,
" My gracious Mistress still is in my sight.
" Her full perfections how shall I displaye ?
" No words the bright IDEA can pourtraye :
" To paint her right, would neede her own sweete lays ;
" None but ELIZA should ELIZA praise.—

  " By you selected from the mimick band,
" So grac'd, so honour'd, by your high command,
" Such was the gratitude that thrill'd my heart,
" My trembling fingers could not play their parte ;
" In vain my faithless lyre I try'd to sound,
" Mute were the strings and unresponsive found.—
" So when some lowly swain essayes to prove
" His humble duty and obsequious love,
" The practised accents in his throat are lost,
" And his best purpose by his virtue crost.—
" Lo, THE DUMB BARD ! the spangled courtier cries,
" And round me speechless, all St. James's flies ;
" Each titled dame deserts her rolls and tea,
" And all the Maids of Honour crye—Te ! He !—
" From the gay tittering throng dismay'd I fled,
" Nor knowe I where to hide my wretched head."

In the original there is a Note, mentioning that this unfortunate miscarriage happened to our poet at a *Breakfast*
given

epistle. Whence is it, that the Lord Chamberlain is introduced here as the person

given by the Queen to a select number of Courtiers of both sexes ; among whom were Lord and Lady Essex, Lord Southampton and the fair Mrs. Vernon, Sir Walter Ralegh, Lord and Lady Hunsdon, Mr. John Harrington, the fair Mistress Bridges, Sir Thomas Heneage, Sir Francis and Lady Knollys, Lord and Lady Howard, Lady Rich, Lord Mountjoy, the Lord Marquis, and many more.

If the simile—" So when a lowly swain," should be said to smell too strongly of one of our poet's plays, and to be faulty in another respect, as being little more than a comparison of a thing with itself, the answer, I suppose, would be, that Shakspeare, when he wrote these lines, had probably recently composed his MIDSUMMER'S NIGHT'S DREAM; and as to the other point, that Addison's celebrated simile of *the Angel* was equally faulty ; neither was the time of Elizabeth an age of such nicety of criticism as the present.

On my objecting to the word *idea* in the fourth line, my friend told me, he had himself made the same objection to the gentleman who had communicated these verses ; on which he said he had made a mistake, and that he had a *better copy* at home, without that word : but as I would not venture to alter any thing that even pretended to be the composition of our immortal bard, I have adhered to the first copy. My friend scrupled a little at the mention of *St. James's*, but there he was certainly in an error ; for Queen Elizabeth sometimes resided at that palace.—The last line but two, is more difficult to be got over; but those who may think these verses genuine, may *very consistently* maintain either that Shakspeare foresaw in this, as in many other instances which might be produced from the MIS-

CELLANEOUS

son through whom these verses reached her
Majesty? No doubt, because the writer

CELLANEOUS PAPERS, what would be written in the
eighteenth century, or, (which is full as probable,) that the
ingenious author of the Epistle to Sir William Chambers
had a peep some years ago at this curious relique in the
dark repository where it has been preserved, and stole from
it one of his best lines.

Other objections were made by my friend to the omission of the good chine and surloin and manchet of Queen
Elizabeth's days, and introducing our fragrant Chinese
beverage, with its proper accompaniment, in their room;
and also to the allusion to Balloons and the Earthquake at
Lisbon, in a subsequent part of these verses, which he had
heard, though he had not obtained a copy of them: but the
good Believer told him, that a Committee having been appointed to consider of these matters, (consisting of Messrs.
B, C, D, E, O, P, Q, and R,) these objections were
over-ruled, and unanimously voted of no weight whatsoever.

The Committee observed, in support of their opinion,
that plays having been formerly performed at the Globe
Theatre ten or twelve times every season by COMMAND of
Queen Elizabeth, as they are at present at our modern
theatres by Command of their Majesties, (which was clearly
proved by a deed that would very soon be *brought forward*,)
the covert allusion to this circumstance in the eighth line,
as well as our author's so happily introducing the terms
of his own profession in a subsequent couplet, (which his
Editors had pointed out as a frequent practice of his,)
stamped these verses with Shakspeare's own seal, and were
equal to a thousand witnesses.

conceived

conceived that this was the proper channel
at the present day :—but had Shakspeare
ever addressed his gracious mistress in
verse, Mr. Tylney the Master of the Revels, and Sir Thomas Heneage the Treasurer
of the Chamber, being the persons from
whom the actors of that time received the
royal mandates and the royal bounties, one
or other of those persons would unquestionably have been entreated to present this
tender of his duty to her Majesty.

4. My last topick is, I will not say the
dissimilitude, but the total and entire dissimilitude of every part of the hand-writing
of this letter (except the signature) from
Elizabeth's genuine hand-writing.—As the
name *Elizabeth* is an adumbration of her
hand-writing, (though a most imperfect
one,) and this forgery may be clearly proved
without deriving any aid from thence, I
might now immediately proceed to examine
the writing of the letter itself : but as I
have been informed that a deservedly eminent barrister, whose great practice makes
him peculiarly conversant with the laws of
evidence, has given some kind of sanction
to these spurious papers, I shall, for the sake
of

of my brethren of the bar, expend a little time on this supposed autograph ; that they may not be induced by so high an authority, on similar occasions, and in matters which to the generality of the world will appear of more importance than the question before us, ever to hazard an opinion without a minute comparison of the pretended and real originals.—In the name which has been exhibited as the hand-writing of the Queen, there are no less than six grofs errors. The firft is, that it is too small for the period to which it must be referred. Sir William Musgrave obligingly furnished me with five autographs of her Majesty, two written in the first, the rest in the fifth, tenth, and fifteenth years of her reign. I am myself possessed of one written in her twenty eighth year; and in the *fac-simile* plate, annexed, two others will be found. From these, and others which I have examined, it appears that her hand-writing gradually enlarged as she advanced in life; and that in the year 1587 or 1588, it was at least a fourth, perhaps a third, larger than her writing when she came to the throne. And though there may have been some slight variation in her hand-writing in the same or nearly the same period,

period, as there is between N°. II. and N°. III. on the *fac-simile* plate, (written at no great distance of time from each other,) yet even the smallest of these is considerably larger than what we are now examining.

The second error is, that the pretended autograph inclines sideways ;* whereas her genuine autographs are *bolt-upright*.

In the print-like hand which she adopted for her sign-manual, she contrived the intricate flourish which she always placed under the first letter, so as to supply the lower stroke, and to render the letter perfect and entire : but in her pretended autograph this not being done, we find an F instead of an E. This is the third deviation.

The fourth is in the letter a. In the early part of her reign she formed the direct stroke of that letter like other persons : but by degrees it became higher than the circular part : it never, however, reached to such a height as in the spurious autograph, nor was it ever open or looped at top : nor ever so disjoined as to appear, as it here does, like an *l*.

* See Plate I. N°. I.

P

In

In all her autographs the *b* is closed at bottom either by being so formed, or by the flourish under it. Here it is open at bottom; this is the fifth deviation : and the sixth is, that the R is not connected with the other letters by a line passing through the *b*.— Such is that *perfect* and *unquestionable* autograph, which satisfied such numerous examiners, many of whom are said to have declared that they had seen several autographs of Queen Elizabeth, and that they were as perfectly convinced of its genuineness, as they should have been if they had seen her Majesty write it.

It is manifest that the fabricator of these papers either was possessed of one of the many autographs of this Queen which are extant, or relied upon a *fac-simile* of it in a book which he was likely to examine for other purposes, (the Antiquarian Repertory,) though he has made so miserable and imperfect an imitation of his archetype ; but having no archetype whatfoever of her running or secretary hand, as it is called, he invented as .well as he could ; sometimes keeping that autograph in his eye, and sometimes deviating from it, just

6   as

as caprice dictated. The genuine and spurious Alphabet which is given in Plate I. will shew at once that he had never seen any of her ordinary hand-writing. When she was little more than sixteen years old, her Master, Ascham, highly praises her for her caligraphy;[54] and from that time to a very late period of her life, a fairer, a more

[54] " Si quid Græce Latineve scribat, manu ejus nihil pulchrius." Ascham. EPISTOL. lib. i. p. 21. edit. 1703.

" There are two original letters of hers [the Lady Elizabeth] yet remaining, (says Burnet,) writ to the Queen when she was with child of King Edward, the one in Italian, the other in English, both writ *in a fair hand, the same that she wrote all the rest of her life.* But the conceits in that writ in English are so pretty, that it will not be unacceptable to the reader, to see this first blossome of so great a princess, when she was not full four years of age: she being born in September 1533, and this writ in July 1537." HIST. OF THE REFORM, vol. i. p. 209.

Burnet subjoins the letter, and does not seem to have once reflected that it might be the composition of another person. It was, without doubt, dictated to her by her governess, or some other person near her. Did ever any child of four years old compose such a sentence as this?— " I much rejoice in your health, with the well liking of the country; with my humble thanks that your Grace wished me with you till I were weary of that countrey. Your highness were like to be combered, if I should not depart till I were weary being with you: *although it were in the worst soil in the world, your presence would make it pleasant.*"

beautiful

beautiful, or more uniform hand-writing than her's will not be found in any of the papers of that age. It very strongly resembles, as has been suggested to me, the very elegant hand-writing of the celebrated Dr. Dee, who occasionally addressed letters to her Majesty, which are still extant.

In Plate I., I have contrasted part of the spurious Letter which has been now examined, with two genuine specimens of Elizabeth's hand-writing. That marked N°. II. is the conclusion of a Letter addressed to the King of Scotland, and dated the 26th of April, 1584. It is among the Cotton MSS. in the British Museum; CALIGULA, C. ix. p. 107. No part of the letter but the conclusion and the signature, (" Your best wischinge Cousin and truely Affectionated Sistar, Elizabeth R.") is in her hand-writing. The other specimen, which, as well as the former, was pointed out to me by the Rev. Mr. Ayscough of the Museum, is still more valuable and curious; because it furnishes us with a trait of manners, and a proof of that condescending familiarity by which she won the hearts of her people. It is taken from an imperfect

paper,

paper, of which the address, whether superscribed or subjoined, is lost ; this fragment
being pasted on a leaf in one of the volumes
of the Cotton MSS. VESPASIAN, F. 3.
p. 13. b. It is highly probable, as Mr.
Planta of the Museum suggests to me, that
it was addressed to Sir Henry Wallop, one
of the ancestors of the present earl of
Portsmouth, and a very distinguished character in that age. At the time her Majesty
appears to have honoured him with this
testimony of her regard, he was Vice-trea-
surer and Treasurer at War in Ireland, and
one of the Lords Justices of that kingdom,
to which last high station he was advanced
on the sixth of the preceding September,
1582, on the recall of Spencer's patron, the
Lord Deputy Arthur Lord Grey. Sir Henry
coming to England in 1591, he was in that
year honoured with a royal visit at his seat
at Farley Wallop, where her Majesty and
her attendants were entertained for some
days. He afterwards returned to Ireland,
where he died April 14, 1599.

" Elizabeth R.

" TRUSTIE and right welbeloved, we
greet

greet you well. having had so long expe-
rient of yor good service done to us in that
place where you are, and nowe of late especially by yor carefull and diligent observation of the affaires not only of that realme
where you remaine as o^r Leiger, but of the
occurrents from other Contries, wch as matters
greatly importing o^r State here at home, and
lykewise ou^r affaires abroade with other
princes, you do alwaie both tymely and at
large advertise hither : we cannot but greatly
allowe and comend this yor faithful service,
and therfore for yor better encouragement
to hould on this course in the same we
thought it convenient by this o^r owne Ire
to signifie o^r good acceptation therof. We
may not likewise forgett to yeld you thankes
for sondrie presents you have heretofore sent
unto us, and namely for yor late newe yeares
gifte. Last of all, towching yor private sute
unto us, we will have the same in such good
remembrance as shall bee you shall hereafter see to yor comfort. Given under o^r
signett at o^r Mano^r of Richmond the xxiiijth
of February in the xxvth yere of o^r raigne
[1582-3]."

THERE being a void space at the top of
this

this paper, her Majesty, probably after she had affixed her sign-manual to it, was pleased with her own hand to write as follows :

" I thāke you good Harry for sōe other Services than Comen Comissiōs for wiche in skroile of other Memorielz I faile not to Locke in my best Memorye."[55]

IN comparing these genuine specimens of Elizabeth's hand-writing with the spurious trash on the same plate, (No. I.) copied faithfully from the late publication, no magnifying glasses or other aids are requisite : it is only necessary for any person, however unconversant with ancient manuscripts, to cast his eye on the *fac-similes* annexed, to be convinced that the pretended Letter of Queen Elizabeth to Shakspeare is a manifeſt and bungling forgery.[56]

ANOTHER

[55] See Plate I. N°. III.

[56] That he that runs may read, and that this forgery may be at once made evident even to those least conversant with such subjects, on the same plate is given an Alphabet taken from her spurious Epistle, exhibiting correctly such of the twenty-four letters as are there found ; contrasted with

ANOTHER specimen of this Queen's hand-writing, in the College of Heralds, has been lately pointed out to me, which, if I had known of it in time, should also have been given on the *fac-simile* plate. I shall however, for the sake of the ortho-graphy, insert here the few sentences of which it consists, which are written in the same elegant hand as all her other writing. They are subjoined to a letter addressed to the earl of Shrewsbury, (who had then Mary Queen of Scots in his cuftody,) dated at the " Castle of Windsor, the xxiith of October, 1572," to relieve him from the apprehension which he had entertained that her Majesty had suffered by the small-pox, from which disease Camden says she was then newly recovered :

" MY faithfull Shrewesbury let no grief touche your harte for feare of my disease for I Assure you if my Creadit wer not greatar than my shewe ther is no beholdar

with her genuine alphabet, copied from the two specimens N°. II. and III., except only the letters *p*, *q*, and *x*, for which the engraver was obliged to have recourse to another MS. in the Museum.

wold

wold beleve that ever I had bin touched
with suche a Maladye

Your faitheful loving

Soveraine

Elizabeth R [56]

HAVING lately met with two other short
Letters from this Queen to two ladies of her
court, I shall subjoin them, for the sake of
the spelling and phraseology :

[To LADY DRURY upon the death of
her husband.] [57]

" BEE well ware my Besse you strive
not with divine ordinaunce nor grudge at
irrimediable harmes leste you offend the

---

[56] From the original MS. in the Heralds-Office; SHREWS-
BURY PAPERS, (in several volumes) vol. i. p. 41. This,
and the letter accompanying it, have been printed by Mr.
Lodge.

[57] Nicholls's PROGRESSES of QUEEN ELIZABETH,
Vol. II. p. 36. F 2. b. Mr. Nicholls cannot recollect from
whence he copied this Letter, but believes he found it in
the Museum.

Sir William Drury, who had been Lord President of
Munster in 1575, was appointed Chief Governor of Ireland in April 1578, and died at Waterford in October,
1579. He was a great favourite of Queen Elizabeth, who
honoured him by standing God-mother to one of his children. I suppose the lady here addressed was his widow.

Q   highest

highest Lord and no whitte amend the
married hap   Heape not your harmes
where helpe ther is none, but since you
may not that you would wish that you can
enjoye with comforte, a king for his power
and a queene for her love, who loves
[leaves] [58] not now to protect you when your
case requires care and minds not to omitte
what ever may be best for you and yours.

Your most loving careful sovraigne

E. R."

[To Lady Paget.]

" A Memoriall. ∫ Elizabeth R.

" Cal to your mynde good Kate how
hardly we princes cā broke a crossing of our
comāndes How yreful wyl the hiest power
be may you be sure whā murmure shal be
made of his pleasing wyl. ∫ Let Nature
therfor not hurt your selfe but give place to
the Givur And thogh this lessō be frō a sely
vikar yet is hit sent frō a Lovinge Souve-
raine." [59]

In

[58] *Loves*, must, I think, have been an error of the original transcriber.

[59] Brit. Mus. MSS. Birch. 4160—23. Dr. Birch's
copy has this title : " Queen Eliz. to Lady Paget on the
death of her daughter Lady Crompton, mother to Lady
Lyttelton, wife of Sir Thomas Lyttelton. Orig at Hagley."

Lady

IN both these Letters, as well as in those to Sir Henry Sydney, Lord Shrewsbury, and Sir Henry Wallop, every reader must be struck by the quaintness of the expression, (the quaintness of the age,) tinctured with good sense, for which we look in vain in the pretended Letter to Shakspeare.

BEFORE I dismiss this epistle, I ought not to pass over without remark the manner in which this and the other pieces in this volume have been published, without the slightest notice of the water-mark on each paper. In the smaller pieces, at least, one might have expected that the example of the late Sir John Fenn in the curious publication of the Paston Letters, would have been followed, and that the several paper-marks in these reliques should have been given; whether the *tankard* of Master

Lady Lyttleton's mother, however, the wife of Sir Thomas Crompton of Driffield in Yorkshire, is said by Collins to have been Muriel, the daughter of David Carey, Esq. The daughter of Catharine Lady Paget (the wife of Henry Lord Paget who died in 1568,) was married to Sir Henry Lee, Knight.—I suspect this Letter was addressed to a Lady Carey.

Some deficiencies in Dr. Birch's transcript have been now supplied, and some errors corrected, from another and more accurate copy.

Richarde

Richarde *Jugge* the Stationer, or any other, might present itself to the prying view of the Antiquary. Of this, however, I shall have occasion to say more hereafter.

II. EXTRACTS FROM MISCELLANEOUS PAPERS.

III. A NOTE OF HAND, AND A RECEIPT.

THE four following pieces are so replete with absurdity and incongruity, that it is scarce worth while to examine them : but being very short, they will soon be dispatched. The first of them is as follows :

" Inne the yeare o Christ

[*hiatus valde deflendus*]

" FORRE oure Trouble inne goynge toe Playe before the Lorde Leycesterre ats house and oure greate Expenneces there-uponne 19 poundes.

RECEYVEDDE. ofs Grace the Summe o 50 Poundes.

W^m. Shakspeare."

As this is the first paper which is pretended to be in our poet's hand-writing, it is necessary to enter into a minute detail respecting the spelling of his name; Mr.

6   Steevens

Steevens and myself having most innocently led the fabricator of all these novelties into a lamentable error, which alone, without any other consideration, would prove beyond a doubt the forgery of the whole heterogeneous mass.

In the year 1776 Mr. Steevens, in my presence, traced with the utmost accuracy the three signatures affixed by the poet to his Will. While two of these [N°. xi. and xii. in Plate II.] manifestly appeared to us *Shakspere*, we conceived that in the third [N°. xiii.] there was a variation; and that in the second syllable an *a* was found. Accordingly we have constantly so exhibited the poet's name ever since that time. It ought certainly to have struck us as a very extraordinary circumstance, that a man should write his name twice one way, and once another, on the same paper: however it did not; and I had no suspicion of our mistake, till, about three years ago, I received a very sensible letter from an anonymous correspondent, [60] who shewed me very clearly

[60] At the same time that I return my thanks to this correspondent, (to whom I wish to be personally known,) I beg

clearly that, though there was a superfluous
stroke when the poet came to write the letter
r in his last signature,* probably from the
tremor of his hand, there was no *a* discover-
able in that syllable ; and that this name, like
both the other, was written *Shakspere.* Re-
volving this matter in my mind, it occurred
to me that in the new *fac-simile* of his name
which I gave in 1790, my engraver had made
a mistake in placing an *a* over the name

which was there exhibited $\boxed{Shakspe^a}$, and

that what was supposed to be that letter
was only a mark of abbreviation, with a
turn or curl at the first part of it, which
gave it the appearance of a letter. I resolved therefore once more to examine the
original, before I published any future
edition of his works ; and (it being very

beg leave to inform him, that I had myself corrected the
error into which I had fallen relative to Shakspeare's
second daughter Judith Queeny, [PLAYS AND POEMS OF
WILLIAM SHAKSPEARE, Vol. I. P. I. p. 175, n. 3.] and
on the very ground he mentions ; as he will find by turning to Vol. I. P. II. p. 158. She was, without doubt,
married to Thomas Queeny with her father's *knowledge,*
though probably without his *approbation.*

* See Plate II. N°. xiii.

material

material in the present inquiry) to take this opportunity of ascertaining my own error, if any error there was.

On the 10th of March 1612-13, Shakspeare purchased from one Henry Walker a small estate in Blackfriars, for one hundred and forty pounds, eighty of which he appears to have paid down; and he mortgaged the premises for the remainder. In the year 1768 the mortgage-deed, which was dated the 11th of March, but without doubt executed on the same day as the deed of bargain and sale, (like our modern conveyance of Lease and Release,) was found by Mr. Albany Wallis, among the title-deeds of the Rev. Mr. Fetherstonhaugh of Oxted in the county of Surrey, and was presented by him to the late Mr. Garrick. From that deed the *fac-simile* above mentioned was made. As I have not the pleasure of being acquainted with Mrs. Garrick, to whom I was indebted on that occasion, Lord Orford, (since I began this Letter,) very obligingly requested her to furnish me once more with the deed to which our poet's autograph is affixed: but that lady, after a very careful search, was

not

not able to find it, it having by some means or other been either mislaid or stolen from her. On the same day on which I received this account, I called upon Mr. Wallis, with whom I am acquainted, and to whom the deeds of Mr. Fetherston-haugh, after having been a long time out of his hands, have been lately restored. among them he luckily met with the counterpart of the original deed of bargain and sale, made on the 10th of March 1612-13, which furnished me with our poet's name, and fully confirmed my conjecture; for there the mark of abbreviation appears at top nearly such as I expected I should find it in Mrs. Garrick's deed, and the poet having had room to write an *r*, though on the very edge of the label, his own orthography of his name is ascertained, beyond a possibility of doubt, to have been SHAK-SPERE. Mr. Wallis having obligingly permitted me to make use of this new autograph of our poet, (which has the additional advantage of having his christian name at length,) a *fac-simile* of it will be found in Plate II. Nº. x. Notwithstanding this authority, I shall still continue to write our poet's name SHAKSPEARE, for reasons
which

which I have assigned in his Life. But whether in doing so I am right or wrong, it is manifest that he wrote it himself SHAKSPERE; and therefore if any original Letter or other MS. of his shall ever be discovered, his name will appear in that form. The necessary consequence is, that these papers, in which a different orthography is almost uniformly found, cannot but be a forgery.

YOUR Lordship sees, that if Mr. Steevens and I had maliciously intended to lay a trap for this fabricator to fall into, we could not have done the business more adroitly. But you will readily acquit us of any such intention.—This, however, was not the only errour into which he has been led. When I had resolved to give, in my edition, our poet's name on the *fac-simile* plate, at length, (to shew how it would have appeared had it been so written, and on paper, instead of parchment,) the Engraver desired me to furnish him with an archetype for one of the concluding letters ; the letter *r*. Inadvertently I took down a MS. of the time, which happened to be near at hand, and pointed out to him a German *r*, (much

R   used

used by Scriveners in the time of Elizabeth
and James,) for which, the printing-house
not being furnished with such a type, I
must refer you to Plate II. where it is
placed close to Nº. x. with a view to the
present reference. The correspondent above-
mentioned very justly observed, that I was
here also inaccurate ; for Shakspeare having
thrice in his Will used a different kind of *r*,
(such as is frequently used at this day,) and
no other specimens of his hand-writing,
containing that letter, being then extant,
there was no ground for supposing that he
had ever employed the German *r*.—Our
fabricator, however, has here also followed
me implicitly ; and as he conceived that the
poet had in his Will written his name twice
Shakspere, and once *Shakspeare*, he resolved
to supply us with equal variations : in his
modern-antique papers therefore we have
the name exhibited in both ways ; and that
no kind of variety might be wanting, we
have one pretended signature with the
chancery-hand *r*,[61] another with this same
German *r*,[62] of which I have been obliged

[61] See the pretended Letter " to Masterre Richard
Cowley," in MISCELLANEOUS PAPERS, &c.
[62] See the pretended Letter to Lord Southampton, Pl. II.
Nº. ix.

to

to give so long a history, and one without
any *r* at all. [63] This canine letter, indeed,
seems to have particularly engaged his attention, and to have been particularly fatal
to him ; for finding in the Paston Letters,
and in Forbes's Collections, (to both of
which, if I mistake not, he has been indebted,) that some persons in ancient times
used what is called the Chancery-hand *r*, [64]
he thought it would give an antique air to
these wonderful discoveries : and therefore
in almost all Shakspeare's pretended writing,
and in one of his autographs, he has made
him employ a letter which is intended to
represent this kind of *r*, but is no more like
it than the first letter of the alphabet is to the
last. [65] The use of this letter was entirely dis-
continued

[63] See the Signature to the " Tributary Lines to Ireland." MISCELLANEOUS PAPERS, p. 50, counting from
the first ; for the book is not paged.

[64] See it in Plate II. N°. X. next to the German *r* already
mentioned.

[65] The reader is desired to cast his eye on the word *Leycesterre* in N°. VII. Plate II. and also a little below on the
true Chancery-hand (*r*), near the edge of the plate under
N°. X. But why, it will be said, could he not imitate this
letter exactly ? Why should he give what looks more like
a *g* than an *r* ? I suppose to elevate and surprise.—Of this,

however,

continued in current writing long before the time of James the First, except in enrolments of deeds, and other legal instruments ; now and then indeed, but very rarely, a signature may be found in which it occurs : but in the ordinary or secretary hand I have never met with it.—These circumstances, alone, therefore, without further examination, would ascertain every one of the papers that have been attributed to our poet, to be forged.

IN copying his *name*, the fabricator had for his direction the autographs with which we have furnished him, and therefore it is not at all surprising that here there should be some little resemblance to the archetypes before him ; though even here the imitation,

however, more will be said hereafter.—He had seen in the *fac-simile* of the Letter of Elizabeth of York to Sir John Paston, this *r* formed very rudely, and probably thought that a good archetype. However, he has gone beyond his original, by giving an open tail to this letter, of which he would find it difficult to produce a single precedent. For the sake of joining it to an *e* or some other letter, they used sometimes to run a stroke from about the middle of the *r* to the next letter; but it was never made as it is here, like a *j* or *g*.—But of these *minutiæ* perhaps too much.

partly

partly from inability and partly from caprice, is bungling and incorrect enough: [66] but to all the other writing attributed to our poet many other objections lie, beside those already made. It is manifest that when in health he wrote a small hand, as was the general mode of that time, at least among authors and actors,[67] and that his writing was neat and uniform; none of which characters belong to the forged scrawls that have been ascribed to him.

[66] It is observable that our poet before he began to form the *W* in his christian name, made a kind of prelude or flourish (See Plate II. N°. X. and XII.): this our fabricator observing, resolved that he would not omit so characteristick a singularity; but in doing it, in order to be quite sure of producing a proper effect, he has made in fact *two W's*. See Pl. II. N°. viii.

[67] See Plate II.—Authors probably adopted a very small hand, for the sake of sparing paper, and compressing a great deal of matter in a little space. Sir William Dugdale, Anthony Wood, and many others in the last age, wrote so extremely small, that their Manuscripts are to a weak sight very difficult to read.—In their signatures our Ancestors, in the age of Elizabeth and James, followed two modes very different; writing either the very small hand now mentioned, (see the signatures of Massinger and Chapman in Plate II.) or a large fair Italian hand, (See the signatures of Nat. Field, Hathwaye the poet, and Lord Leycester, ibid. :) and this latter was the more common among the nobility.

BUT

But it is time to return to his Account
of Lord Leycester's great bounty to him,
for playing before him, which we are told
was no less than " the summe o 50 Poundes."

In this paper, as in all the rest, we have
the spelling of no time. The corner of the
paper is very dextrously wanting, so as
to deprive us of the date, after the word
Christ: devoured, we may suppose, by
mice in that dark repository from whence it
came. It is, however, ascertained to have
been prior to September, 1588. As her
Majesty knew not how to spell the name of
her favourite Leycester, one might forgive
Shakspeare for writing his name in a manner in which neither that nobleman nor
others in that age wrote it, if the poet had
not lived within fourteen miles of Kenelworth Castle from his infancy, and from
his early years been acquainted with the
troop of actors who served Lord Leycester.
But these are but trifling objections to the
manner in which the sums are here specified, I mean in Arabick numerals; a mode
which those who have the slightest knowledge of former times know not to have been
the practice of that age. If any exceptions
can

can be produced, (which I much doubt) they
will but confirm the general rule. In several
hundred Accounts of that age which I have
perused, the sums mentioned are marked
by Roman numerals. [68] The sum therefore
here stated, should have been written xix^{li}.
Thus, in " the Accompte of John Gibbes,
one of the Chamberlains of Stratford-upon-
Avon from the fowerth day of october 1589,

[68] In the Collection of Ordinances and Regulations for
the Government of the Royal Housholds, printed by the
Society of Antiquaries in 1790, we find under the head of
" The Annual Expences of Queen Elizabeth" all the sums
specified in Arabick numerals. But this paper was copied
from the DESIDERATA CURIOSA of Mr. Peck, who
printed from a MS. in his possession. I have not the
smallest doubt that he adopted this mode as least troublesome, and that his original, like all the accounts of that age
which I have seen, had Roman numerals.

In confirmation of my opinion I may observe, that in
the same volume of ORDINANCES are given the Establishments of Henry Prince of Wales in 1610, and
various other Royal Houshold Establishments, from MS.
Harl. N°. 642, and all the sums are printed by the editor
in Arabick figures: but on examining the MS. itself, I
find the sums are there all specified in Roman numerals:
as is the case in every money-account of that age that I
have seen. At the head of different sections of Establishments, they used Arabick figures, 1, 2, &c. so also in
expressing the year of our Lord: but not in sums —The
modern fashion of printing has been adopted merely to save
trouble. 7l. 8s. 4d. is much shorter than vii *li*. viii *s*. iiij *d*.

I   to

to St. Thomas thapostle in the same yeare,"
(in the Archives of Stratford,) I find at the
bottom of the first page, " Some vii.[lb] 11s.
vd. ob. ; at the foot of the second,—
" Some xiiij.[lb] vs. ; and subjoined to the
third,—" Some xx.[lb] vs. viiid."—I will
not trouble you with any more instances:
almost every book of that age in which any
accounts are given, will prove that this was
the ordinary practice of the age of Elizabeth.
Even when the sums specified were very
large, they still adhered to this tedious and
troublesome mode. Thus, in a MS. receipt now before me, dated the xii[th]. of
November 1586, the sum which in the body
of the paper is stated to be " the som of
two thowsande two hundrethe threeskore
and seven powndes, nyne shyllings, sixe
pence sterlinge," is in the margin expressed
thus : " M[li]. M[li]. ccLxvij[l]. ix[s]. vid."

IN the HISTORY OF THE STAGE I
ascertained the payment of a play at Court,
when the actors were called upon to go into
the country to perform at any of the royal
palaces, to have been, in the time of Charles
the First, twenty pounds ; and I conjectured
that the same sum was probably paid by
Elizabeth.

Elizabeth. But I have since found from authentick documents that this was not the fact ; and that in her time the sum paid for each representation at Court was no more than ten pounds. My error, however, in this instance was the foundation of the sum here charged to Lord Leycester in Arabick numerals (19 poundes) : and, to mend the matter, that nobleman in his great liberality is made to pay thirty-one pounds more for his entertainment than was charged to him, and to exceed her Majesty's bounty on similar occasions in no less a sum than forty pounds. Whether Shakspeare and his troop were Lord Leycester's servants, or, if they were not his servants, how they came to be preferred to that company which were immediately under his patronage, very prudently has not been told.

To add to all the other denotations of forgery in this paper, our incomparable poet is represented as so grossly ignorant as not to know an earl's proper title. It is scarcely necessary to observe, (the fact having been of late so particularly noticed,) [69] that the

69 PLAYS and POEMS of WILLIAM SHAKSPEARE, 1790, vol. x. p. 3. n. 2.

most

most common address to peers under the
degree of a Duke, was in that age *your
honour*. His *grace* (here applied to Leycester) was then, as it is now, appropriated to
dukes, and at an earlier period was given
even to the person on the throne. Henry
the Eighth is mentioned in some of the
statutes of his reign by the appellation of
" the king's *Grace*." This title was also
occasionally given to Elizabeth. Nor was
our author ignorant of this circumstance :
of what indeed was he ignorant ? In the
First Part of HENRY THE FOURTH, in
the scene where Falstaff and the Prince
amuse themselves by alternately represent-
ing the King, " I would," (says Falstaff,
in the person of the Prince, and addressing
Henry as King) " your *Grace* would take
me with you : What means your *Grace ?*"—
The same title we find also given to the
princes and princesses of the blood.[7a]

THAT in our poet's time, as well as at

[7o] So in Sir Thomas Pope's Letter from Hatfield to the
President of his newly founded College, dated the 22d of
August, 1556 :—" and at my lady Elizabeth her *Grace*
desier, and at my wiffes request, they were receyved into the
house again." Warton's LIFE of Sir THOMAS POPE,
2d edit. p. 88.

present,

present, your *grace* was the proper and usual
mode of address to dukes, might be proved
by innumerable instances. I shall only give
one from Shakspeare himself. In the very
first scene of the first act of HENRY THE
EIGHTH, the Dukes of Norfolk and Buckingham are introduced meeting each other :

BUCK. Good-morrow, and well met. How have
    you done,
Since last we saw in France ?

NOR. I thank your *Grace :*
Healthful, &c.

Our next curious relique is this :

" FORRE our greate trouble inne getting
alle inne orderre forre the lord Leycesterres
comynge ande oure moneys layde oute
there upponne 59 shyllinges.

" Receyved o Masterre Hemynge forre
thatte Nyghte 3 Poundes.

" Masterre Lowine 2 shyllynges moure
forre his Good Servyces ande welle playinge."

W^m. S.

ON this nonsensical and unintelligible
trash I will not detain you long. All the
observations already made on the orthogra-

phy,

phy, and the Arabick numerals, apply to the words *forre*, *alle*, *inne*, *moure*, &c. here found, and to the sums here specified. Where my lord Leycester was to come, who at this time was principal and who subordinate, some one better versed in de-cyphering nonsense than I am, must deter-mine. Concerning " Master Lowin," I shall have occasion hereafter to speak more particularly. At present it is only necessary to observe that he was born in the year 1576, as appears from the inscription on his portrait in the Ashmolean Museum at Ox-ford [71] (given, I believe, with many other portraits by Mr. John Aubrey): so that allowing to this paper the latest date it can bear, that of 1588, when he was rewarded for these " his good servyces ande welle playinge," he was just *twelve* years old.

He might, however, without doubt we shall be told, perform the part of Arthur in King John, or the Duke of York in King Richard III. But there is good ground for believing that those plays were not

[71] From this portrait an Engraving was made, which was given in the edition of Shakspeare, 1790.

written

written till about eight years afterwards.
" Well then, he might have acted the part
of a young prince, or of a young woman in
some other play."—Undoubtedly he might,
had he been then on the stage, or had he
been in the early part of his life in the same
company with Shakspeare, Heminges, and
Burbadge; but unluckily, (as I shall shew
presently,) he does not appear to have joined
their troop till after the Accession of King
James.

THE two following papers relate to money, which Shakspeare *promises to pay* to
John Heminges, for so his name should be
written.

" ONE Moneth from the date hereof I doe
promyse to paye to my good and Worthye
Freynd John Hemynge the sume of *five
Pounds and five shillings* English Monye as
a recompense for hys greate trouble in
settling and doinge much for me at the
Globe Theatre as also for hys trouble in
going downe for me to statford *Witness my
Hand*   Wm Shakspere.
    *September
    the Nynth* 1589.
                              " RE-

" RECEIVED of Master Wm Shakspeare the sum of five Pounds and five Shillings good English Money thys Nynth Day of October 1589.

Jn° Hemynge."

HERE we find, I think for the first and last time, the poet's name spelt in his own genuine manner; yet even that circumstance will not give any authenticity to this paper.—We have here fortunately a date, which beside the other uses it may serve, may prevent your lordship from supposing that you are reading some tradesman's promissory note of the year 1796. — It is observable that the old spelling, some of which is of no age, is here almost entirely deserted, and the orthography of about Charles the Second's time adopted. We have no *poundes*, no *shyllynges*, no *Masterre*, no *moure*, &c. But then on the other hand we have several very striking novelties. The first is our bard's *new* hand-writing, which you will perceive, if you look on the *fac-simile*, is as different from what we had before, as both are from the poet's true hand-writing. But what is most worthy of remark is, that Shakspeare, having been,

we

we are to suppose, some eight or ten years
in London, and now at the head of an established company of comedians, has quite
forgot the name of his native town, for
which he writes *Statford* (for the letter *r* is
still to be a stumbling-block). Need I call
your attention to the sum of five guineas,
here in fact, though not in words, promised
to be paid? Some persons have sagaciously
remarked, in defence of this paper, that in
old accounts such sums as five pounds and
five shillings sometimes occur.[72] Who ever
maintained

[72] Since this was written, as a *decisive proof* of this fact, the
following extract from the Royal Houshold Establishments,
4to. 1790, has been produced. (*Comparative Review,* &c.
ut supr. p. 55.)

	£.	S.	D.
" P. 255.—Joyners fee - -	19.	19.	0.
Record - - -	16.	16.	8."

How this last sum, which I cannot find in the page
mentioned, illustrates the question, I am unable to discover. I wonder the writer did not also give us such sums
as—20l. 4s. 6d.—30l. 16. 4d. &c.—The sums required
are those which *exactly* represent a certain number of
guineas of the present day; of which without doubt in the
infinite combinations of sums entered on ancient rolls,
instances may be found, without in the smallest degree
diminishing the suspicion that the sum specified in Shakspeare's *Promissory Note* naturally suggests.

The sums above stated, and all others in that paper, which
is an Account of Q. Elizabeth's Annual Expences Civil and
Military

maintained that in the infinite combinations
which sums are capable of, such payments
may not occasionally have been made as five
pounds and five shillings, or one pound and
one shilling ?—Yet even in these instances
the usual mode of ancient times was,
to write—xxi shillings; or cv shillings.
But the question is not, whether some very
rare instances of the kind above-mentioned
do not occur : though twenty such should
be pointed out, this circumstance in the
paper before us, when *accompanied with
many other suspicious circumstances*, must have
weight, because it is highly probable that so
very ignorant a person as the fabricator of it
might have thought that pieces of the same
precise value as our guinea then subsisted.

THE word *recompence*, though it was in
use at that time, would not have been the
word employed here, but *reward*; and
settling [73] for adjusting is equally suspicious;

Military about the year 1578, should have been printed in
Roman Numerals, which are found in all the accounts of
that age. (See n. 68.) The other mode has been adopted
in modern publications merely to save trouble.

[73] " In Minsheu we have only—" To settle, set or sit
down. - - - Lat. *residere.*"

more

more especially as the great trouble taken by
John Heminges " in settling and doing much
for Shakspeare," was at the GLOBE Theatre,
which I have shewn was not built for
some years after 1589. But we want no aid
from these minute observations. The whole
is an evident forgery : and the Receipt
signed with the name of John Hemynge was
manifestly done by the same person who
has attempted to exhibit the hand-writing of
Lord Southampton.[74]

WHEN I first looked on the *fac-simile* intended to represent Heminges' hand-writing,
though I was not then possessed of his autograph, it was manifest from the unsteadi-
ness and irregularity of the strokes, that it
could not be the genuine hand-writing of
any one. Dr. Johnson, as some others do,
inclined all his letters towards the left, as
the hand-writing of most persons on the
contrary inclines to the right : but no hand-
writing was ever yet found, except that of a
drunkard or a madman, that inclined alter-

[74] See Plate II. N°. iv. (Superscription of the pretended
Letter of Southampton,) and N°. v. (John Heminges' Receipt,) which I have placed together, to shew that these two
were the performances of the same hand.

T   nately

nately each way, as that now before us does. I determined, however, in every part of the present inquiry, not to rely on any general reasoning, but, whenever I could, to get at facts : and therefore spent some time at the Prerogative-Office with the hope of finding the original Will of this Actor. Unluckily that which is preserved in the Office as an original, though it has both the *Probat* and what is called the *Jurat*, is not an original ; having neither the testator's name nor that of the witnesses. By the means however of a deed executed by John Heminges, Feb. 10th, 1617–18, in performance of a trust reposed in him by Shakspeare, with which I have been furnished by Mr. Albany Wallis, and which will be found in the Appendix, (N°. III.) I have obtained his Autograph, which is given in Plate II. N°. vi. It proved, as I expected it would, to have no more resemblance to the signature subscribed to this forged receipt, than Hebrew or Chinse characters have to English.

In the spelling of this actor's name, as in that of Shakspeare, I have led the fabricator into another error. It was a very frequent practice in the last age to add a
final

final *s* to proper names ;[75] which, though at first a mere corruption, in process of time became so inveterate that the true name was lost. Thus, our author's friend, John *Combe*, was more frequently called John-a-*Combes*; Lord Clarendon always calls Bishop *Earle*, Earle*s*; and the great Bacon is in the modern editions of his printed Works called St. *Albans*, as was his successor in the title, Henry Jermyn, though both he and Jermyn always wrote *St. Alban*.[76] The corruption of the name of Heminge, [*Heminges*] (for so it appeared to me, and I accordingly always printed it Heminge,) was, we find, adopted by himself, and accordingly in this his genuine autograph it is written *Heminges*, as it is also in the margin of that Will which is preserved in the Prerogative-Office as an original. Our forger, however, has given us *Hemynge*.

ON examining the Register of the parish

<hr>

[75] See POEMS and PLAYS of WILLIAM SHAKSPEARE, 1790, Vol. I. Part ii. p. 177, n. 1.

[76] See his Signature subscribed to his Confession, presented to the House of Lords in 1621. PARL. HIST. Vol. V. p. 415.—The autograph of Henry Jermyn, Earl of St. Alban, I have seen.

of

of Aldermanbury, since I began this Letter, I found an entry of this actor's marriage, which had escaped me on a former search. He was married on the xth of March 1587–8, to Rebecca Nuell, Widow.—It was certainly a great mark of his friendship to our poet to leave his bride in the following year, to go down to this *terra incognita*, STATFORD: but how far the lady may have relished such a desertion, I have no means of ascertaining.

I have already noticed the form of this promissory note, which is so completely modern, that the doubters concerning the mistake of five pounds five shillings might, methinks, give the forger credit for that absurdity, when they see such plain marks of fraud and folly in every other part of the paper. I run no rifk, when I assert that no such form of promissory note existed at that time, because luckily I am able, from an old theatrical register, to give the forms then actually used in bills of debt, (the promissory note of that time,) payable both on demand, and one month after date; which I beg leave to recommend as precedents to all persons who may hereafter have occasion to *make* old MSS.   M. [*Mem^m*]

[141]

M. [*Mem^m*] That I Gabrell spencer the 5 of apell. have borowed of phillippe henslo the some of thirtie shellynges in Redy money to be payed unto hime agayne *when he shalle demande yt.* I saye borowed—xxx^s· Gabriell Spencer."[77]

THE above, we see, is the true promissory note on demand, of that time. The following is a Note or bill of debt payable one month after date, signed by an actor, who at one period performed in our author's company:

" THE 1 and twentie daye of septtember a thousand six houndard borrowed of Mr. Henshlowe in Redie monie the som of fortie shellings to be paid the twentie daie of october next folleinge the date her of *in witnes her of I set to my hand.*
John Duke.[78]

ANOTHER form was,—" Received 30 die Januarii 1598, of — the sum of — to

---

[77] A player; one of the Lord Admiral's Servants.
[78] Henslowe's Register, MS.—From this autograph the fac-simile in Pl. II. N°. xv. has been made. The note, as well as the signature, is in the handwriting of John Duke, who was at this time one of Lord Worcester's Servants.

be

bee repayed unto him or his assignes upon
the last of February next ensuinge, for payment whereof I bind me, my heires, executors and administrators."—But none of these,
whether entered in the book of the lender,
or written on separate slips of paper, were
indorsable over, nor could an action at law
be maintained on them.[79]

IV. A Letter from Shakspeare to Anna Hatherrewaye.

But now I ought in due form to invoke
Venus, and her son, and all the Loves and
Graces, to listen to my tale; for lo! I am
next to present you with a letter from the
Stratford youth to the lady whom he after-

[79] Being fully convinced, on general recollection, that no
such Promissory Notes as that which has been here
examined, were in use in the time of Shakspeare, and
having produced examples of the kind of unnegotiable
paper-security, or bills unsealed, then given for money due,
I did not think it neceſſary to turn over my law-books, or
to go deeper into the subject : but some very judicious
observations, communicated by a friend, furnish so clear
and satisfactory a history of the origin and gradual exten-
sion of Bills Ob'igatory, of which our present Promissory Notes are the genuine offspring, that my readers, I
am confident, will be pleased with their insertion. Being
too long for this place, they will be found in the Appendix, No. I.

wards

wards married. Though love, like death,
levels all distinctions, yet as that passion,
which the poet tells us first invented verse,
certainly exalts the mind as well as improves
the heart, and makes almost every man eloquent, what may we not expect from the tender effusions of such a soul as Shakspeare's
in such a situation!—Prepare then, my
lord, to behold our bard in circumstances in
which he has never before been viewed.

THIS precious letter is accompanied with
a lock of the poet's hair, " too intrinse to
unloose" and most curiously braided, [80] in
speaking of which he assures his DEAR-

[80] To the following lines in our author's beautiful poem
entitled The LOVER's COMPLAINT, (edit. 1790.) we
are, without doubt, indebted for this *braided lock :*

" Look here, what tributes wounded fancies fent me
" Of paled pearls, and rubies red as blood :
" And lo! behold these talents of their *hair*
" With twisted metal *amourously impleach'd,*
" I have receiv'd from many a several fair," &c.

A person who viewed this lock of hair, observed that it
has a wonderful property belonging to it, of retaining the
same *close* and *compact* appearance which it had when originally discovered, though since that time it is said to have
furnished materials to ornament several rings, decorated
with proper inscriptions in honour of our immortal bard.

ESSTE ANNA, that " no rude hande hathe
knottedde itte, thye Willys alone hathe done
the worke. Neytherre the gyldedde bawble
thatte envyronnes the heade of Majestye noe
norre honourres moste weyghtye wulde
give mee halfe the joye as didde thysse
mye lyttle worke forre thee. The feelinge
thatte dydde neareste approache untoe itte
was thatte whiche commethe nygheste
untoe God meeke and Gentle Charytye."—
I shall not at present trouble you with any
more of this soft epistle than what I have now
transcribed. At the bottom of the page
we find, ANNA HATHERREWAYE, which
is meant for the superscription, the poet foreseeing that two centuries afterwards it would
become the fashionable mode to discard the
superfluous *To* or *For*, with which fuch ad-
dresses were formerly introduced. But
how far the lady here meant was entitled
to this address, or how probable it was that
this letter should ever reach her hands, may
be worth our inquiry. The truth is, she
had no title whatsoever to either of those
names: she was christened plain Anne, and
her name was not HATHERREWAYE,
as fhe is here absurdly called, but HATH-
AWAY.

YOUR

YOUR lordship well remembers the first rise of the yet prevailing passion for long and sonorous christian names, instead of the more familiar appellations with which our simpler ancestors were contented. The Lady Elizas, Lady Matildas, and Lady Lousas, have now gained a complete ascendency, and a Lady Betty or Lady Fanny is no where to be found. Lady Betty Germaine was, I believe, the last in this country ; and you have, I think, still in Ireland, one Lady Betty, of the noble house of Cavendish, who keeps up the memory of the *olden* time. But to talk of ANNA *Hatherrewaye* in 1582, is truly ridiculous. Master Slender, and " sweet ANNE Page, might have taught the fabricator better. In the Indexes of the Prerogative Office, in which the entries are made in Latin, and in some old Parish Registers, where the entries have been made by clergymen in the same language, we find ANNAS and MARIAS enough; and so also in some of our oldest poets, in imitation of the Cynthia and Delia of Propertius and Tibullus, and in order to give a dignity to their verse : but in plain prose the most diligent researcher will, I am confident, not discover a single Anna in the sixteenth cen-

U tury.

tury. The name of the father of this
lady, here absurdly called *Hatherrewaye*,
was, as Mr. Rowe long since mentioned,
Hathaway; and the tradition which he
received from Stratford upon this subject,
is confirmed by the Will of Lady Barnard
our poet's grand-daughter, which I discovered and published some years ago;
and by a deed executed by her, in my possession. She in her Will expressly notices
several of her relations of the name of
Hathaway. As to the true orthography of
both the christian and surname of the person to whom this letter is pretended to be
addressed, we need only consult the Register of Stratford, where the following entry
occurs under the head of Marriages in
1579-80. " Jan. 17. William Wilson
to ANNE HATHAWAY of Shotterye." I
once thought it not improbable that the lady
whose marriage is here recorded, afterwards
became the wife of our poet; but that could
not have been the case for a reason which
I have assigned in his Life. However it
sufficiently establishes the forgery before
us. [81]

I CANNOT

[81] I suppose it will be asked, why could not the fabricator

I CANNOT dismiss the first two words of this Epistle without observing that *dear* and *dearest* was not so common an address at that period as at present. Had the fabricator of this letter given us—" My *sweet* Anne," it might have passed well enough. Thus, Sir John Harrington begins his Letter to his lady, dated Dec. 27, 1602, with the words —" *Sweet Mall,*" for which, if the maker of these MSS. had invented an epistle for that Knight, we undoubtedly should have had—*My dearest Maria.*

THOUGH, after what has been now stated, it may seem superfluous to animadvert fur-

tor as well have written this name *Hathaway* as *Hatherrewaye?* To these and other questions of a similar kind it is by no means necessary to give any answer. He *has* written it falsely : Shakspeare could not have written it so ; and the consequence necessarily follows, that the paper is forged.——If, however, it were necessary to assign a reason for this misnomer, it would not be very difficult. It might have arisen from caprice, and a foolish notion that this sort of variation in this and other instances would give an air of truth to these papers : or it might have arisen from mere ignorance, and the vulgar or inaccurate pronunciation of one person dictating to another. But speculations of this kind are endless, and in the present case wholly unnecessary. Whatever the cause or motive may have been, the forgery is proved by the *fact*.

ther

ther on this spurious paper, I muſt not omit
to observe that the word *themselves* is here
(as in other places), contrary to the practice
of that age, spelt as one word inſtead of
two [thenne indeede shalle Kynges *themme-
selves* bowe ande paye homage toe itte]:
nor can I dismiss it without particularly
noticing the other sentence which I have
transcribed from it.

WHENEVER hereafter any light shall be
given that may lead to a discovery of the
now unknown hand that has dared to fabri-
cate this tissue of imposture, the vulgarisms,
and the sentiments found in it, may be worth
attending to, as they may aid the detection.
Thus, from the present contemptuous mention of KINGS, it is no very wild conjecture
to suppose that the unknown writer is not
extremely adverse to those modern republican zealots who have for some time past
employed their feeble, but unwearied, endea-
vours to diminish that love and veneration
which every true Briton feels, and I trust
will ever feel, for ROYALTY, so happily
and beneficially inwoven in our inestimable
constitution. Such, however, was his ignorance of the period to which the Letter
before

before us must be referred, that, for the sake of the sentiment, the contemptuous language of the present day is introduced at a time when it was as little known, as the orthography and phraseology which the writer has employed.

OUR author was married to Anne Hathaway in or before September, 1582. We will suppose this love-letter to have been written a few months before, in the April or May of that year, at which time he was just eighteen years old. Of the Queen, who had then sat on the throne above twenty-three years, it is not necessary here to give any minute delineation. However the splendour of her character may have been a little abated by the lapse of time, the inquisition that has been made into the history of that age, and the more definite notions of the prerogatives of the crown and the rights of the people now entertained and happily established, it is certain that her virtues gave her an unbounded ascendant over her subjects ; and though few of our princes have exercised a more arbitrary dominion, the boundaries of our admirable constitution not being then, as at present, nicely

nicely ascertained, she unquestionably was
not in that age thought to infringe the
liberties of the people. No stronger proof
of this can be produced than her great popularity. Every act of her reign appearing to
spring from a regard to the welfare and
happiness of her subjects, imperious as she
was in many instances, she was almost
idolized by them. At once dignified and
familiar, respected and beloved, she almost
every year of her reign made a Progress
among them, and won their hearts by her
affability and condescension.[82] — " There
was no Prince living, (says a good observer,
who lived near the time,) who was so tender of honour, and so exactly stood for the
preservation of sovereignty, that was so
great a courtier of her people, yea of the
commons, and that stooped and descended
lower in presenting her person to the publick view, as she passed in her progresses
and perambulations, and in the ejaculation
of her prayers for her people."[83]—The de-

[82] In one of these Progresses she visited Leycester at
Kenelworth Castle, in 1576, when our youthful bard, among
the crowds that flocked thither from all the neighbourhood,
might have seen her.

[83] Naunton's FRAGMENTA REGALIA, p. 12.

testable

testable doctrines of French Philosophy and the imaginary Rights of Man, had not yet been inculcated; nor had Englishmen yet been sedulously taught to throw away " respect, tradition, form, and ceremonious duty," and to accept of *French liberty* and *French equality*, instead of that beautiful and salutary gradation of ranks, which forms an essential part of our admirable constitution; where the distinction of conditions is so easy and imperceptible, that almost every man under the first personages of the land places himself, in his own estimation, without offence, in a somewhat higher order than that to which he is strictly entitled; and where men of the lowest origin may always by their own merit attain the highest honours and emoluments of the state.—A due subordination then everywhere prevailed; which naturally produced a profound reverence for persons distinguished by their noble birth and the offices they held, from the *worshipful* Justice of the Peace to the grave counsellors and splendid courtiers who surrounded the throne. " It was (as has been truly observed) an ingenuous uninquisitive time, when all the passions and affections of the people were lapped up in

such

such an innocent and humble obedience,
that there was never the least contestations
nor capitulations with the Queen; nor,
though she very frequently consulted with
her subjects, any further reasons urged of
her actions than *her own will.*[84]

ADD to this the powerful operation produced in the minds of the people at that
time by the alterations in religion. " As
they had been lately made," (I use the
words of a learned writer yet living,) as
their importance was great, and as the
benefits of the change had been earned at
the expence of much blood and labour, all
these considerations begot a zeal for religion
which hardly ever appears under other circumstances. This zeal had an immediate
and very sensible effect on the morals of the
reformed. It improved them in every instance; especially as it produced a cheerful

[84] THE DISPARITY (written by Lord Clarendon in his
youth). RELIQ. WOTTON. 1685, p. 189.
Happily for us, no such reason of action can now be
urged by our Kings, the boundaries between the prerogatives of the crown and the privileges of the people having
since the period here described been nicely ascertained, so
as to leave the executive branch of our Constitution no
power but what is salutary and beneficial for the the people.
submission

submission to the Government, which had rescued them from their former slavery, and was still their only support against the returning dangers of superstition. Thus religion acting with all its power, and that too heightened by gratitude and even self-interest, bound obedience on the minds of men with the strongest ties. [85] And luckily for the Queen this obedience was further secured to her by the high uncontroverted notions of royalty which at that time obtained amongst the people." [86]

To prevent these notions from fading from their minds, the Homilies, which were published by authority and enjoined to

[85] " One of these (says this writer) was the prejudice of education; and some uncommon methods were used to bind it fast on the minds of the people.—A book called EIPHNAPXIA, *sive* ELIZABETHA, was written in *Latin* verse by one Ockland, containing the highest panegyricks on the Queen's character and government, and setting forth the transcendent virtues of her ministers. This book was enjoined by authority to be taught, as a classick author, in grammar-schools, and was of course to be gotten by heart by the young scholars throughout the kingdom.— This was a matchless contrivance to imprint a sense of loyalty on the minds of the people." Hurd, *ubi supr.*

[86] MORAL and POLITICAL DIALOGUES, by the Rev. Mr. Hurd, (now Lord Bishop of Worcester,) vol. ii. p. 27.

be

be read every Sunday by the Clergy in their
respective churches, inculcated unconditional
and passive obedience [87] to the prince on the
throne, which on no account or pretence
whatsoever was it lawful to infringe.

Such was the period, when our Stratford
youth, whose tender mind was probably
impressed with a sense of loyalty on each
day of the week employed in the acquisition
of learning, and who was further confirmed
in the same sentiments by the doctrines enjoined to be taught on the day devoted to
the functions of religion, is made to express
himself concerning the diadem of kings, in
the style which one of the Regicides would
have used in the following century, or one
of the Rulers of France would employ at
this day.

When Cromwell had no further use for
the Rump Parliament, and kicked them, as
they well deserved, out of doors, he desired
one of his Janizaries (as Whitelocke tells us)
to take away that *fool's-bauble*, the Speaker's

[87] The Homilies, it has been observed, contain more
precepts in support of this vile and slavish doctrine, than all
the writings of Filmer and his followers.

I   mace."

mace."[88]   A bauble, in ancient time, had
various significations.   It originally meant
a jewel,[89] and afterwards a temporary scaf-
fold for any scenick exhibition or pageant.[90]
It also signified the truncheon which licensed
fools used to carry in their hands.—In a secondary and derivative sense deduced from
the original barbarous term *baubellum*, (a
jewel,) in process of time the word in
popular language came to signify any slight
toy, gewgaw, or trifling piece of finery;
and in this sense it is employed by our poet
himself in several of his plays : but I have
some doubt whether the word had obtained
that signification so early as the middle of
the reign of Elizabeth.   Be that as it may,
the sentiment before us may have been suggested either by the following passage in
a Letter of Cromwell's to his Secretary

[88] Hume, and some other Historians, make him say—
" What shall we do with *this bauble ?*" here, take it away :
by which the point of the allusion is lost.—The *fool's bauble* was a short truncheon with a carved head and ass's
ears.

[89] Roger Hoveden, as Minshieu, and (after him) Dr.
Johnson, observe, has the word *baubellum* in this sense:
" *Omnia baubella sua dedit Othoni.*" fol. 449. b.

[90] Barrett's ALVEARIE, 1580, in v.

Thurloe,

Thurloe, relative to a petition presented to
his HIGHNESS! by the wife of William
Beacham, mariner, which was printed about
thirty years ago,—" I have not the particular
shining *bauble* or feather in my cap for
crowds to gaze at, or kneel to, but I have
power and resolution for foes to tremble
at ;"" or (which is still more probable) by
these satirical verses of Swift :

> " A prince, the moment he is *crown'd*,
> " Inherits every virtue round,
> " As emblems of the sovereign power,
> " Like other *baubles* of the Tower." [92]

CROMWELL, or some of his flagitious
colleagues, if I remember right, speaking
of Charles the First, said that he considered
him only as the HIGH CONSTABLE of the
nation. If, in the present passage, we had in
the more measured language of our modern
republicans—" Neither the gilded bauble

[91] GENTLEMAN's MAGAZINE for 1766, p. 412. This
Letter had, I believe, appeared in the ANNUAL REGIS-
TER, a few years before.

[92] ON POETRY, A RHAPSODY. 1733.

that

that environs the head of the CHIEF MA-
GISTRATE," &c. all would have been
uniform and complete.

THE *counterfeit* ornament with which the
fabricator of this paper has environed the
head of Majesty, is perfectly in unison
with all the rest of these factitious manuscripts. IT is, however, worthy of remark,
that our poet was better acquainted with the
diadem, than to call it a *gilded* bauble ; in
every place where he mentions a crown
(that I can recollect) describing it, truly, as
made of gold. Thus in his K. RICHARD II.

" Now is the *golden crown* like a deep well,—."

Again, in K. HENRY IV. P. II.

" Why does the *crown* lie there upon his pillow,
" Being so troublesome a bed-fellow !
" O polish'd perturbation, *golden* care," &c.

Again, on the same occasion, after his
son has taken the crown away, the king
exclaims,

" How quickly nature falls into revolt,
" When *gold* becomes her object !"

So

So also, in MACBETH :

" ———— Hie thee hither,
" That I may pour my spirits in thine ear ;
" And chastise with the valour of my tongue
" All that impedes thee from the *golden round*,
" Which fate and metaphysical aid doth seem
" To have thee *crown'd* withal."

Again, in the same play, where the eight kings appear :

" Thy *crown* does sear mine eye-balls :—And
thy air,
" Thou other *gold-bound* brow, is like the first." *

IF it should be said that in his earlier days he was unacquainted with this circumstance, the answer is, that at that period of his life, instead of supposing the diadem to have been a piece of gilded metal, he was much more likely to have fancied it still more rich and resplendent than it really is,

* At the opening of the Session in 1614, King James told the parliament that his integrity was like the whiteness of his robe, and his purity like the metal of *gold* in his crown. PARL. HIST. vol. v. p. 273.

and

and to have emblazoned it in his youthful
imagination with all the precious stones of
the East.

I HAVE but one or two observations more
to make on this love-epistle. It has not
been proved that our poet wrote any of his
admirable plays while he was yet at school,
or recently after he had left it, though with
due diligence some discovery of this kind
may be furnished from the inexhaustible
store-house of curiosities already in part
exposed to the publick view. However,
when he wrote to his *dearesste Anna* that
" the feelinge that dydde neareste approache
untoe itte was thatte which commeth nygheste untoe God, meeke and gentle charytye,"
it is evident that the sentiment of his own
PORTIA was passing through his youthful
mind :

" The quality of *mercy* is not strain'd ;
" It droppeth, as the *gentle* rain from heaven
" Upon the place beneath : - - -
" 'Tis mightiest in the mightiest ; it becomes
" The throned monarch better than his crown :
" His sceptre shews the force of temporal
     power,
                 " The

" The attribute to awe and majesty,

" Wherein doth sit the dread and fear of kings;

" But mercy is above this scepter'd sway,

" It is enthroned in the hearts of kings,

" It is an attribute to God himself;

" And earthly power doth then shew *likest God's,*

" When *mercy* seasons justice." [93]

IT is observable that our author here speaks with somewhat more respect of the *sceptre* of kings, than the writer of the epistle before us has done of the " precious diadem" with which their brows are environed; and in one of his early historical plays his veneration for Majesty is still more apparent. The unhappy Richard the Second asserts, that

" Not all the water in the rough rude sea

" Can wash the balm from an anointed king;

" The breath of worldly men can not depose

" The deputy elected by the lord."

[93] It may be worth remarking, that in my edition the writer might have found at the bottom of the page, where this encomium on mercy occurs,

" And kings *approache the nearest unto God,*

" By giving life and safety unto men."

AND

AND in the same play we find the Bishop
of Carlisle expressing the same sentiments :

" What subject can give sentence on his king ?
" And who sits here, that is not Richard's sub-
ject ?
" Thieves are not judg'd, but they are by to
hear,
" Although apparent guilt be seen in them :
" And shall the figure of God's majesty,
" His captain, steward, deputy elect,
" Anointed, crowned, planted many years,
" Be judg'd by subject and inferior breath,
" And he himself not present ? O, forbid it,
God!"

Thus also, the King in HAMLET :

" Let him go, Gertrude ; do not fear our
person ;
" There's such divinity doth hedge a king,
" That treason can but peep to what it would,
" Acts little of his will."

WITH the truth or rectitude of these
sentiments we have at present nothing to
do : they are produced solely to shew the
prevalent opinions of our author's age, and
that, I conceive, they do most effectually.

OUR

OUR youthful lover's last compliment to his mistress is couched in the following terms : " I cheryshe thee in my hearte, forre thou arte ass a talle Cedarre stretchynge forthe its branches ande succourynge smaller Plants fromme nyppynge Winneterre orr the boysterouse Wyndes."

As Shakspeare is known to have been a curious observer of nature, we might suppose that this description was suggested by what he had himself seen : but as it has been shewn that there were no Cedars in England till after the Restoration,* where could this image have been presented to our Stratford Youth ? In the Bible, without doubt we shall be told. In Holy Writ we find that the Cedar of Lebanon was " exalted in height above all the trees of the field ;" that it had " fair *branches*, and a shadowing shroud : the waters made him great, the deep set him up on high with her rivers running round about his *plants* [his *own* plants] : all the fowls of heaven made their

* Mr. Evelyn is on good ground supposed to have first brought the Cedar tree into England, about the year 1662. See a curious Memoir on this subject, by the late Sir John Cullum, in the GENT. MAGAZINE for 1779, p. 138.

nests

nests in his boughs, and under his shadow dwell all generations."*—But where did our author discover that the wide-spreading branches of this goodly tree protect the smaller plants under it from the nipping blasts of winter? In some Natural History, I suppose, that will shortly be *brought forward*: but till it appears, it may be safely asserted that the very reverse of this is the truth, and that an " umbrageous multitude of leaves," instead of succouring, destroys all vegetation under it.

V. Verses by Shakspeare, addressed to Anna Hatherrewaye.

We are at length arrived at the Verses pretended to have been addressed by Shakspeare to his mistress. As a specimen of them, take the first stanza. Is there, says the lisping poet,

> Is there inne heav-enne aught more rare
> Thanne thou sweete nymphe of Avon fayre
> Is there onne earthe a manne more trewe
> Thanne Willy Shakspeare is toe you

* Ezek. c. 31.

Y 2

Is

Is this, I know you will say, a love-
sonnet, or the posy of a ring? I shall not
therefore sicken your Lordship with any
more of this namby-pamby stuff. Let me
however draw your attention to the rhythm
of the first line, on which we have the
decision of Spencer: " *Heaven* being used
short as one syllable, when it is in verse
stretched with a *diastole*, is like a lame dog
that holdeth up one leg."[94] In our poet's
genuine compositions we never find any
such hobling metre.

VI. Letter from Shakspeare to
the Earl of Southampton.
VII. The Earl's Answer.

The Letters which are pretended to have
passed between our poet and his patron,
Henry Earl of Southampton, if possible
surpass in absurdity any thing we have yet
examined: for there is not a single circumstance belonging to them, that is not so
evidently fraudulent, that the mere statement of them, without any amplification or
colouring whatsoever, will be sufficient to
detect and expose the imposture.

[94] Letter to Gabriel Harvey, 10 April, 1580.

In

In my edition of our poet's works, I endeavoured to do all honour to this highly distinguished and most amiable nobleman, by collecting some Memoirs of his life, which I have since enlarged; and if they should not become too bulky for an episode, they may perhaps be interwoven in the Life of Shakspeare. Having been sedulously, though at intervals, employed on that work for two years past, and collected more materials for it than the most sanguine expectation could have hoped to procure, to say nothing of the time which I had previously expended (perhaps idly, but certainly agreeably to myself, and I hope not wholly unprofitably to the publick,) on the illustration of both his works and his history, I could not help smiling at the observation of some of the criticks of the day, that I had shewn great temerity in thus hastily deciding on the authenticity of these Manuscripts. When I tell your Lordship that in the course of my inquiries, I have, with the aid of authentick and indisputable documents, overturned almost every traditional story that has been received concerning Shakspeare for near a century past, need I employ many words to shew that I was at

least

least not unconversant with the subject of
the late spurious publication ? The truth is,
that a single perusal of it was sufficient;
and in one hour afterwards the entire foundation of the Letter I am now writing was
laid, and all the principal heads of objection
briefly set down. The expanding of the
topicks, and the minute examination of
authorities, necessarily required some time.

I HAVE already observed, that several of
these papers have been formed either on
some existing archetype, or some received
tradition concerning Shakspeare ; which
was considered as a canvass which might
commodiously and plausibly be wrought
upon and filled up : and if the artist, or
rather artists, had known any thing of
drawing, had not all their colours been made
of brickdust, and the whole piece crowded
with distorted and disgusting figures,
without any regard to nature, or truth, or
costume, there might have been some difficulty in distinguishing the copy from the
original.⁹⁵

THE

---

⁹⁵ Even where the task is undertaken by persons of talents
much superior to the miserable and bungling artificers employed

THE fabrication we are now considering,
took its rise from a tradition, first mentioned by Mr. Rowe, and transmitted to
him (though not immediately) from Sir
William D'Avenant,—that Lord Southampton gave our author, to complete a purchase, no less a sum than one thousand
pounds, which was then certainly equal
to five thousand at this day. Having the
highest veneration for this nobleman, I am
far from wishing to diminish his well-
earned fame ; and I have not the smallest
doubt that he was extremely liberal to
Shakspeare : he appears indeed, from
every circumstance that I have collected
concerning him, to have been the very
soul of bounty and of honour: but still I
am possessed of indisputable documents,

ployed in the present fabrication, happily for mankind they
cannot guard themselves on every side against detection.—
It is extremely difficult, (as Archbishop Tennison has
justly observed,) " to imitate such great authors in so lively
and exact a form, as without suspicion to pass for them.
They who are the moſt artificial counterfeits in this way,
do not resemble them as the son does the father, but, at
best, as the dead picture does the living person."—BACO-
NIANA, 8vo. 1679.—The resemblance in the present
case is that of a weather-beaten alehouse' sign in a country
village to a portrait by Titian or Sir Joshua Reynolds.

which

which prove decisively that his liberality
to our poet must have been greatly magni-
fied, and that this story in all its parts cannot be true. True or false, however, it
was thought, to be a good subject for a
correspondence between the patron and the
poet to be engrafted upon. In such a
correspondence, what would have been
the natural order of things? First, would
pass a Letter in which this amiable en-
courager and patron of talents, wherever
they were found, would offer to bestow a
sum of money on his humble follower,
either in return for the poems dedicated
to him by Shakspeare, or from an admiration of those inimitable dramas which he
and his friend the Earl of Rutland used
to see with such pleasure.[96] The poet's
Letter of thanks would follow of course.
Such, I say, would have been the natural
order, if any such correspondence had really
passed between them. But this order
would not at all have suited our fabricator;

[96] " My Lord Southampton and Lord Rutland come
not to the Court [at Nonesuch]. The one doth but very
seldome. They pass away the tyme in London *merely in
going to plaies every day.*—Strand, this thursday the 11 of
october, 1599." SYDNEY PAPERS, ii. 132.

for

for then, in making the offer on the
part of the patron, a specifick sum must
have been mentioned; and if some in-
quisitive researcher, like myself, should
happen to be possessed of documents that
ascertained this bounty to have been very
different from the sum fixed upon, detection would instantly follow. To evade
this difficulty, though the fabricator had
certainly never heard of the ὕϛερον πρότερον
of the Rhetoricians, it was in fact adopted:
and hence the preposterous order of the
two letters which I ſhall now transcribe;
in the firſt of which the poet thanks his
patron for his "great bounty" already
bestowed on him, and in the other the
patron, in reply, tells the poet what he
knew already;—but that was not sufficient for our schemer; it was necessary
that *the reader should know it also.*

" *Copye of mye Letter toe hys Grace offe*
Southampton.

" Mye Lorde,

" DOE notte esteeme me a sluggarde nor
tardye for thus havynge delayed to answerre
or rather toe thank you for youre greate

z   Bountye

Bountye I doe assure you my graciouse ande good Lorde that thryce I have essayed toe wryte and thryce mye efforts have benne fruitlesse I knowe notte what toe saye Prose Verse alle all is naughte gratitude is alle I have toe utter and that is tooe greate and tooe *sublyme a feeling* for poore mortalls toe expresse O my Lord itte is a Budde which Bllossommes Bllooms butte never dyes itte cherifhes sweete Nature and lulls the calme Breaste toe softe softe repose Butte mye goode Lorde forgive thys mye departure fromme mye subjecte which was toe retturne thankes and thankes I Doe retturne O excuse mee mye Lorde more at presente I cannotte

Yours devotedlye and withe due respecte

Wᵐ Shakspeare."

" Deare Willam

" I CANNOTTE doe lesse than thanke you forre youre kynde Letterre butte whye dearest Freynd talke soe muche offe gratitude mye offerre was double the somme butte you woulde accepte butte the halfe thereforre you neede notte speake soe muche onn thatte subjectte as I have beene thye Freynd

Freynd soe will I continue aughte thatte
I canne doe forre thee praye commande mee
ande you shall fynde mee

Julye the 4   **Yours**

                    Southampton."

[*Superscribed*]
" To the Globe Theatre
Forre Mast^r Willam
Shakspeare."

HERE, as in all the other papers, the proofs
of fraud are so numerous, that they produce
conviction on the first view. The orthography, the phraseology, and hand-writing,
all betray the imposture, and render it almost
superfluous to say a word on the subject.—
However, I must go through my task.

To take these Letters in their order.
The handwriting of the first has not the
slightest resemblance to that of Shakspeare.
The spelling is the spelling of no time.
The writer however, it is observable, though
he retaines his *ande*, forgets to spell *for*
with the duplication observed in other
inftances (*forre*); but, by way of compen-
z 2   sation

sation, gives us *bllossomes* and *bllooms*, [97] a combination of consonants of which no example can be produced in the English language, from the time of Robert of Gloucester to this day.

NEED I insist on the improbability of our careless poet ever keeping a *copy* of any Letter he wrote, or of this being the copy of a Letter addressed to his GRACE of Southampton. He well knew, as I have already shewn, that this was not the proper designation of an Earl; and no very uncommon book, which I suppose will presently be produced from Shakspeare's newly discovered library, with sundry annotations by our poet, might have taught the writer to have avoided this absurdity. Whitney concludes the Epistle Dedicatory to the earl of Leycester, prefixed to his EMBLEMS in 1586,—" Your *Honours* humble and faithfull Servant, Geffrey Whitney." So also in the concluding Emblem addressed to the same nobleman :

[97] It has been justly observed, that Shakspeare was too good a naturalist not to know that a bud first *blooms*, and then *blossoms*. *Free Reflections*, &c. 8vo. 1796.

" Which

" Which if you shall receive with pleasinge looke,

" I shall rejoyce, and thinke my labour lighte ;

" And pray the Lorde your *Honour* to preserve,

" Our noble Queene and countrie long to serve."

BUT were I even to allow that GRACE, instead of being in those days the usual address to Dukes, and sometimes to the Queen[98] and the princes of the blood, was also used in speaking to or of Earls, it would not exempt this Letter from the charge of forgery : for the phrase—*his Grace of Norfolk*, or *his Grace of Bucks*, is much posterior to the sixteenth century.

INSTEAD of " Mye Lorde," with which words this Letter commences, we ought to have had—" Right Honorable ;" which, though it was not the only mode of that time, (the other being sometimes used,) was the more ordinary mode, especially from an inferior to a superior; and certainly was our

[98] " Her Ma.[tie] remeaneth here at Nonsyche as yet, but mindeth to remove to Otlands about a senight hens. Hir *Grace* liketh well of this place." Letter from Lord Talbot to his father the Earl of Shrewsbury, dated " frō the Couert at Nonsyche the xxiii.[th] of June, 1580." SHREWS-BURY PAPERS, ii. 228.

author's

author's mode, as appears from his Dedications to this nobleman.

THE origin of the indefinite words—
" youre greate bountye," has been already
pointed out.—When the following words
were written," *thryce* I have *essayed* toe write,
and *thryce* mye efforts have been fruitlesse,"
it requires no great sagacity to discover that
Ovid suggested this thought :

" Ter conata loqui, ter fletibus ora rigavit :"—

but I entirely acquit the author of having
ever read the original. He was without
doubt indebted to Milton's imitation of
his favourite poet :

" *Thrice* he *essay'd*, and *thrice*, in spight of scorn,
" Tears, such as angels weep, burst forth." 99

A SUBSEQUENT passage is still more

99 He might likewise have remembered Dryden's translation of the sixth Æneid :
    " He twice *essay'd* to cast his son in gold,
    " Twice from his hands he dropp'd the forming mould."

    " Then *thrice* around his neck his arms he threw,
    " And *thrice* the flitting shadow slipp'd away,
    " Like winds, or empty dreams that fly the day."

worthy

worthy of remark ;—I mean where the poet tells his patron that " gratitude is a budde which bllossommes, bllooms, butte never dyes ; itte cherishes sweete *Nature*, ande *lulls* the calme breaste *toe softe softe repose*."—

Of all the editors of our poet's works, Dr. Warburton is, I believe, the last person that he would consider as his *fidus Achates*.— Yet were this letter genuine, it would do the Bishop more honour than perhaps all his other literary triumphs ; for it would prove that he read the very soul of Shakspeare ; or rather that the bard two centuries ago expressed himself in exactly the same language as the editor in the middle of the present century employed in his Commentary, without the slightest communication with each other, or either knowing what the other wrote.

In the fifth act of Antony *and* Cleopatra, (scene ii.) the Egyptian Queen, when she is in the monument, thus reflects upon the suicide she was about to commit :

" My desolation does begin to make
" A better life : 'tis paltry to be Cæsar ;

" Not

" Not being fortune, he's but fortune's knave,

" A minister of her will ; And it is great

" To do that thing that ends all other deeds ;

" Which shackles accidents, and bolts up change ;

" Which sleeps, and never palates more the dung,

" The beggar's nurse and Cæsar's."

BUT, says the Commentator, we should read thus :

" —————————— And it is great

" To do that thing that ends all other deeds ;

" Which shackles accidents, and bolts up change,

" [*Lulls* wearied *Nature to a sound repose,*]

" Which sleeps, and never palates more the *dugg,*

" The beggar's nurse and Cæsars."

" THAT *this line in hooks* (he adds) *was the substance of that lost*, is evident from its making sense of all the rest ; which are to this effect : It is great to do that which frees us from all the accidents of humanity, *lulls our over-wearied nature to repose*, (which now sleeps and has no more appetite for worldly enjoyments) and is equally the nurse of Cæsar and the beggar."

WOULD your Lordship desire better

1   sympathy

sympathy than this ? Whether Shakspeare, when he told Lord Southampton that " gratitude cherishes sweet *nature*, and *lulls* the calm breast *to soft repose*," foresaw what would occur to Dr. Warburton a hundred and fifty years afterwards ; or the Doctor dived into the poet's bosom, and there found that sentiment which has lain so long concealed in the bottom of an old trunk ; which ever way this marvellous coincidence is viewed, it reflects the highest honour on the sagacity of one or the other : but whether the laurel crown is to be adjudged to the poet or the commentator, I shall not presume to determine.

It is not necessary to take notice of any other part of this Letter, except the conclusion, which is completely modern : " O excuse me, mye Lorde, more at presente I cannotte."

Yours devotedlye and with due respecte."

Almost every word here deserves to be particularly attended to. Though " *no more at present*" might pass well enough in a modern epistle, however spurious, it will not do here. The phrase of the time was

not " at present," but, " at *this* present;"[100]
and—" with due respecte" is equally modern, and equally objectionable. There is a
fashion in the style, and particularly in the
conclusion, of Letters, as in most other
things. As the writer of the present day
assures his correspondent that he is his
faithful, or *affectionate*, or *obedient servant*,
(as the case may be,) so, in the times we
are now treating of, the mode between equals
was—" Your Lordships assuredly," or
" Your good Lordships assured loving
frend," or " your Lordships most assured
to comande," or " your assured frende to do
you service :"—and from an inferior the
customary expressions were—" Your honours most humbly at comandmente ;"—or
" Your good lordships most readie in all
service ;" or " Your honours most assured
and ready to be used ;" or " Your honours
most humbly to use and commande ;" or
" Your honours most humble poore frende,
assured, and at comandement."[101]—Such, I
say,

---

[100] " And many a man there is, even at *this present*,—."
WINTER'S TALE.
" Thy letters have transported me beyond
" *This* ignorant *present* ;—." MACBETH.
[101] SYDNEY and SHREWSBURY PAPERS, *passim*.

The

say, were the modes of those days, of which our fabricator appears to have been completely ignorant.—Whenever any example shall be produced of a person in so low a situation as that of a player was then esteemed to be, presuming to conclude a letter to a nobleman with the modern familiar assurance of attachment—" Yours," and of his adding also that he is *devotedly* attached to the person thus addressed, (a word certainly used in the same sense in that age, but which I have not found in the conclusion of letters, though at a subsequent period it became common,) and when all the other absurdities and incongruities of this Letter are also done away, then may it pass for the composition of our poet; " but in such a *then* I write a *never*."

Permit me now to take a view of Lord Southampton's Answer to this epistle.

The writer might also have found an apt conclusion for this fabrication, in a Letter from Sir John Harrington to the Lord Treasurer Burghley, Nugæ Antiq. ii. 84; " In all dutie I reste your humble well-wisher:"—but he appears to have been as little acquainted with the writings as the manners of the time.

Henry

HENRY, the third earl of Southampton, was born October 6, 1573; [102] so that he was not twenty years old, when our poet selected him for his patron by the dedication of his earliest poem. It is not necessary for me here to enter minutely into his history; nor do I wish to anticipate my future work by stating the circumstances which led our poet to place himself under the patronage of this nobleman, or which shew how well he merited the encomiums that Shakspeare has bestowed upon him. At once accomplished, literate, brave, and liberal, all the poets and artists of the time looked up to him as their protector. Whatever donation he gave to Shakspeare, it is highly probable that it was given in return for his dedications, according to the established practice of that age. This circumstance would fix the date of the Letter before us to 1594. Let us, however, suppose it to have been written either then or at any subsequent period that its partisans may choose to fix upon, previous to the death of the poet in 1616. Lord Southampton was then in his forty third year.

[102] Esc. 24 Eliz. p. 1. n. 46.

To

To pass over the Orthography, (which is not only not that of Lord Southampton, as we shall presently see, but not the orthography of any age whatsoever,) and to come to the Phraseology, the first badge of literary fraud in this piece is found *in limine ;*— " DEARE Willam." I will not take up your Lordship's time on this inauspicious commencement, which every one, at all acquainted with the manners of that day, knows was not the language of a nobleman to a person at the immeasurable distance at which Shakspeare stood from Lord Southampton. Had he condescended to write to our poet, he would without doubt have begun with " Mr. Shakspeare," or " Good Master Shakspeare," or " Good William ;"[103] or some other similar form.—The christian name, William, was sometimes at that

---

[103] So, in the Queen's Letter already given,—" I thanke you, *Good Harry*," &c. So also, Lord Essex, writing to his dependant, Mr. Combe, in 1599, (Harrington's *Nugæ Antiq.* ii. 8.) " *Good Thomas.*"—And Lord Burghley to Mr. (afterwards,) Sir John Harrington, when a boy at Cambridge, in 1578 : " I thancke you, *my good Jacke*, for your lettres," &c. *Ibid.* p. 282.—See also SYDNEY PAPERS, i. 389, Sir Philip Sydney to Edward Waterhouse, (28th April, 1578,)—" *My good Ned*, never since yow wente," &c.

period,

period, as now, written contractedly, W^m,
as Shakspeare himself has once written it :
but the more ordinary abbreviation was
Willm̄; which I have found in several hundred papers of the age of Elizabeth, and
is employed by our poet in his will. *Willam*,
as here given, is the pronunciation of a
vulgar illiterate female of the present day.

LORD Southampton's telling Shakspeare,
whom he is here absurdly made to call his
dearest *freynd*, (which, by the way, we shall
presently find was neither his mode of spelling the latter word, nor the spelling of the
age,) that he had *offered him double the sum*,
will naturally remind your Lordship of
those inartificial soliloquies on the stage,
where a gentleman is introduced very grave-
ly telling himself a long story, of which
the poet wishes the audience to be informed.
But it was quite necessary here ; for though
Shakspeare knew of this generous offer,
how should the reader have known any
thing of it, if the patron had not reminded
the poet of his own liberality ? and the
words—" double the somme," and " you
woulde accepte butte the halfe," leave the
matter involved in that mist of uncertainty
and

and obscurity, which on this occasion was so desirable, for the reason I have already stated.

BUT I hasten to the conclusion :—" As I have beene thye freynde, soe will I continue aughte thatte I canne doe forre thee: praye, commande mee, and you shalle fynde mee Yours, Southampton."

HERE, in the true style of Mr. BAYS, we have " flash for flash, and dash for dash." As the poet concludes with the most familiar assurance of regard, *(Yours,)* the patron will not be outdone by him, and adopts the same mode; scorning the ordinary forms of—" Your assured wellwisher," or " Your ready friend to do you service," &c. as trite and vulgar.—The preceding words, " Pray, command me," (to say nothing of their modern air, when thus used imperatively,) considered as the language of a nobleman to a player, harmonize perfectly well with the rest of this spurious epistle.

BUT the signature, " Southampton," requires a more minute examination. This circum-

circumstance, and Lord Leycester's being mentioned in the Queen's pretended Letter addressed to Shakspeare as master of a company of comedians, of which I was informed soon after this wonderful discovery was announced, gave me a perfect insight into the nature and quality of these manuscripts. In the reign of Elizabeth, as your Lordship knows, noblemen in their signatures usually prefixed their christian name to their titles; as their ladies, and my lords the Bishops, do at this day. This, I say, was the ordinary practice, though a few peers deviated from that mode, and subscribed their titles only; as they now do universally. In the time of James the First, the general mode continued the same, though it was then also occasionally departed from; and in the time of his successor the present mode seems to have prevailed rather more than the other, though it was not generally established till after the Restoration. But whatever examples of the modern practice may occasionally be found in ancient times, Henry Lord Southampton prefixed his christian name to his title; a practice which seems to have been hereditary in his family; for the autograph of his father (H.

ɪ   South-

Southampton) is in the Museum; [104] and his son, the Lord Treasurer, even some years after the Restoration, (June 26, 1666,) signed T. Southampton, as appears from an autograph in my possession. This circumstance therefore, even if it stood alone, would be fatal to this spurious epistle.

NOTHING more now remains on this part of my subject, but to prove what I have asserted, by producing two Letters written by Lord Southampton, the only Letters of his known to be extant; [105] which, while they ascertain this point, will shew

---

[104] MS. COTTON. Titus. B. vii. Letter the fourth, dated July 26, 1572. This Nobleman, who wrote a very good hand, formed his autograph, (as was much the fashion formerly,) so as to make the first letter of *Southampton* serve for half of the initial letter of his christian name (Henry). This was a common practice in the last century. Antony Wood almost always, in writing the initials of his christian and surname, made the second stroke of the A serve as the first of the W.

[105] Mr. Astle very obligingly, at my request, searched the State-Paper Office, with the hope of finding some other specimens of Lord Southampton's hand-writing; but in vain. I had also hoped to have found some of his Letters among the papers belonging to the Ordnance-Office; but was there also disappointed.

B B   that

that not one word of this nobleman's hand-writing had ever been seen by the fabricator of the Letter before us, in which the miserable scrawl of a paralytick man of fourscore is attributed to a young peer probably of one and twenty, but certainly not more than forty-two.

THE first of these Letters, which I found near a year ago in the Museum, (MSS. Harl. 7000, p. 46,) has no date, but was written to the Lord Keeper in the latter end of July, 1621. In the parliament which met January 30, 1620-21, Lord Southampton took a very active part; and in a debate on the 14th of March, relative to an illegal patent granted to Sir Giles Mompesson, the profits of which were shared by Sir Edward Villiers, he called the Duke of Buckingham to order, for speaking twice on the same subject; which created such confusion in the House, that the Prince of Wales thought it proper to interpose, and reconciled them.[106] This reconciliation, however,

---

[106] Camden. Regn. Reg. Jacob. ANNAL. p. 69. 4to. 1691.—According to the Parliamentary History, this altercation happened on the 22d of March. "A debate arising

however, should seem not to have been very
sincere on the part of the minifter; for on
the 16th of June he caused Lord Southampton to be taken into close custody,[101] and
confined under the care of the Dean of
Westminster (Dr. Williams), who in the following month was made Bishop of Lincoln,
and Lord Keeper of the great Seal, in the

arising in what manner to proceed against the said Sir
Giles, whether by indictment in that house or otherwise;
and there being some confusion amongst the Speakers, the
Prince of Wales, who constantly attended this business
morning and afternoon, made a motion, ' That by the
ancient orders of the House no Lord was to speak twice,
though to explain himself, except some other Lord mistake his meaning in any part of his speech.' This was
commanded to be entered, and ordered to be observed."
PARL. HIST. V. 371.

[107] Camden. *ut supr.* p. 72. The altercation however
in March was not the only cause of Lord Southampton's
being taken into custody, as appears from his Examination,
preserved in the Museum, (MSS. Harl. 161. art. 8.) and
published by Mr. Tyrwhitt, at the end of the DEBATES of
the HOUSE OF COMMONS in 1621, 8vo. 1766. Two
of the questions put to him were these: " Whether in the
time of Parliament some of the lower House did not usually
come up into the Committee-chamber of the upper House,
upon design and plot *to receive a direction* from him what
to do in their House?"—" Whether he did not say, they
had like to come to blows?" ANSWER. " He said, that he
saw that heat in the House, that, if the Prince had not been
there, they had like to have come to blows."

room of Bacon, who had been degraded
on the 2d of May. On the 18th of July,
Lord Southampton was liberated from his
confinement in the house of the Lord
Keeper,[108] but was not ſuffered to appear
at court, being commanded to retire to his
country-house at Tichfield. In the latter
end of that month he wrote the following
Letter[199] to the Lord Keeper, Williams : [110]

" My

[108] *Ibid.* p. 73.

[109] This Letter is very inaccurately printed in the CA-
BALA, p. 359, edit. 1663, where also is the Lord Keeper's
answer, dated August 2, 1621. On the preceding day he
had written to the Duke of Buckingham in favour of Lord
Southampton. " This enclosed (says the Bishop) will
let your lordship understand, that somewhat is to be finished
in that excellent piece of mercy which his Majesty (your
hand guiding the pencil) is about to express to the earl of
Southampton. It is full time his attendant were revoked,
in my poor opinion, and himself left to the custody of his
own good angel."—CABAL. p. 285. On the 22d of
July, he thus expresses himself in a letter to the same person: " With my trueſt affection and thankfulness pre-
mised, I do not doubt but his Majesty and your Lordship
do now enjoy the general applause of your goodness to
the Earl of Southampton. Saturday last he came and
dined with me, and I find him more cordially affected to
the service of the King, and your Lordship's love and friend-
ſhip, then ever he was, when he lay a prisoner in my house.
Yet the sunshine of his Majesties favour, though most
bright

" My Lo:

" I HAVE found your lo: alredy
so favorable & affectionate unto mee that
I shall bee still hereafter desirous to acquaint
you wth what concernes mee, & bould to
aske your advice & counsell, which
makes mee now send this bearer to give
your lo: an account of my answer from
Court, wch I cannot better doe then by
sendinge unto you the answer it self, w^{b}
you shall receave heere enclosed, wherin
you may see what is expected from mee
that I must not only magnifie his ma^{ties}
gracious dealings with mee, but cause all
my frendes to doe the lyke, & restrayne
them from makinge any extenuation of my
errors, w^{h} if they be disposed to doe or

bright upon others (more open offenders), is noted to be
somewhat eclipsed towards him. What directions soever
his Majesty gave, the order is somewhat tart upon the Earl.
The word *Confinement* spread about the city, though I observed not one syllable so quick to fall from his Majesty,
his Keeper much wondered at. The act of the Councel
[was] published in our names, who were neither present
thereat, nor heard any word of the same : yet upon my
credit the Earl takes all things patiently, and thankfully,
though others wonder at the same." IBID. p. 283.

[110] See Plate III. N^{o}. xxiii. where a *fac-simile* of part
of it is given.

not

not to doe is unpossible for mee to alter,
that am not lykely for a good time to see
any other then my owne famely. for my
self I shall euer be ready as is fitt to ac-
knowlege his ma^{ties} favor to mee, but can
hardly perswade my self that any error by
mee cōmitted deserved more punishment
then I haue had, & hope his Ma^{ty} will
not expect that I should confess my self
to have beene subject to a starchamber
sentence, w^h God forbidd I should euer
doe. I haue & shall doe accordinge to
that part of my lo: of Buckingams aduise
to speake as little of it as I can, & so
shall doe in other thinges to meddle as
little as I can. I purpose God willinge
to goe to-morow to Tichfield the place of
my confinement, there to stay as long as
the Kinge shall please. Sir Will. Parkurst [111] must goe wth mee, who hoped to
[have] been discharged at the returne of
my messenger from Court, & seames
much trobled that hee is not, pertendinge
that it is extreeme inconuenient for him in
regard of his owne occations. hee is fear-

[111] Sir William Parkurst was the *attendant* mentioned
by the Lord Keeper in his Letter to the Duke of Buckingham. See n. 109.

full

full least hee should bee forgotten, if there.
Wherfore when your lo: writes to the
Court, if you would putt my lo: of
Buckingham in remembrance of it, you
shall I thinke doe him a favor. for my part
it is so little troble to mee & of so small
moment, as I mean to move no more for
it ; when this bearer returns I beseech you
returne by him this enclosed lēr, & be-
leeue that whatsoever I am I will ever bee
your lo :

  most assured frend to doe you seruice

    H Southampton."[112]

THE following Letter, written by the
same nobleman, of part of which a *fac-
simile* is also given,[113] was obligingly
pointed out to me by Mr. Planta of the
Museum. It has no date but that of

[112] Lord Southampton, not having room to conclude
this letter at the bottom of the page, was obliged to turn the
paper, and to write the words—" ever bee," &c. on the side
margin ; in consequence of which, having very little space
for his name, he wrote it in a smaller size, and could not
make the first stroke of the letter H in what appears from
his other autograph to have been his ordinary manner.
See the signatures, Plate III. N°. xxiii. and xxiv.

[113] BRIT. MUS. MS. Cotton. F. xiii. p. 311.—See
Plate III. N°. xxiv.

     " the

" the 17 of october ;" nor have I been
able to discover the undertaking alluded to,
in which Lord Chandos was engaged,
and which might serve to ascertain the
date ; but Grey, Lord Chandos, the person
here meant, (who was commonly called
the KING OF COTSWOLD,) having died
at Sudeley in Glocestershire, on the 10th
of August, 1621,[114] this Letter must have
been dated in some year between October
1620 and the accession of King James to
the English throne.

" I HAVE sent you heerewith a petition delivered unto mee in the behalf of
certayne poore men dwellinge att Gosport
who have been hardly used by *winter*,[115]
who under coller of beeinge Captayne of

[114] Esc. 19 Jac. p. 1. n. 103.—Camden says in his
Annals of King James, that Lord Chandos died at Spa in
Germany, Aug. 5, 1621 ; but the Inquisition which was
taken at Winchcombe in Glocestershire, close to his house,
Jan. 11, 1621-2, shews that the Annalist was misinformed.
George, the eldest son of Grey, Lord Chandos, (who had
succeeded to the title in 1602,) was only one year and one
day old at his father's death.

[115] Perhaps a descendant of William Winter, Esq. who
(as appears from Forbes's STATE PAPERS) was much employed in the early part of Queen Elizabeth's reign in furnishing the Navy with Ordnance stores.

the

the Kinges Pinnace hath comitted mayny insolences ; as also a noate of divers other his misdeamenors, wth the neglect of his duty & charge; all w^{ch} & much more (as I am informed) will be proued against him, if it will please my Lo. Priuy Seale to appointe some to examin the parties that complayne, and some other dwellinge thereaboutes, who will bee redy to iustify these thinges and more; but they beeinge poore men would bee utterly undoone if they should goe to London, to bee examined. Wherfore, my lo. weare best to appoint any who hee shall thinke fitt, to take their examinations heere in the contry. My lo: Shandos hath fayled, for I heare no newes of him, & am therfore uncertayne of my cominge into the playnes,[116] but if I come you shall heare from mee, otherwiss I hope wee shall meete att your returne; till when wishinge you good sport I rest

your assured frend

" the 17 of Octob."   H Southampton."

[116] Probably Salisbury Plains.—In the preceding part of this letter in p. 192, (which is on a different sheet,) an error happened at the press, which I did not discover till the sheet was worked off. For *coller*, the original has *collor*; and for *have*, we should twice read *haue*.

C C   THESE

THESE Letters require no comment or
observation. One glance on the plate
where *fac-similes* of both of them are given,
will at once establish the spuriousness of
the pretended correspondence between this
nobleman and our poet. There are some
peculiarities in Lord Southampton's hand-
writing; one of which is his formation of
the letter *f*, in which he is uniform throughout ;—but neither this circumstance, nor
his using the letter *u* where we should now
write *v*, (as was common at that time,)
nor his signature, nor the orthography of
both these genuine letters, though totally
varying from the modern-antique exhibited
in a former page, (where we find the *r*
used in the old chancery-hand, *notte, forre,*
&c.) none of these, I say, are wanting
to prove what the entire dissimilitude of
the hand-writing ascertains beyond a doubt,
—that the whole is " false and hollow," a
miserable, bungling, nonsensical forgery.[117]

VIII. SHAK-

[117] I cannot dismiss this part of my subject without laying before my readers the following observation, as a *literary
curiosity:*

" The comparison of signatures is not always satisfactory proof of authenticity, on account of diversities which
occur

VIII. SHAKSPEARE'S PROFESSION OF FAITH.

ON the PROFESSION OF FAITH, which is the next article of this extraordinary Miscellany,

occur in the same person's writing at different times. In the British Museum are to be seen three signatures, *unaccompanied by any date*, of the Earls of Southampton ; one of the father, and two said to be of the son, the friend of Shakspeare : the two latter on comparison appear to be widely different from each other, and from Mr. Ireland's MSS. [With respect to the assertion that Lord Southampton's two signatures differ widely from each other, the reader has only to cast his eye on Pl. III. to be convinced that it is wholly unfounded. They differ only in *size*. The cause is assigned in p. 191, n. 112.]

" In general, however, (proceeds this writer,) signatures, though agreeing perhaps upon the *whole*, have some individual distinctions more or less minute, according to the different circumstances which may have affected them." COMPARATIVE REVIEW, &c. p. 26.

As it has been very generally known that specimens of Lord Southampton's genuine hand-writing were speedily to be produced, it is not unreasonable to suppose that the foregoing observation was made with a view of meeting with this evidence, and diminishing its force by anticipation.

Let us then see what kind of illustration the subject may derive from this remark. In examining affidavits, which are frequently made by the contending parties in the course of legal proceedings, Judges make it a rule to throw out of their consideration every thing that is irrelevant to the question before them, to use legal language, or in plain English, nothing to the purpose. If such a process were used here, I fear the residue would be a mere *caput mortuum*. For

what

Miscellany, I have very little to say.   There
being no note of time to ascertain when it
was

what is the state of the question ?—A Letter is produced
pretending to be the hand-writing of Henry Lord Southampton, the patron of Shakspeare, but exhibiting the scrawl of
a man drunk or paralytick.   To this are opposed two
genuine letters of the same nobleman, in a fair, regular hand,
and no more resembling the forged scrawl than Chinese
characters resemble English.—What is the Answer ? It is
not precisely in the words of Fluellen—" There is a river
in Macedon, and there is also moreover a river at Monmouth,—and there is salmons in both ;" but the reasoning
is nearly as good. " There is a signature in the Museum,
written by Henry Lord Southampton the father, [and it
might have been added, *in a strong, free, and fair hand,
July 26, 1572,*] and two by the son [*equally fair, and
differing from each other only in size*], and all totally
differing from the pretended letter. *Ergo,* the pretended letter may be genuine, *because* signatures, though
agreeing on the whole, have minute and individual distinctions."—If the foregoing deduction be not intended to be
drawn, I know not what the writer had in view. The
concluding paragraph I do not well understand, but suppose it was meant to support and strengthen what went
before.

I do not conceive that on a question of evidence this reasoning would appear quite satisfactory to my lords the
Judges in Westminster Hall ; and, though only an adopted
son, I have so high a respect for the University of OXFORD,
that I cannot suppose any such logick is taught by that
learned body in their Schools. Certain it is, that neither
Crakanthorp, Wallis, or Aldrich, furnish any examples of
it. It is not, however, wholly without precedent ; for I
am

was written, no argument can be grounded on its date. The same objections, however, founded on the orthography, the language and phraseology, and the dissimilitude of the hand-writing to that of the person to whom it is ascribed, lie to this paper as to all the former.

I HAVE already had occasion to observe that several of these fictions were founded on, and grew out of, either tra-

am told that several instances of this species of argument are to be found in the DIALECTICKS of PIGROGROMITUS, (a well-known sciolist of the sixteenth century,) which were translated into English from the original Vapian language by a great admirer of his, Sir Topas, a country curate, of Queubus near Leeds in Yorkshire, and published in 1590, by John Trundle, Stationer in Barbican, at the Sign of NO-BODY. This tract consists of two hundred pages, or 3980 lines (the lines being *numbered* throughout, and twenty lines in every page but the first and the last): It is of such extreme rarity, that no copy of it is known to be extant, except one said to have been lately discovered in Shakspeare's library, which is proved beyond all question to have belonged to our incomparable poet, by his having written his name in it exactly SIX HUNDRED TIMES, that is, on the top and bottom and side margin of every page, with all the variety and diversity that the most wanton caprice could dictate. In the last leaf, there being a vacant space, he observes that he and his friend Cowley, the player, had many a hearty laugh over the paralogisms in this book.

ditional

ditional stories concerning our author, or
papers which had previously appeared in the
account of his Life. The Profession of
Faith before us was manifestly formed on a
Confession of Faith written by one John
Shakspeare, which I published for the first
time in the end of the year 1790.[118] It was
found about the year 1770, by one Mosely,
a master bricklayer, who usually worked
with his men, being employed by Mr.
Thomas Hart, (the fifth descendant in a
direct line from our poet's sister, Joan Hart,)
to new-tile the old house in Stratford, in
which Shakspeare, on no good authority, is
supposed to have been born. The paper
was discovered between the rafters and the
tiling of the house; and the evidence respecting its authenticity transmitted to me
by my friend the Rev. Dr. Davenport, Vicar
of Stratford-upon-Avon, appeared to me sufficiently satisfactory to warrant its publication. But in my conjecture concerning
the writer of that paper, I certainly was
mistaken; for I have since obtained documents that clearly prove it could not have

[118] PLAYS and POEMS of WILLIAM SHAKSPEARE,
1790. Vol. II. P. II. p. 162, and p. 330.

been

been the composition of any one of our poet's family; as will be fully shewn in his Life.

However, here was a ground to work on; and accordingly we have before us a second and similar paper, the fabricator of which does not seem to have once reflected how extremely improbable it would appear that *all* the Shakspeare family should be CONFESSORS of their FAITH.

Of this mystical rhapsody I shall only quote a few passages, adhering closely to the absurd orthography that has been employed. It begins thus :

" I BEYNGE nowe off sounde Mynde doe hope that this mye wyshe wille atte mye deathe be ACCEEDED toe." " - - - I doe fyrste looke toe oune lovynge and great God ande toe his gloriouse sonne Jesus I doe alsoe beleyve thatte thys mye weake ande frayle Bodye wille returne to duste but *forre* my soule lette God judge that as to *hymsselfe* shalle seeme meete."

- - - - whenne the teares offe sweete repentance bathe hys *wretched* pillowe - - -
" O Manne,

" O Manne, - - - where are thye greate
thye boasted attrybutes buried loste forre
everre inne colde Death - - - more thou
attempteste more arte thou loste tille thye
poore weake thoughtes arre elevated toe
theyre summite ande thence assnowe fromme
the leffee tree [119] droppe ande distylle themselves tille theye are noe more - - - -

" - - - greate God receyve me toe thye
bosomme where alle is sweete contente ande
happynesse alle is blysse

" - - - O cherishe usse like the sweete
Chickenne thatte under the coverte offe herre
spreadynge Wings Receyves herre lyttle
Broode &c."

THIS last passage has evidently been
formed on Holy Writ,[120] where the kindness

---

[119] It has been justly observed, that this epithet is unfortunate, trees being generally denuded of their foliage when
snow falls. Letter to George Steevens, Esq. &c. by James
Boaden, Esq. p. 44.

[120] " O Jerusalem, Jerusalem, - - - how often would I
have gathered thy children together, even as a hen gathereth
her chickens under her wings, and ye would not."
ST. MATTHEW, xxiii. 37.
" —O thou that savest by thy right hand them which put
their

ness and pity of our merciful Creator are
represented under the familiar image of a
hen protecting her little brood under her
wings. But whence the absurd introduction
of a *chicken*, (which is here by courtesy
to pass for the mother bird,) to perform this
parental office? Whence, but from the same
caprice and refinement of folly which dictated his *Grace* of Southampton, and twenty
other fooleries, which it was supposed would
give an air of originality to the whole, on
the principle that a *forger* would not have
so departed from verisimilitude; and that
therefore the conclusion that the MSS. were
genuine would necessarily follow; for in this
fabricator's mind, absurdity and authenticity
seem to have been terms precisely synonymous and equipollent.

IT is observable, that in this paper the poet
deserts the old *r* used in the chancery-hand,
of which he was before so prodigal, and
which is presented to us in every page of

their trust in thee, from those that rise up against them,
keep me as the apple of the eye, *hide me under the shadow
of thy wings.*" PSALM xvii. 8.

" He shall *cover* thee with his feathers, and under his
wings shalt thou trust." PSALM xci. 4.

the

the factitious copy of KING LEAR. Without, however, resting on the hand-writing, or the orthography, (which is of no age,) The " *wretched* pillow," and the modern duplication without a connecting particle,—" buried, lost,"—" all is sweete contente, alle is blysse," &c. might enable any reasonable man to form a decided opinion upon it : but when I have added that the word *hymsselfe* is exhibited in this pretended ancient MS. as one word,[121] and that the word ACCEDED is found in it, I conceive it would be a perfect waste of time to detain your lordship any longer on this head.

THE word *accede* Dr. Johnson supposed to have been originally a diplomatick word, and it is of so recent an origin that no example of it is found in his Dictionary. It came into use, I believe, within the present century ; and was probably employed in State-papers and parliamentary speeches, before it became a word of ordinary use. It is unnecessary here to refer to Barrett, Bullokar, Minshieu, or any of our elder lexicographers. It is remarkable that Edward Philips, Milton's nephew, who was a good scholar,

[121] See p. 80.

as

as appears by his Latin Treatise on Dramatick Poetry,[122] has not this word in his Dictionary, though he has the kindred word
concede ; and what shews decisively that the
word did not exist when he published his
book, (1659,) is, that he mentions and explains the two law-writs, *Accedas* ad Curiam,
and *Accedas* ad Vice-comitem ; so that he
could not possibly have over-looked the
English word *accede,* had it been then in
use. This is decisive. Its non-existence

---

[122] An anonymous Annotator on Dr. Johnson's Life of
Milton, as exhibited in the collection of his works, supposed that the Biographer was in an error when he described Philips as the author of " a small History of Poetry
written in Latin," and that he had mistaken his THEA-
TRUM POETARUM, (which is written in English, and is
only a list of poets Ancient and Modern, with a short
account of their works,) for a Latin Treatise. But the
Annotator is himself in an error, and Dr. Johnson was
perfectly correct. Philips's treatise, of which I have a
copy, is entitled, *Tractatulus de Carmine Dramatico Poetarum
Veterum, præsertim in Choris tragicis et veteris comædiæ.
Cui subjungitur compendiosa enumeratio poetarum (saltem
quorum fama maxime enituit) qui a tempore Dantis Aligerii
usque ad hunc ætatem claruerunt,* &c. He published another short Latin tract in 4to. entitled *Tractatulus de modo et
ratione formandi voces derivitivas Linguæ Latinæ,* &c. of
which I have never seen a copy except that in the Bodleian
Library.

is

is further confirmed by Coles' Latin Dictionary, 1679, who thus interprets the word *Accedo :* " To come, approach, resemble, *assent*, to be added, increased, included in." Here we do not find *accede*, an unquestionable proof that the word was then unknown. Blount in the fifth edition of his GLOSSOGRAPHIA, (1681,) though professing to " interpret the *hard words* of whatever language now used in our English tongue," has it not ; neither is it found in so late a book as Kersey's English Dictionary, 1708.— We have here therefore a word unknown to our language for near a century after the death of the person by whom it is pretended to have been used. If this be not a decisive proof of forgery, I know not what has a title to be considered as one.

EVEN the French, who perhaps adopted this word from the Latin before us, had it not in Shakspeare's time, for it is not noticed by Cotgrave in 1611, nor by Howel or Sherwood in 1650 ; so that probably it was introduced even among them, after the Restoration.

IX. X. XI.

IX. X. XI. A LETTER FROM SHAK-SPEARE TO RICHARD COWLEY, &c.

THE piece next presented to us in this Miscellany, is a pretended Letter from Shakspeare to Richard Cowley, a low actor who played the part of Verges in MUCH ADO ABOUT NOTHING; and who, if we are to credit these papers, was our poet's bosom friend. Like the greater part of these fictions, it (very prudently) has no date, except *Marche nynthe*. In this epistle Shakspeare says to his *worthye freynde*,—" Havinge alwaye accountedde thee a Pleasaynte ande *wittye* Personne and oune whose Companye I doe muche efteeme I have sente thee inclosedde *a whymsycalle* conceyte." - - - - I do not think it necessary to proceed any further.

WIT, in our author's time, being the general term for the intellectual powers, a *witty* person then signified either a man of cunning and shrewdness, or one of sound understanding, of considerable intellectual endowments; not, as it is here used, a man of lively

lively fancy or imagination. Thus Buckingham is characterised by Richard, as " the deep-revolving, *witty* Buckingham."[123]

THE *whymsicalle* conceit will demand a more particular examination. WHIM, according to Dr. Johnson, " is derived by Skinner, from a thing turning round, nor can I (adds that lexicographer) find any etymology more probable." But there is here certainly some mistake ; for Skinner seems to think that the word *whimzy* (he has not *whim,*) comes from the French *Quint,* originally a fifth in musick, and afterwards used metaphorically, as Cotgrave has stated, for " a fantasticall humour or veine, a foolish giddinesse of the braine." Skinner's etymology is surely very far-fetched. The English word WHIM in its present sense, without doubt was a mere contraction of

[123] So, in THE OVERTHROW OF STAGE PLAYES, 4to. 1599 ; Pref. " Maister Dr. Gager is likewise, I understand, a *man of giftes,* a good *schollar,* and an honest man, and, (as it should seeme by Maister Rainoldes his severall aunsweres and replies,) hath saied more for the defense of plaies than can be well saied againe by any man that shall succede and come after him. So that the cause being thus *wittely* and *schollerlike* maintained," &c. See also PLAYS and POEMS of WILLIAM SHAKSPEARE, vol. vi. p. 561.

I

whim-

whim-wham,[124] a child's toy, which being of some fantastical form, (perhaps of the shape of a wind-mill,) gave birth to the secondary sense in which WHIM is used at this day. Though this secondary sense had come into use before Shakspeare's death,* the adjective WHIMSICAL, most assuredly, was not employed till long afterwards. Neither Bullokar, nor Minshieu in his first or second edition, nor Sherwood in 1650, nor Philips in his third edition in 1671, nor Blount, nor Skinner, have the word. It first appears in Coles' Latin Dictionary in 1679,[125] and Dr. Johnson could find among our English writers no authority for this word higher than Addison.

[124] See Cotgrave's DICT. 1611. " BABIOLE. A trifle, a *whim-wham,* guigaw, or small toy for a child to play with."

* *Whimsey* is used by B. Jonson, VOLPONE, (1607,) Act III. sc. i. (The quotation is Mr. Waldron's.)

" ———— my most prosperous parts
" They do so spring and burgeon, [*germinate*] I can feele
" A *whimsey* in my blood."

[125] Coles seems to have derived his conception of this word from Skinner's definition of *whimzy,* for he renders it by *morosus,* and *whim* or *whimzy* by " *Morositas ; impetus morosus* et anomalus ; chimæra."

He has likewise *whim-wham,* but its original meaning (a child's toy) seems to have been forgotten, and it had assumed a new signification. Coles' interpretation of this word is—*fabulæ ; nugæ aniles.*

A COL-

A COLLATERAL proof of its non-existence may be drawn from the French and
Italian Dictionaries of our poet's time. The
French words now ordinarily used to express what we call *whimsical*, are *fantastique*,
capricieux, *bizarre*; the Italian, *capricioso*,
fantastico, *ghiribizzoso*. Had the word
whimsical been then known, unquestionably
under one or other of these words it would
have been found. But *fantastique* is inter-
preted by Cotgrave in 1611, " fantasticall,
humorous, new-fangled, giddie, skittish,
invented, conceited. *Capricieux*, " capricious, humorous, fantasticall, conceited, gid-
die-headed." *Bizarre* is explained by
" fantasticall, toyish, odde, humorous, gid-
die-headed, selfe-conceited, haire-brained;
also divers or diversified in fashion or in
colour." Thus also Florio in his Italian
Dictionary, 1611 : " *Capricioso*, humorous, fantasticall, toyish, conceited, wavering
in minde."—" *Fantasia*, A fantasy, a humour, a conceit."—" *Fantastico*, fantasticall,
humorous." " *Ghiribizzoso*, humorous, fantasticall, full of sudden toyes or humours."—
I may add, that in Howel's improved edition
of Cotgrave's book in 1650, all the same
definitions appear, without any addition.

So

So much for this rare and " *whymsycalle* conceyte,"which is addressed " To Masterre Richard Cowleye dwellynge atte *oune* [126] Masterre Holliss a draperre inne the Watlynge Streete Londonne." The " inclosedde conceyte" is indeed most truly whimsical, being a miserable drawing of our poet done by himself with a pen, from Martin Droeshout's print of him engraved seven years after his death, and prefixed to the first folio edition of his works. Could any thing be devised more novel and truly whimsical than this ? Lest there should be any doubt on this subject, the inventor and fabricator of this ingenious conceit has taken care that the light should fall, in the drawing, on the narrow side of the face, as it does in Droeshout's print, as well as in the Chandos picture ; otherwise the likeness might have escaped him, and our author might have lost the credit to which he is entitled for being able, in addition to all his other great powers, to delineate himself after he was dead.[127]

XII. A

[126] *Oune* for *one* is the spelling of no time whatsoever : but amidst such a host of absurdities it is hardly worth notice.

[127] On the reverse of this portrait I expected to have found a group of loggerheads ; but though Shakspeare says

in

XII. A DEED OF GIFT TO WILLIAM HENRY IRELAND.

HAVING now dispatched all the ſmaller fry, we come to the great "Triton of the minnows," Masterre William Henry Ireland, a most expert swimmer, and one whom, if we are to give credit to this deed, our poet "wore in his heart of heart." In plain language, we are presented with a deed of gift from William Shakspeare to his friend and neighbour in the Blackfriars, William Henry Ireland, as a reward for his having saved our poet from being drowned in the Thames. —But let our author speak for himself.

"I WILLIAM Shakspeare of *Statford on*

in his letter to his friend Cowley, that if he should not be able to discover his whimsical conceit, he shall be set down in the poet's table of loggerheads, neither group nor table is given : an omission much to be lamented, as the fabricator had here so fair an opportunity of furnishing us with what one of our modern Auctioneers would call a proper companion to the wooden exhibition at the other side.—Instead, however, of these, we have only a few scrawls, such as a boy of eight or nine years makes on the back of one of his exercises, when dismissed by his writing-master from his task.

AVON

Avon butt nowe livyng in London neare untoe a Yard calledd or knowne bye the name of Irelands yarde in the Blackfry*a*rs *London*," &c.

" Whereas onne or abowte the thyrde daye of the laste monethe beyng the monethe of *Auguste* havynge withe mye goode freynde Masterre William Henrye Irelande ande otherres *taen boate* neare untowe myne house afowersayde wee didd purpose goynge *upp Thames* butte those thatte were soe to *connducte* us beyng muche toe merrye throughe Lyquorre theye did *upsette* oure fowresayde bayrge all butte *myeselfe* savedd *themselves* bye swimmyng for though the Waterre was deepe yette owre beynge close nygh toe shore made itte lyttel dyffyculte for them knowinge the fowersayde Arte Masterre William henrye Irelande notte seeynge mee dydd aske for mee, butte oune of the Companye dydd answerre thatte I was drownynge onn the whyche he pulledd off hys Jerrekynne and Jumpedd inn afterre mee withe much paynes he draggedd mee forthe I beynge then nearelye deade and soe he dydd save mye life and for the whyche I

doe

doe herebye give hym as folowithe ! ! ! [128]
fyrste mye writtenn Playe of Henrye fowrthe
Henrye fyfthe Kyng John Kyng Leare as
allsoe mye written Playe neverr yett impryntedd whych I have named kyng henry
thyrde of Englande alle the profyts of the
whych are whollye toe bee for sayde Ireland ande atte hys deathe thenne toe hys
fyrste Sonne namedd alsoe William henrye
and atte hys deathe toe hys brother ande soe
onne butte inn case of faylure of Issue thenne
toe the nexte of kynn ande soe on for everre
inn hys lyne.   Ande I doe alsoe give untoe
sayde Ireland the Sum of ten Pounds, as a
preesaunte oute of the whyche I doe require
hym toe buye oune Rynge as a remem-
braunce."—This very curious deed, we are
afterwards told, was executed on the 25th
of October, 1604.

IT has been a common practice with our
English writers to borrow titles for their
pieces from their predecessors. Thus we had
a SHEPHERDS CALENDER long before Spencer's, and a TALE OF A TUB long before Swift
produced his ingenious Allegory.   But the

[128] So the original.   See p. 231, n. 139.

piece

piece before us is quite new; and the thought certainly has not been derived from any other writer ancient or modern. If, however, the old Satire of COCKE LORELLES BOTE, printed by Wynken de Worde, or the later TALE OF TWO SWANNES, should ever again be reprinted, the TALE OF A BOAT, or THE TALE OF THE SWAN OF AVON HALF DROWNED IN THAMES, or by whatever other name it may be called, will make a most happy accompaniment to those rare pieces; and the Collection may very properly be bound up with one of those GAR-LANDS OF DELIGHT, which were formerly sold for two or three pence, and may now be had at any of our principal booksellers for as many guineas.

THIS is the first deed that I have ever perused, (though I have examined not a few,) in which a story, with all its circum-stances, was regularly told. It is, however, we must acknowledge a very pretty story, and almost as interesting as some of our modern novels.—The circumstance that de-mands our attention in the outset, is our author describing himself as living in the Blackfriars in October, 1604. It is mani-fest

fest from the licence granted May 19, 1603,
to Shakspeare and others, (procured without doubt by the favour of the Earl of
Southampton, for the grant was made twelve
days after the King arrived in London, and
three days after Lord Southampton's own pardon passed the seals,) that the King's Servants
were not then possessed of the Blackfriars
Theatre ; for by that grant they are authorized—" the said comedies, tragedies, &c.
to shew—as well within their *nowe usuall
house* called the GLOBE, within our county
of Surrey, as also within anie toune halls,"
&c. [129] But in 1625, when they had been
long in possession of the other theatre also,
the words of the licence are—" the said
comedies, &c. to shew as well within those
two theire most usuall houses called the
GLOBE, within our county of Surrey, and
their private houses situate within the precinct of the *black Fryers*, within our city of
London," &c. [130] Even in April in the following year, they had not got possession of the
theatre in the Blackfriars, where the children
of the Revels had performed, till they were

[129] Pat. 1. Jac. p. 2. m. 4.
[130] Pat. 1. Car. p. 1. m. 5.

devested

devested of it by the King's Servants ; for I
have before me a Letter directed to the Lord
Mayor of London, and to the Justices of
the Peace in the Counties of Middlesex and
Surrey, ordering them " to permit and suffer
the three Companies of Plaiers to the King,
Queene, and Prince, to exercise ther plaies
in ther severall and usuall howses, the
GLOBE, - - - the Fortune, - - - and the
Curtain—." This paper being dated April
9th, 1604, it appears that Shakspeare's company were not then possessed of the play-
house in Blackfriars ; but probably, in the
winter of that year, and before the 24th
of March, 1604-5, they purchased it ; for
Marston's MALECONTENT appears to have
been acted there some time in that winter.—
We see from hence that Shakspeare had no
motive to reside in the Blackfriars before
this period. The truth indeed, I believe,
is, that he never resided in the Blackfriars
at all. From a paper now before me, which
formerly belonged to Edward Alleyn, the
player, our poet appears to have lived in
Southwark, near the Bear-Garden, in 1596.
Another curious document in my possession,
which will be produced in the History
of his Life, affords the strongest presumptive

sumptive evidence that he continued to reside
in Southwark to the year 1608, which is
four years after the date of this pretended
deed ; nor is there any ground for supposing
that he ceased to reside there, till he quitted
the stage entirely ; for he did not purchase the
tenement in the Blackfriars till March 10,
1612-13, (about which time he probably
retired to Stratford ;) and soon after he got
possession of it, he appears to have made
a lease of it for a term of years to one John
Robinson, who is mentioned in his Will three
years afterwards as the tenant in possession.
Supposing he had not then retired from the
stage, his residence on the Bankside could
be no inconvenience to him, the passage
from thence to Puddle Wharf, near the
Blackfriars theatre, being very short.

So much for that part of this deed which
describes our author as a resident in Blackfriars in the year 1604. Let us now
examine the curious tale contained in it.
Shakspeare, we find, being *on Thames* with
his friend, *his* Ireland, (who bore, we are
told, the two christian names of WILLIAM
HENRY, which are likewise the baptismal
names of the son of the Editor of these
deeds

deeds and papers,) and other friends,—by
some mismanagement in consequence of
the boatmen being " toe merrye throughe
liquorre," the boat was *upsette*, and our poet
would have been drowned, had not his life
been most happily saved by Mr. William
Henry Ireland.—Whether Shakspeare could
swim, I have no means of ascertaining. I
think it, however, extremely probable, from
his admirable lines in the TEMPEST, that
he was well acquainted with that useful
art. [131] This, however, is mere conjecture,
which certainly can have no weight if the
deed before us be genuine : for here we find
that the hapless bard was as ignorant in this
respect as those little wanton boys whom
he describes, that, trusting to bladders, are
sometimes carried beyond their depth. It

[131] " I saw him beat the surges under him,
  " And ride upon their backs ; he trod the water,
  " Whose enmity he flung aside, and breasted
  " The surge most swoln that met him : his bold head
  " 'Bove the contentious waves he kept, and oar'd
  " Himself with his good arms in lusty stroke
  " To the shore, that o'er his wave-worn basis bow'd,
  " As stooping to relieve him : I not doubt,
  " He came alive to land."
See also JULIUS CÆSAR, Act I. :
  " For once upon a raw and gusty day," &c.

is

is worthy of notice that when all his friends, as well as the boatmen, had got safe to shore, and saw the poor poet drowning, not one of them offered him any assistance, except Master WILLIAM HENRY Ireland. Most fortunately this kind act was left to him alone. Shakspeare, in similar circumstances, I have no doubt would have " plunged in, accoutred as he was;" but his friend, warmly as he was attached to our author, though this accident happened close to the shore, which he had just reached by swimming, would not venture again into the water, till he had " takenne offe his Jerrekynne,"which we may suppose was made of blue velvet, drawn out with white sattin, and given him by *his* friend, *his* Shakspeare, out of that splendid wardrobe, an account of which is reserved for a subsequent page. As for the other expert swimmers, they most unfeelingly stood stone-still, one only of them observing that Shakspeare was drowning.—Some of the occurrences mentioned in these papers are so extremely curious and picturesque, that one naturally is induced to wish that they may be delineated by some of our excellent modern artists. The *drowning poet* will make

make a very proper companion for his sup-
perless editor, as exhibited by the admirable
pencil of Hogarth.

BUT to return once more to verbal disquisition.—The word UPSET is " a word of
exceeding good command," and requires our
particular attention. It is perfectly a seaman's word, and was without doubt first
introduced by that brave and honest class of
men, to express shortly and clearly one of
those unfortunate accidents to which the
uncertain element on which a great part of
their lives is passed, exposes them. So far
from being found in any ancient vocabulary,
it has not a place even in Johnson's Dictionary. It has crept into our language, I
think, within these few years, but certainly
within this century ; and I do not recollect
ever to have seen it in print, except in a
newspaper, before the present publication.
The word indeed was so little familiar to
me, that, till I sat down to examine these
spurious papers, I had not a precise idea of
its signification. It denotes, as I now understand, a particular species of misfortune
to which seamen are liable. When a boat
is turned keel-upward by the mere force of

the

the waves, it is in the seaman's language *upset* ; when a similar accident happens by mismanagement of a sail, or the force of the wind, the boat is then said to be *over-turned*. Here, therefore, we find an accident not very likely to happen on the Thames, where we seldom have such boisterous waves, expressed by a word unknown to our language for above a century afterwards.

THERE are several other circumstances belonging to this deed, that must not be passed over. The editor in his preface mentions, that "amongst a mass of family papers the Contracts between Shakspeare, Lowine, and Condelle, and the lease granted by him and Hemynge to Michael Fraser and his wife, which was first found, were discovered ; and *soon afterwards* the deed of gift to William Henry Ireland." When the believers in the authenticity of these MSS. were first informed of this deed, they can best ascertain. I certainly never heard it mentioned by any of those who were in the habit of inspecting these papers, till May last, about FOUR MONTHS after they were first announced ; and lately on

my

my questioning a very accurate friend on
this subject, who, from time to time, had a
very early view of all of them, as they
were *brought forward*, he told me that my
recollection was perfectly correct. The
words, however, *soon afterwards*, being
indefinite, perhaps may have been intended
to apply to the period which I have mentioned. In the intervening time every one
was naturally curious to know from what
quarter they were derived. A plausible
story was circulated, (but I know not on
what authority,) that our poet's associate
in the theatre, John Heminges, having died
intestate, his papers fell into the hands of
an artful attorney, from whom they descended to the *unknown* gentleman, in
whose house they were discovered; to
which there was no objection but that
Heminges had made a Will, which I published a few years ago. This circumstance, I remember, I mentioned to the
gentleman from whom I received the foregoing account, and from that time I never
heard more of John Heminges. But
the time when his eldest son, William,
died, being unknown, the *true believers*
were obliged to rest their faith on him for
a while;

a while; till at length a kind of obscure
twilight was thrown upon the subject by
the lucky discovery of the deed before us:
which certainly furnishes a very plausible
ground for the unknown gentleman's so
liberally bestowing all these treasures (this
valuable relique among the rest) on the
son of the editor, who most fortunately
bears the same two christian names. The
only difficulty is, that it has not yet been
quite satisfactorily proved that any such
man as *William Henry* Ireland ever existed
in the days of Shakspeare; though there
are unquestionable proofs that a *piece of
him*, (as Horatio says,) one *William Ireland*,
did live at that period: an honest tradesman who kept a shop in the Blackfriars,
and whom, about five years ago, I had the
honour of first introducing to the world.

In March 1612-13, as I have already
mentioned, Shakspeare purchased from
one Henry Walker a house in the Blackfriars.[132] This house Walker had bought

[132] It is observable, that this modern spelling is constantly
employed in this and all the other deeds where Blackfriars
is mentioned, except one. But the spelling and phraseology of Shakspeare's time was—*the* black-*fryers*.

in

in Oct. 1604, from Mr. Mathew Bacon of Gray's Inn, as appears by a conveyance among the Fetherstonhaugh Deeds now before me; at the bottom of which I find this same William Ireland as an attesting witness. He appears to have been no great clerk, but made as handsome a *mark* as can well be desired.—In the Conveyance to Shakspeare, which in honour of this person will be found in the Appendix, (N°. II.) the tenement which he purchased is described as having been " sometymes in the tenure of James Gardyner Esquier, and since that in the tenure of John Fortescue Gent. and now or late being in the tenure or occupation of one WILLIAM IRELAND, or of his assignee or assigns." From the prefix *one*, the want of the addition of *Gent.* and the word *occupation*, which at that time was a term that denoted trade,[133] I had no doubt that he was a tradesman: and I found my conjecture confirmed by a Lease of a stable in Blackfriars, which

---

[133] So, in CORIOLANUS :

" ———— you that stood so much
" Upon the voice of *occupation*, and
" The breath of garlick-eaters."

was

was made to him by John Green in 1602, (now in the possession of Mr. Wallis,) in which he is expressly styled a Haberdasher. Some time after Henry Walker had purchased the house in Blackfryars in 1604, this haberdasher appears to have become his tenant at will, previous to which time the premises were occupied by one William Robinson. Notwithstanding the great intimacy which, we are told, subsisted between this tradesman and our author, as soon as he purchased this house, he turned Ireland out; for on the subsequent day after it was conveyed to him (or more probably on the same day) in addition to the mortgage made to Walker for sixty pounds of the purchase-money unpaid,—" to make assurance double sure," he also made him a lease of the premises for one hundred years at the rent of a pepper-corn, (March 11th, 1612-13,) with a proviso that on the payment of the sum above-mentioned the lease should be void: [134] and afterwards, when he had paid off the whole of the

[134] This deed is among the other title-deeds of the Rev. Mr. Fetherstonhaugh, in the custody of Albany Wallis, Esq.

pur-

purchase-money, he made a lease for a term of years to John Robinson, the son probably of William.[135]   Whether the William Henry Ireland mentioned in the deed now before us, as the bosom-friend of Shakspeare, was intended to represent this Haberdasher, and we are to suppose that the scriveners who drew the several instruments forgot one of his christian names, or we are to believe that Mr. William Henry Ireland, the friend of Shakspeare, was the father, or son, or brother, or uncle, of the other, I know not; but it seems it was WILLIAM HENRY *alone* that gave the name to a yard in that quarter called *Ireland's Yard*, and the poor Haberdasher, though he appears to have lived a long time there, had no title to so honourable a distinction.[136]

IT

[135] See APPENDIX, N°. III.

[136] To *A* VIEW *of the House of this Mr.* WILLIAM HENRY *Ireland* (which will be *reviewed* presently) the editor of these treasures has subjoined the following observations : " The house here sketched by the hand of Shakspeare, and situated in Blackfriars, became his property. The yard adjoining, at this hour, bears the name of his *friend*, Ireland, who *occupied* it, and is pointed out to the

G G   passenger

IT is not very easy to conjecture on what principle the unknown gentleman (for in this case none of his ancestors or their attorneys can bear any part of the burthen) could have proceeded, when he fabricated this deed. Whether he had never read the Mortgage-deed which I published in 1790, in which WILLIAM IRELAND is mentioned as a person who had for a time occupied the house in the Blackfriars, previous

---

passenger by two painted boards, one at each end, bearing the inscription of *Ireland's Yard.* The Fetherstonhaugh family, to whom it now belongs, [whether the *house* or the *yard* is here meant, is not very clear,] were in Shakspeare's time, it is presumed, the *ground landlords :* [See the Conveyance to Shakspeare, Appendix, N°. II. " — and also the *soyle* whereuppon the said tenement standeth ;"] and the editor has the satisfaction of informing the publick, that he has been favoured by Albany Wallis, Esq. of Norfolk street, the Agent of that family, with a ground-plot of this estate, *taken in the year* 1672, in which it appears that the passage leading to this house, there described as Ireland's house, and whose name is there also given to a small street adjoining, constitutes a part of *Ireland's Yard.*"—This reasoning is so very clear and conclusive, that no reasonable man, I think, can doubt—that there is such a place as *Ireland's Yard,* and that it derived its name from a person of the name of *Ireland.* But as for our WILLIAM HENRY, I fear, notwithstanding his great expertness in swimming, he must still remain in the mire of the neighbouring Fleet-ditch, where for the present we shall leave him.

to

to Shakspeare's purchase, and merely by
accident or out of zeal to do honour to
the son of the editor, stumbled on the name
of WILLIAM HENRY Ireland; or whether he supposed that no one would examine
that original and authentick deed, and discover that WILLIAM, was not WILLIAM
HENRY, Ireland; or whether, finally, he
supposed that one of these persons might
very well pass for the other; (as a mere
misnomer, arising from a clerical error of
so trivial a nature as the omission of a christian name,) on which of these various grounds
he proceeded, I have no means of ascertaining; but certain it is, that his zeal to serve
his friend, (enkindled by so valuable an
acquisition as that good estate which he has
lately *recovered*, or *discovered*,) greatly out-
ran his discretion, and that no other three
words in the language could been selected
more unpropitious to the cause of imposture
than the names—WILLIAM HENRY Ireland.—The deed in which they are found is
so perfectly a *felo de se*, that were there no
denotations of fraud in the other instruments
and papers, (as they are spangled all over
with them,) the whole would " take corruption

From

" From this particular fault : *this* dram of base
" *Would* all the noble subtsance of worth dout,
" To his own scandal."

IT will not require a long dissertation to
shew that in the beginning of the last century, and long afterwards, persons of the
first rank in England were contented with
one christian name, though this haberdasher
in the Blackfriars has been decorated with
two. As the House of Commons is usually
composed of the most respectable gentlemen
in every county, if any one at that time had
been baptized with two christian names, he
might naturally be expected to be found
among the Members of that house. In the
first parliament of King James, which met
in 1603, one year before the date of this
pretended deed, I find four hundred and
sixty seven persons returned ; and among
them one only with two christian names,
not, however, analogous to those now under
consideration. [137]   In the List of Baronets
created

[137] PARL. HIST. vol. v. p. 11.   In this parliament
Sir Thomas *Posthumus* Hobbey sat for Scarborough : but
this, as I have observed above, is not properly an exception.   When a son was born after the death of his father,
it was common in that age to add *Posthumus* to the name
given

created by King James between May 1611
and August 1623, containing two hundred
and five names, I find not one : among the
Knights of the Bath made at the creation
of Henry Prince of Wales in 1610, and
of Prince Charles in 1616, not one. In a
word, neither the parliament that met in
1621, nor that which assembled in 1627,
nor the long parliament of 1640,[138] furnishes
a single example of a gentleman distinguished by a second baptismal name. Even
the House of Peers during this whole period, nay, the heirs apparent of the crown,
Henry and Charles, could boast of no such
distinction : it was reserved alone for this
worthy haberdasher of Blackfriars, the *jerre-*
kynned Nautilus of the Thames, the pre-

given him at the font, merely to denote this circumstance.
So Dudley *Posthumus* Lovelace, (brother of the Poet,) and
many others.—This is not a second christian name in the
sense now under consideration.

[138] Even in the Restoration Parliament there was but
one member who had two christian names ; Sir Francis
Henry Lee. In the parliament which met in 1661, and
continued till 1678, there was not one : at least I do not
find one in Chamberlaine's List, printed in 1673. See
also Dugdale's ORIG. JUD. and Wood's ATH. OXON where,
if I mistake not, not a single lawyer or academick with
two baptismal names is to be found.

server

server of Shakspeare's life, the renowned and never-to-be-forgotten Mr. WILLIAM HENRY Ireland.

LEAVING him in full possession of his honours, let us take one other glance at the curious deed where alone they are recorded. In recitals in pleadings, &c. in the courts of law and equity, when a Will is mentioned, lawyers, with their usual caution, commonly state that the testator died *on or about* a certain day (named), and that previously *on or about* another certain day, which is also named, he made his Will. But where a man has been near drowning, and he is going to reward the friend who saved his life, it is somewhat remarkable that he should not remember the precise day on which he had so providential an escape, though not two months had elapsed from the time when this disaster happened. So very careful a chronicler as Shakspeare, who on the backs of all his papers, we find, wrote a short account of them or some injunction touching their preservation, might, methinks, have made a little minute concerning this watry escape. I have stated that not two months had elapsed, because the deed

I   is

is said to be made on the 25th of Oct. 1604,
and the accident to have happened " onne
or abowte the thyrde daye of the *laste*
monethe, beyng the monethe of *August*."
Here indeed is another small difficulty to be
got over; for the poor half-drowned poet is
made to know so little of the ordinary divi-
sions of the year, that he conceives the
month of October to follow immediately
after that of August; a circumstance not
very easy to be accounted for, unless we
suppose, that when he made this deed he
was as much distempered with liquor as
his boatmen were, when, like his own Falstaff, he was soused into the Thames; or that
some Macclesfield of ancient days persuaded
the people of England to annihilate the ill-
fated month of September in that year.

THE particular species of gift which our
poet's gratitude dictated on this occasion
next demands our attention:—" for the
whyche service I doe herebye give hym
as folowithe ! ! ! "[139] fyrste mye written playe
of

[139] No punctuation whatsoever is employed in deeds.
These three notes of admiration (of which even the printed
books of former times furnish no example,) are therefore
here

of Henrye fowrthe, Henrye fyfthe, Kyng
John, Kyng Leare, as allsoe mye written
playe neverr yett impryntedd whych I have
named Kyng henrye thyrde of Englande
alle the profytts of the whych are whollye
toe bee for sayde Ireland ande atte hys
deathe thenne toe hys fyrste sonne namedd
also William henrye;" for this name of
WILLIAM HENRY is to be continued,
like an heir-loom, in the family, to the
third and fourth generation.

FROM his mentioning his " *written*
playe of Henrye Fowrthe," &c. one not
particularly conversant with the various
editions of our poet's works might suppose
that neither KING HENRY IV. nor HENRY
V. had been printed in 1604; but the first
part of the former had appeared in 1598,
the second in 1600, and HENRY THE
FIFTH in the same year. KING JOHN
indeed was not then printed; and what is
somewhat unlucky, KING LEAR was not

here faithfully preserved, not only as what Dogberry would
call a most graceful and senseless ornament, but because
they render this instrument what the collectors of coins and
other rarities so highly estimate, *unique*.

written

written till after the 24th of October, 1604,
as I have shewn in the Essay on the Chronological Order of our author's plays. [140]
The

[140] PLAYS and POEMS, &c. 1790. vol. i. p. i. p. 353.
The following *shrewd* remark on this subject is worth
notice : " Mr. Malone shrewdly guesses - - - that it
[K. LEAR,] was not written till after the *accession* of
James the First to *the crown of England*, which happened,
says Mr. B, on the 24th of October, 1604 ; but which
happened, *says History*, on the 24th of March, 1602-3.
So much for accuracy of dates, and skill in comparison."
COMPARATIVE REVIEW, &c. p. 54.

It is an old remark, which can never be too often repeated, that those who write, should read. It is, however, very clear, that the writer of the above passage,
though he refers to my Essay at the bottom of the page,
had not read it, or did not understand it.—Not one word
will be found there concerning this play being written after
the accession of King James to the throne ; neither did the
gentleman who relied on my authority, say a word of his
Accession. What I *have* said, and what I was quoted
as saying, was, that the play of KING LEAR was written
after James was *proclaimed* King of GREAT BRITAIN ;
and that was not on the 24th of March, 1602-3, but on
the 24th of October, 1604. " *So much for accuracy of
dates, and skill in comparison.*"

In fixing the date of this tragedy I had less difficulty
than in almost any of Shakspeare's plays, and was not re-
duced to *guessing*, as the author would have found if he had
looked at what he has referred to. My words are,—" This
play is *ascertained* to have been written after the month of
October, 1604," &c.

H H   " The

The present deed bears date the following day : to reconcile these dates therefore we have only to suppose that Shakspeare rose early on the 25th ; and considering the wonderful facility with which he wrote, it will not be extravagant to suppose that he began and finished that sublime tragedy in one morning, previous to the Scrivener's engrossing this deed.—Leaving this play to shift for itself, it must be remembered that our poet had already sold to the theatre such of the plays here enumerated as were then written, as was the constant practice of that time, and had no property whatsoever in them : and had he ever mentioned his historical play of Henry the Fifth, he would have written it, not as we find it here, but *Fift*,[141] as it is printed in the early quarto edition of that piece, and in the folio copy

[141] "The Chronicle History of Henry the *fift*," &c. 4to. 1600. And so in the folio, 1623, "The Life of Henry the *Fift.*" See also Stowe's ANNALS, 4to. 1605. p. 557 : King Henry the *Fift*, born at Monmouth," &c. William Basse's Epitaph on Shakspeare ascertains the ancient pronunciation of this word, which remains the same at this day in many parts of England:

" To lodge all four in one bed make a *shift*
" Until doomsday ; for hardly will a *fift*," &c.
        SHAKSP. *ut supr.* Vol. 1. P. I. p. 198.

I   published

published by Heminges and Condellin 1623;
as he himself unquestionably pronounced
the word, and as half the people of England
pronounce it at this day.

OF the play of " Henrye thyrde of Englande," I have only to say, that I make no
doubt it is as good a piece as any that has
been or ever will be drawn from the same
repository.—Before however we fling this
instrument after all the rest, it may not be
without use to take a slight view of the
indorsements on it. They are these: " Sealed
and delyveredd in the presaunce of us Jo:
Edwards—Jos. Byggett.—Deede of guyfte
from Shakspeare to *Irelaunde*—2 James."

THOSE who are conversant with deeds of
that period know, that the Scrivener who
drew them, and his servant or apprentice,
were almost always witnesses to them. On
neither this deed, however, nor any other
that has been produced on the present occasion, does the name of a Scrivener appear
as a subscribing witness.—But this defect on
the back of this and all the other deeds is
not half so fatal as that indorsement which

the

the ignorance of the fabricator has placed on them : the year of the king's reign in English. If the maker of these instruments had even been what, I think, Lord Camden called a *sucking* lawyer, he would have learned, before he had turned over a few leaves of Sir Edward Coke's First Institute, that some ancient feofments had been discovered to be forged by their having livery of seisin indorsed on them ; [142] and would not have fallen into a similar error.—— In the time we are now treating of, it was by no means common to write either the year of the king's reign, or the year of our Lord, on the back of a deed. I have very

[142] " For certainly (says this great lawyer,) the witnesses named in the deed were witnesses of both [the delivery of the deed and livery of seisin]; and witnesses either of delivery of the deed or of livery of seisin by expresse tearms, was but of later times ; and the reason was in respect of the notoriety of the feofment. - - - [So] if a deed, in the style of the king, name him *defensor fidei* before 13 H. 8., or *supreme head* before 20 H. 8., (at which time he was first acknowledged supreme head by the clergy, albeit the king had not the style of *supreme head* in his charters, &c. till 22 H. 8.) or *king* of Ireland before 33 H. 8., at which time he assumed the title of *King of Ireland*, being before that called *Lord* of Ireland, it is certainly forged : *et sic de* SIMILIBUS." Co. Litt. 7. Hargrave's edit.

seldom

seldom found more than a short note of the purport of it, (as, " A Deed belonging to the house in Blackfryers,"—or " A deed of bargain and sale from Walker to Shakspeare,") and often not even so much as that : but when the year of the king's reign *was* indorsed, it was always written in Latin (2 Jacobi, or 2 Jac. &c.) ;[143] and this continued to be the uniform practice till the statute 4 Geo. II. c. 26. was made, which directing that all the proceedings at law should be from thenceforth in English, naturally produced an alteration in this minute particular also. The indorsement, therefore, on this and all the other deeds before us, containing the year of the king's reign in English, instead of Latin, is a decisive proof of forgery ; and the two words " 2 *James*," are as fatal on the outside as WILLIAM-HENRY are within this instrument.—Thus we see that the spirit of Horace's precept,—*talis ad imum*, operated

---

[143] So the Statutes were formerly always referred to in Latin : 10 Jac. , 4 Car. &c. And Sir George Croke's Reports in the time of Elizabeth and the two succeeding princes, are constantly cited in the same language : Cro. Jac. Cro. Car.

through

through every part of these fabrications, however little the letter of it may have been known to the fabricator.

XIII. Tributary Lines to Ireland.

XIV. View of William Henry Ireland's House and Coat of Arms.

XV. Engraved Portraits of Bassanio and Shylock.

I may now congratulate your Lordship on being within sight of land; for after I shall have dispatched the foregoing—what shall I call them?—" unreal mockeries," which will be quickly done, we have only three or four deeds left to examine.

On the " Tributary Lines" to the renowned William Henry, I shall not detain you long, contenting myself with a short extract, by way of specimen:

" O Modelle of Virretue Charytyes sweeteste
" Chylde thye Shakspeare thanks thee
" Norre Verse norre Sygh norre Teare canne
" paynte mye Soule norre saye bye
" halfe howe muche I love thee."

Is

Is this the composition of Shakspeare, or
of a young lady of fifteen, after reading the
first novel that has fallen into her hands ?—
But I beg pardon of all the young ladies of
Great Britain and Ireland; there is not one
of them that would not, even at that early
age, produce something more in character
than the tender effusion of one man addressing another, which is here stuck in between
the verses and tears of our blubbering
poet.

THE next paper is briefly, and in the true
modern style, entitled — " VIEW of my
Masterre Irelande's House," &c. with two
coats of arms beneath it, *trick'd* (as, I think,
the heralds call it,) and most beautifully
linked together; the one of Shakspeare, the
other of our hero, William Henry Ireland.—
The VIEW is a miserable exhibition of an
old-fashioned tenement, with the modern
improvement of windows down to the
ground, done with a pen and ink by our
immortal bard. The only objection to it is,
the title; the word *View*, in the sense of a
delineation of a house or any other object,
either on canvass, paper, or copper, being
unfortunately wholly unknown to our ancestors,

cestors, and so completely modern, that it is not found in any one of the various vocabularies which I have mentioned in the course of this inquiry. Had the word borne this signification in the last century, we should have had here—*A* VIEW," &c. not the clipt language of the present day.

I HAVE not met with many delineations of this kind so early as the time of our author; but when such *Views* came to be commonly delineated and engraved, they were called PROSPECTS, or PROSPECTIVES, or PICTURES. Thus we have " PROSPECTS of remarkable places in and about the city of London,"—sold by Overton, after the Restoration. " The South-east PPOSPECT of the Church of St. Dunstan's." " The South PROSPECT of the Citie of London, (after a print by Hollar,) R. P. *excudit*;" in which many heads appear on London Bridge, and old St. Paul's without a spire. " A PROSPECT of London and Westminster, taken at several stations to the southward," sold by Robert Morden, at the Atlas in Cornhill, and Philip Lea, at the Atlas in Cheapside. " The PICTURE of the most famous City of London, as it appeared in the night in the height of its
ruinous

ruinous condition by fire, September 2,
1666."—Engraved by Sherwin. "TheWest
Prospect of the Cathedral Church of St.
Paul," engraved by Daniel King.[144] In 1693
was published, in folio, Slezer's " Thea-
trum Scotiæ, containing the Prospects
of his Majesty's Palaces, Castles, and most
considerable towns in Scotland." And even
within this present century have appeared
" A Prospect of the seat of Sir William
Ashhurst, Knight, at Highgate," (Member
of Parliament for London, in the reign of
Queen Anne,) and " A South Prospect
of Pancras Wells."[145] The word View,
as now used, came to us from the French,
(Veuë et Perspective) if I mistake not, in the
beginning of the present century.[146]—So
much

[144] All the Prospects here mentioned, are in a volume
in the Library of the Society of Antiquaries, marked London Plans, &c. The names of the Sellers and Engravers of them have been specified, as they contribute in
some measure to fix the dates.

[145] *Ut supr.*

[146] In 1710 appeared " The View of the inside of the
Quire of St. Paul's Cathedral, Queen Anne, and the noble
House of Lords," &c. engraved by Du Guernier, a Frenchman. In a Volume belonging to the Society of Antiquaries, given by Lord Coleraine.—The French used the word
veuë, in this sense, early in the sixteenth century.

much for this curious VIEW, which was
done by our author in order to win a wager
of five shillings. [147]

As for our Blackfriars' *Marksman* and
Haberdasher, when he got these arms
which our poet has so gracefully tricked,
I am altogether ignorant. Certain however

In Lord Orford's Catalogue of Engravers, p. 61, I find—
" VIEW of York from the Water-House," &c. by William Lodge, (who was born in 1649, and died in 1689.)
But this description was given by Virtue, who employed
the language of his own day (little thinking that he was
laying a trap for our forger) ; for on examining the original in the very valuable topographical Collection of John
Symmons, of Paddington, Esq. I find that Lodge knew
nothing of this VIEW. His prints are entitled, " The
ancient and loyal City of York ;" by William Lodge. [De-
dicated to the Hon. Sir John Broeke, Bart.]—" From the
old Water-house in York." By W. L.

[147] Here we have another proof of several of these fabrications having been founded on archetypes furnished by the
edition of Shakspeare's Plays and Poems, published in 1790.
See Vol. I. P. II. p. 323, where I have given a Letter
addressed to Edward Alleyn, the Player, who was requested
to play, for a *wager*, some part in which Knell, or Bently,
(the Garrick and Barry of their day,) had excelled :

" Deny me not, sweet Ned ; the wager's downe,
" And twice as muche commaunde of me or myne ;
" And if you wynne, I swear the half is thine,
" And for an overplus an *English crowne.*"

it

it is, that in those days armorial bearings were thought a very honourable distinction; and that it was not quite so common at that time as it is at present, for a haberdasher to walk to the College of Heralds, and as soon as he had learned what were the arms of an ancient family whose name he happened to bear, to assume them without further ceremony.

THE originals of the two following coloured prints, one of which presents us with the portrait of an actor, (Shakspeare, if you will,) in the part of Bassanio, in THE MERCHANT OF VENICE, and the other with that of Shylock in the same play, I have not seen; and if I had seen them, I am not entitled, by any knowledge of the art, to decide upon their merit or authenticity. But by those who are perfect and indisputable judges in such matters, I have been informed, that in spite of the process of discoloration by tobacco-water and of fumigation by smoke and brimstone, which they appear to have undergone in that unknown repository in the country from whence all these curiosities have been

issued,

issued, they are manifestly washed drawings of a recent date. The Dutch Shylock,
with his blue night-cap, and his hands in his
trowsers, will, I am told, be easily recognized by any one who has either visited
Holland, or seen any representation of the
natives of that country.

XVI. AGREEMENT BETWEEN SHAK-SPEARE AND LOWINE.

THE sixteenth article of this Miscellany
is an Agreement between our poet and John
Lowin, the player, made on the 7th of
November, 1608 ; by which Mr. Lowin
binds himself for four years " to playe upon
the stage, (what stage is not mentioned,) [148]
as well in those comedyes and tragedyes
which he [Shakspeare] has alreadye produced, as those which he may at anye time
hereafter *brynge forward*, ande likewise any
other Playes which he the saide Wm Shakspeare maye at anye tyme cause to be

---

[148] In the real stage-contracts of that time, the theatre
on which such of the actors as were called *Hirelings* were
engaged to play, was always mentioned either by name or
description ; and they covenanted not to play in any other
publick or common playhouse. See the next note.

played,

played, not written or composd bye *hymselfe*, but whiche are the Writyngs or *composityons* of others." The actor's salary, it is agreed, shall be (not one guinea per week, as was maliciously reported, but) the summe of " *oune* pound ande ten shillings per week."

THE phrase *to bring forward*, which occurs in more places than one in this volume, is now a very common theatrical expression, being presented to us almost every morning at breakfast in the play-bills of the present day : but how *ancient* it is, I shall leave to the partisans of these manuscripts to ascertain. In the History of the Stage I have shewn, that the principal actors formerly played on Shares, as it is called ; that is, they divided the profits of the exhibition daily in various proportions among them ; as is yet the practice in itinerant companies in the country. Other inferior actors were retained by the name of HIRELINGS,[149] at a weekly salary of from

---

[149] " Md yᵗ this 8th of December 1597 my father Philip Hinshlow hiered as a covenaunt servant willyam Kendall for ij years after the statute of winchester wᵗʰ ij single penc A [he] to geve hym for his sayd servis everi week of his playing

from six to ten shillings a week, which was paid by the Sharers; and each Sharer was entitled to have a boy, [150] who played either young or female characters, for whose services he received from three to six shillings a week. The mode frequently was, for some speculator to build a theatre, which he conducted, dividing the emoluments into shares, and retaining to himself the receipts of the Galleries or half the Galleries, [151] to reimburse him for all expences,

playing in London x s. & in yᵉ cuntrie vs. for the wᶜʰ he covenaunteth for yᵉ space of those ij yeares to be redye at all Tymes to play *in yᵗ howse of the said Philip* & in no other during the sayd Terme.

Wittnes my self the writer of This—E. Alleyn."
Henslowe's Register. MS.

See also PLAYS and POEMS of SHAKSPEARE, Vol. I. P. II. p. 311.

[150] Hart, the celebrated tragedian, had been Robinson's boy or apprentice, at Blackfriars, and Mohun was Beeston's boy, at the Cockpit.

[151] " Item, he [Philip Henslowe] agrees with the same Companie, that they should enter bond to plaie with him for three yeares at such house and houses as hee shall appoint, and to allowe him *half galleries* for the said house and houses, and the other halfe galleries towards his debt of 126ˡˡ. and other such moneys as hee should laie out for playe-apparel duringe the space of the said three yeares agreeinge with them, in consideracōn wheareof to seale each of them
a bond

pences, of which he kept an account; such
as dresses, &c. for new plays, the purchase
of the copies of such plays as a certain
number of the Sharers should think fit to be
bought, and all other incidental charges.
At a certain period he settled accounts with
the company; [152] and if the receipts appropriated

a bond of 200[ll]. to find them a convenient house and houses,
and laie out such moneies as fower of the Sharers should
think fitt for theire use in apparel, which at the three yeares
end being paid for to be delivered to the Sharers; who ac-
cordinglie entered the said bonds, but Mr. Henchlowe and
Mr. Mead deferred the same, and in conclusion denied to
seale at all."

From a paper, entitled ARTICLES OF GRIEVANCE
against Mr. Hinchlowe. MS.

[152] " Reckned wth the company of my lorde the earle of
notingames men to this place, & I have layd owte for them
the some of vi hunderd & thirtie two pownds & they have
payd unto me of this deatte iij hunderd & fiftie & eyghte
powndes to this daye beinge the 13 of october 1599."

Henslowe's Register. MS.

" Merd. That the fulle some of all the deabtes w[ch] we
owe unto Mr. Henslow to this xvi of m[r]che 1603, cometh
to juste the some of 140[ll]. 1s. ood. w[ch] some of 140[ll].
ois. ood. we whose names are here under wrytten do
aknowledge ower dew deatte & promysse trewe payment.
Thomas Blackwood." *Ibid.*

" Caste up all the acowntes frome the beginninge of the
world untell this daye beinge the 14 daye of marche 1604
[1604-5] by Thomas Dowghton & Edward Jube for
the

priated to him were not sufficient to defray
the charges he had been at, the balance was
paid him by the company in various proportions according to the shares they held;
who thus acquired a property in the plays
and dresses which had been purchased.

I HAD been induced by a passage in an
old Collection of Epigrams printed in 1614,
to suppose that there were sometimes *forty*
sharers in a company : but this was certainly a mistake; and I have now good
reason to believe that the sharers were
usually not more than *twelve*. These shares
were again often divided into two and
sometimes into four parts : and the owner
of the share, whether an actor or proprietor
of the house, made a lease of such part of
it as he chose to dispose of, to an actor,
who paying a certain rent was thereby entitled to play in the company, to receive
his dividend daily, (proportionable to what
he held,) and to a share also in the property

the company of the Princes men and I Philipe Henslow
So ther reastethe dewe unto me P. Henslow the some of
xxiiij." all Reconyngs conservnynge the company in stocke
generall descarged, and my sealfe descarged to them of all
deat." *Ibid.*

of the cloaths and other stage-necessaries, [153] which having been paid for out of the receipts of the house, or the pockets of the Sharers on settling accounts, became their own. What I have now stated is not conjectural, but is ascertained by a Lease intended to have been made by Philip Henslowe and Edward Alleyn in the year 1608, (the very year in which the deed before us is said to have been made,) to Thomas Downton, an actor; [154] and by other documents in my possession, which have been given in the notes. This explains the following passage in the Will of John Heminges : " And I do hereby will and appoint that the moiety or one half of the yearly benefit and profit of the several *parts* [155] which I have by *lease* in the several playhouses of the Globe and Black-fryers, - - - be from time to time received and taken up by my executor."

[153] On this ground the Sharer, when he came into the company, laid down a sum of money, which was paid in to the general stock.

[154] See the APPENDIX, N°. IV. He had originally been a Hireling, but afterwards became a Sharer.

[155] In a subsequent part of his Will he uses the technical term: " — the yearly profit and benefit which shall arise or be made by my several *parts* and *shares* in the several playhouses called the Globe and Blackfriers." SHAKSP. Vol. I. P. II. p. 194.

K K   JOHN

JOHN Lowin, whose name was formerly sometimes written *Lewin*, but never *Lowine*, as it is exhibited in this deed, was born, as I have already mentioned, in 1576. He probably went on the stage before the end of that century : but he was not in the Company of the Lord Chamberlain's Servants, to which Shakspeare belonged ; and in 1603, when he was one of Lord Worcester's servants, he was in so low a situation, that in that year he was under the necessity of borrowing a very small sum of money from the Proprietor of the Rose Theatre, where he then played, to enable him to go with a strolling party into the country. This fact is proved by the following memorandum :

" LENT unto John Lowyn the 12 of marche 1602, [1602-3] when he went into the contrey with the company to playe, in Redy mony, the some of——vs." [156]

SOME time in the following year he joined our author's Company who then had become the King's Servants, and appeared

[156] Henslowe's Register. MS.

personally

personally in the Induction to Marston's
MALECONTENT, which was played at the
theatre in the Blackfriars then newly taken
by that company.[157]   He was at this time
without any doubt a subordinate actor, and
did not get into the first rank till after the
death of Shakspeare and Burbadge, and the
retirement of Heminges and Condell, in or
before 1623.[158] The progress of this actor's
reputation

[157] He likewise appears in the list of the performers of
Ben Jonson's SEJANUS, which he informs us was acted
by the King's Servants in 1603 ; but the year then extending to the 25th of March, this piece must have been produced in 1603-4.—That Lowin was not of their company
in 1603, is proved not only by Henslowe's MS., but by
the Patent granted to Shakspeare, &c. May 19, 1603,
where, though we find the names of the obscure Cowley
and William Sly, Lowin's name does not appear.

[158] That Condell had retired before 1623, is ascertained
by the title-page of Webster's DUCHESS OF MALFY,
printed in that year.   Heminges without doubt retired at
the same time, or before ; for in the next year Lowin and
Taylor stand at the head of the List of the King's Servants.
See PLAYS and POEMS of Shakspeare, Vol. I. P. II.
p. 208.

Heminges, however, it appears from Sir Henry Herbert's
MS. took some concern in the management of the theatre,
and used to present Sir Henry, as Master of the Revels,
with his New-Year's gift, for three or four years afterwards.
—Shakspeare died in 1616, and Burbadge in 1619: thus,

there-

reputation I have thought it necessary to
mark particularly, because in another deed,
that shall very soon be *brought forward*,
dated 20 Feb. 1611-12, we shall find him
called OUR BEST ACTOR, when he was
only emerging into notice. Our fabricator
was led into this errour by two lines which
I have quoted from an old lampoon written
on Ben Jonson :

" Let Lowin cease, and Taylor scorn to touch
" The loathed stage, for thou hast made it such :"

and by another quotation from Wright's
HISTORIA HISTRIONICA, in which it is
said that " before the Wars he used to act
Falstaff with mighty applause." But this
undoubtedly relates to the period between
1623 and 1641, as the preceding verses
have a reference to the year 1632, when
Jonson's MAGNETICK LADY was played,
which the writer asserts had rendered the
stage loathsome. Accordingly, in 1625,
Lowin had attained to so high a rank as to
be named together with Taylor in the Patent
granted to the King's Servants by Charles

therefore, about the period I have mentioned, an open field
was left to Taylor and Lowin.—Taylor, from 1612 to
1616, appears to have played with another Company.

the

the First, immediately after Heminges and Condell, who though they appear to have ceased to act, preserved a property in the theatre ; and not long before, (Dec. 20, 1624,) on the Master of the Revels expressing his disapprobation at the play of the SPANISH VICEROY having been performed by that company without a licence, the submission made on that occasion was signed by the ten principal actors in the King's Company, at the head of which list stand the names of Joseph Taylor and John Lowin. [159]

BUT though Lowin in 1608 was only in the second class, there is no reason to suppose that a man who afterwards attained to such eminence was then an annual hireling. He without doubt had a half share, or some other portion of one, even then : a fatal circumstance for the deed before us. It is indeed, like the rest, a *felo de se* ; for here we find him, like one of our modern actors, engaged for three years at a salary of one pound ten shillings a week. The actor is to receive his salary even when he is pre-

[159] SHAKSPEARE, Vol. I. P. II. p. 208.

vented

vented from playing by sickness or any
other impediment; and, like one of our
modern taylors or shoemakers, he is to
receive his thirty shillings every *Saturday
night before twelve o'clock*. In the Appendix
will be found a genuine stage-contract of
this very period, that renders it quite
unnecessary to say more on this part of the
subject; from which I shall only quote one
passage that may serve to throw some light
on this Saturday-Night-Clause. The deed,
which was intended to have been executed
in 1608, after informing us that Philip
Henslowe and Edward Alleyn, in consideration of twenty pounds and ten shillings,
had demised to Thomas Downton [an actor
then in the Prince's Company, who played
at the FORTUNE Theatre,] " one eight parte
of a fowerth of all such clere gaynes in
monye as shall hereafter duringe the terme
hereunder demised [thirteen years] arise,
grow, accrew, or become dewe, or properly
belonge unto the said Phillip Henslowe and
Edward Alleyn, - - - - - for or by reason
of any stage - playing or other exercise,
comoditie or use whatsoever, used or to be
used or exercised within the play-house of
the

the said Phillipp Henslow and Edward
Alleyn, comonly called the Fortune, situate and beinge betweene Whitecrosstreet
and Golding Lane,"—proceeds thus : " And
the said eight part of a fowerth parte
of all the saide clere gaynes properly belonginge to the saide Phillipp Henslowe
and Edward Alleyn to be paide by the saide
Phillipp Henslowe and Edward Alleyn, or
one of them, their or one of their executors
or assignes, unto the saide Thomas Downton,
or his assigns *every day that any play or other
exercise shal be acted or exercised* in the play-
house aforesaide, *upon the sharing of the mo-
nies gathered and gotten at every of the same
playes and exercises*, AS HERETOFORE HATH
BEEN USED AND ACCUSTOMED." Mr.
Downton covenants to pay Henslowe and
Alleyn a Rent of ten shillings a year during
his term ; to defray his due proportion of
whatever expences may be incurred by the
repairs of the play-house ; to exercise during the said term his faculty or quality of
playing in the said house " to the best and
most benefit he can," unless he should be
disabled by sickness, or should obtain the
consent of the Lessors ; and that he will not

ɪ   during

during the said term act in any common play-house in London or within two miles of it, except the Fortune, without the special licence of Henslowe and Alleyn (or one of them) in writing under their hands and seals.

HERE we have a true stage-contract of precisely the period in question, and as decisive a proof of the forgery of the deed which I have been obliged so minutely to examine, as can be conceived.

To furnish us, however, with additional proofs, if they were wanting, the fabricator has introduced the word *composition*, as descriptive of a written work. The word undoubtedly signified in our author's time the act of forming or composing a work, being used in that sense by Spencer ; [160] but I do not believe that it then bore the signification of a written work. Our author has it not, I think, in either sense. [161] The

highest

160 " Simple is the device, and the composition meane; yet carrieth some delight." Epistle Ded. to MOTHER HUBBERD'S TALE, 4to. 1590.

161 " There is no *composition* [that is, congruity or consistency]

highest authority Dr. Johnson could find
for this word, with the signification here required, is L'Estrange. Cawdrey in 1604 defines it, " A making or mingling together ;"
Bullokar in 1616, " a joining or putting together." From Cotgrave's Dictionary in 1611,
it appears, that the French long before us
employed this word in the sense required
to justify its use in the deed now under consideration. " *Composition*. A composition,
[here clearly in the sense given by Bullokar
and Cawdrey,] a making, framing, a con-
fection, compositure, compounding : also a
worke or *book*, or the writing of a work or
book ; also accord," &c. Here we see he
uses the English word as synonymous to
the French in the first clause, which relates
to *compounding*, &c. but when he comes to
give that sense of the French word which
we are now considering, he explains it by
booke or *work*, not as before by the English
word, *composition* ; a proof that it was not
then in use, in this latter sense. Cockeram
in 1655 gives only the old interpretation,

sistency] in these news," says the Duke, in OTHELLO.
This is the only place in which I recollect the word to
have been used by Shakspeare.

" a join-

" a joining or setting together :" but some years afterwards Philips in his WORLD OF WORDS, (3d Edition, 1671,) affixes to this word the signification which it now bears : " A setting together ; also *a work set forth* in any piece of learning or art."—Thus therefore, I think, we are furnished with strong presumptive evidence that this word in the sense we are now speaking of, came to us from the French about the time of the Restoration.

IN all the instances of modern language which I have produced, I am perfectly aware of the impossibility of proving a universal negative : but I have, I apprehend, *brought forward* evidence enough to satisfy any reasonable inquirer, and which at least is entitled to be received as true, till some proof of the existence of the contested words shall be produced from a book of Shakspeare's age, by those who may differ from me in opinion.

THE Will of John Lowin (if ever he made one) not being extant, I am not furnished with his autograph, so as to prove

the

the signature to this deed a forgery. But the other circumstances attending it render any additional proof of that kind quite unnecessary. The reader has only to compare the forged name of John Heminges with his true autograph, and then apply the old adage—*crimine ab uno disce omnes*. The names of his friend Joseph Taylor and the other comedians in Plate II. may also throw some light on the *fancy-scrawl* of this " our best actor."—Before, however, I dismiss this stage-contract, I must draw your Lordship's attention to Master Lowin's SEAL, which is well worthy of inspection with a magnifying-glass ; being a well-formed head, copied, if I mistake not, from the representation of some of our Saxon Monarchs, among the engravings of Virtue.

I HAD almost forgot to mention, that though the Scrivener who drew this deed has written our poet's christian name very correctly, the poet himself had either quite forgot it, or to keep his *booby* patron in countenance, mis-spells it—WILLAM.

XVII.

XVII. Agreement between Shakspeare and Henry Condell.

We now come to similar articles of Agreement between Shakspeare, who is the grand proprietor and sole mover of the theatrical machine, and his fellow Henry Condell, executed on the 20th of May, 1610; by which he covenants " for the further space or terme of three years to play upon *the* stage for the s^d W^m. Shakspeare alle comedyes *ande* tragedyes whiche he the s^d. W^m. Shakspeare may at any tyme during the s^d terme cause to be played *not written or composed by hymselfe butte are the writings or composytyons of others.*"

His salary is to be a *guinea* a week, not indeed in express words, being only " oune pounde and oune shillynge per weeke." Like Lowin, he is to be paid every Saturday night before twelve of the clock, sick or well, and whether he plays or not. If we add to this that he is to forfeit a hundred pounds if he does not perform the covenants expressed,[162] we have the whole of this deed.

[162] This penalty was copied from the contracts which I published between Philip Henslowe and those low actors whom

deed. And surely he must be a most unreasonable fellow not to perform them, the
only covenants being that he shall play on
the stage certain plays, and that whether he
plays or not, he shall receive " oune pounde
and oune shillynge" *every week in the year*.

In this deed, as in the former, we find
the word *composition* in the sense of a written
work ; and it also informs us that Condell
was one third lower in estimation than
Lowin. In what manner or by what arts
the latter contrived thus to leap over the
head of our poet's friend, Condell, whom
he has particularly remembered in his will,
and was the joint-editor of his Plays, we
are not told. Certain however it is, that
when Lowin was under the necessity of
borrowing a crown to go a strolling into the
country, Condell was in such repute that

whom he engaged to perform in his playhouse at a weekly
stipend, as hirelings: and the same contracts also suggested
the term of *three years*. [See SHAKSP. 1790, Vol. I. P. II.
p. 311.] But actors of Condell's rank, who had a property
in the house in which they were Sharers, entered into no
bonds, as the hirelings did, for performance of Covenants,
unless when a Company was *first* formed by a Speculator
like Henslowe, when the contracting parties mutually tied
themselves to each other.

in

in the patent granted to Shakspeare and others in 1603, his name stands immediately after that of Heminges, and that so far from being a weekly hireling, he was a principal sharer of the profits made by the performances exhibited at the Globe and Blackfriars theatres, from that time to 1627, when he died.

THERE are several other curious circumstances belonging to this agreement. The first is, that poor Condell is made to covenant, not that he should exercise his faculty or quality of playing in a certain theatre called the Globe, &c. as we have just seen was the mode of the time, but that he should outdo even the aspiring BOTTOM, and *perform an entire comedy or tragedy himself.* In Lowin's Agreement, it is observable that the same covenant is found. To reconcile therefore the two deeds, we must suppose that Condell, the Hotspur of those days, performed, as a mute, on the shoulders of his plump fellow-comedian, a species of exhibition to which Lowin was familiarized by occasionally playing the part of Falstaff, as the *double* of Heminges.—The next observable circumstance is, the mortal antipathy which our author appears

appears to have taken to his own dramas;
for Condell is tied down to play only the
comedies and tragedies written by other authors ; so that we must suppose either that
Shakspeare would never suffer one of his
own pieces to be performed in his own
playhouse, or that he bore such enmity to
Condell, that he had made a fixed resolution that this actor should not *discharge*
any part in them. The salary, " oune
pounde and oune shillynge," is a very proper
periphrasis for that coin which was running
in the head of the fabricator of this deed,
and accords extremely well with the other
ridiculous covenants ; and that all should be
in perfect harmony, the whole is concluded
with a pretty fiction of a trim boar's head,
which is intended to pass for Shakspeare's
seal, and which we are to suppose he employed the Marchant of that day to engrave
for him, in honour of the fat knight who
in three of his plays had afforded to number-
less spectators inexhaustible entertainment.

Some years ago I published a copy of Henry
Condell's Will, extracted from the Registry in
the Prerogative-office : but the bundle of original Wills for the year 1627 being unfortunately

tunately lost, I have not been able to procure the autograph of this actor : [163] happily however the deed itself sufficiently ascertains the nature of the fictitious signature affixed to it. If there be any such letter as is here made to represent an *H* in the signature " H^y Condell," it has escaped not only my researches, but those of a very diligent examiner of ancient hand-writing, in whose work entitled COURT-HAND RESTORED,[164] it is not found. It was manifestly formed on the ninth capital *I* found in the eighteenth Plate of that work, by a reversal and slight change of the letter.

THE indorsement on the deed now before us—" 20th Maye 9th: Iam^s :" is at least as curious as any thing that is found in the

---

[163] As Condell lived, when he was in town, in Aldermanbury, where he served some of the parish offices, I hoped to have found his signature in the Register of that parish, but was disappointed. I was equally unsuccessful at Fulham, where he had a country house. The old Register of that parish is lost, but several of the Vestry Proceedings of a very ancient date are extant ; in none of which, however, the name of Henry Condell occurs.

[164] Published by Mr. Andrew Wright of the Inner Temple, 4to. 1776.—The eighteenth Plate contains " A general Alphabet of the old law hands."

inside

inside of it ; for to say nothing of its being
in English, (which I have already noticed
as a circumstance fatal to all these instruments,) or of the unnecessary *th* after 20,
(which Scriveners never wrote,) the deed
itself has already informed us that it was
made on the " twentieth day of Maye in
the *eyghth* yeare" of King James. When two
such *great authorities* differ, to which of
them are we to give credit ? I conceive,
in the present instance it will be safest to
believe *neither*.

XVIII. A Lease to Michael Fraser and his Wife.

The following deed was one of the
earliest, if not the very first of all these
instruments, which was exhibited to those
" ingenuous, intelligent, and disinterested
persons," on whose shoulders the weighty
load of all this motley mass of trumpery
has been laid. It is a Lease pretended to
be made on the 14th of July, 1610, (8 Jac.)
by which Shakspeare and his friend John
Heminges (by the name of John *Hemynge*)
demise to one Michael Fraser and his wife
" *his* two messuages or tenements (to which

M M   of

of the two lessors the word *his* refers does not appear,) *abutting* close *to* the Globe theatre by Black Fryers London,"- - " and also all those two Gardens on the North side of the same which appertayne or belong thereto, and whiche conteyne *six Acres and an half* be they more or less," for a term of sixty four years from the 29th of September next ensuing, at a rent of forty four pounds a year, to be paid half yearly, and the first payment to be made on the said 29th day of September.

However our modern conveyancers may surpass their predecessors in the number of covenants or provisos, it will, I believe, be found that our ancient deeds, though brief and simple, were at least as clear, explicit, and correct, particularly in the description of the thing sold, demised, or granted, as the more ample and voluminous indentures of the present day. Here, however, we have a description of six acres and a half of land *abutting* close *to* the Globe theatre by Blackfryers ; which is about as good a description, as if the ground on which the house of the present Earl Bathurst is built had been conveyed to the late earl, as

ι   " a certain

" a certain piece of ground containing in front ninety feet, and in depth one hundred and twenty feet, on which the Inn known by the name of the HERCULES' PILLARS now stands, *abutting close* to *Hyde - Park Corner by* WHITECHAPEL."

IN detecting the fabrications of Chatterton it was curious to trace the mistakes he fell into, up to the authors from whose blunders they were derived. The present ridiculous blunder appears to have been derived from a mere error of the press in a book which our fabricator was very likely to examine, the BIOGRAPHIA DRAMATICA, published in 1780, where, under the article "ROBERT ARMIN," he found the following words : " This author was an actor at the *Globe, Black-Fryers,* and was living in 1611," &c. The conjunction *and* having been inadvertently omitted by the compositor at the press, the theatre in Southwark was conceived to be close adjoining to Blackfriars, or this latter was supposed to be a larger and more general description of the quarter where the Globe theatre stood ; as we now say—Duke Street, St. James's Square. It is observable, that in this deed *Blackfryers* is spelt rightly,

as

as it is in the book that led the fabricator into this error : whereas in the other deeds where that district is mentioned, he has spelt the word in the modern fashion, (as far as relates to the vowel in the second syllable) Black*fryars*, contrary to the mode of orthography which prevailed in our author's time, and which was nearer to the etymology of the word *(frere)*; this district being then constantly written with an *e* in the second syllable,*—Blackfryers; or in two words, *blacke ffryers*.

THE phrase abutting *to*, here employed, is unknown to our language, abutting *upon* having been invariably the legal and colloquial language from the time of Shakspeare to this hour. On the phrase—the Globe *theatre*, having omitted to take notice of it where it was first introduced, (in the Promissory Note to Heminges,) I shall not insist here, reserving it for another place. It is only necessary now to mention, that the

---

* See the title-page of OTHELLO, 4to. 1622; the Conveyance from Walker to Shakspeare in the APPENDIX, Nº. II. or any book or MS. of the time of James the First in which this place is mentioned.

GLOBE,

GLOBE, not the Globe *theatre*, was the uniform language of the time.[164]

As it is not very easy to know on which
side of the Thames these six acres and a
half are supposed to have lain, it is necessary to take a view both of the district of
the Blackfriars and the Bankside. In 1596
there was certainly in Southwark some
ground unoccupied by buildings ; but it was
chiefly in that part of it which lay more to
the West than the Globe theatre, and which
afterwards became the property of Thomas,
Earl of Arundel, whose gardener, Cuper,
renting the ground, it took the name of Cuper's Gardens.   Even at an earlier period of
the reign of Elizabeth the ground near where
the Globe stood, seems to have been almost
all occupied, though I do not doubt there
may have been then some small gardens in that quarter. With respect to the
Blackfriars, there were in that district
some void spaces certainly, as is proved
by the Conveyance to Shakspeare, already
mentioned : but in general (as appears from
ancient maps,) the ground on the east side
of Fleet Ditch (where the theatre stood)

[164] See APPEND. N°. I. note.

was

was almost wholly occupied by houses. To the west there appears to have been a considerable space of void ground about forty years before the date of this pretended Lease; but this was in *Whitefriars*, with which we have no concern.—In six acres and a half there are thirty one thousand four hundred and sixty square yards, a space on which above three hundred houses might have been built; as appears from a cause [165] of much celebrity which was tried in the last century, and which I shall presently have occasion to mention more particularly. Most assuredly neither near the Globe, nor in the Blackfriars, was there in the year 1610 void space sufficient to contain the fourth part of the number of edifices above mentioned. If however I were to allow that there might have been such an immense void space as would contain three hundred houses, either adjoining to the eastern end of Maiden-lane in Southwark, where the Globe stood, or in the precinct of the Blackfriars on the other side of the river, it would contribute nothing to the establishment of this fabricated instrument; for till such an ancient build-

[165] Lady Ivy's case, 1684.

ing

ing as *the Globe theatre by Blackfriars* shall
be proved to have existed in the reign of
James the First, together with six acres and
a half adjoining to it, this deed must share
the same fate with the rest.

Mr. Pope, speaking of the early publishers of Shakspeare's works, has observed
that their French is as bad as their Latin,
and even their very Welch is false. A
similar observation may be made on the
papers and deeds before us. One finds it
difficult to say in what circumstance the
fabricator of them displays the most ignorance; whether his spelling is worse than
his phraseology, or the incongruity of his
fictions with the history and manners of the
time be more observable than either. Even
his law is all false.—" Provided always (says
this lease) that if the s^d. Mich^l. Fraser and
Elizth. hys Wife theyr Ex^s. Ad^s. or Affigns
or any of them do well and truly perform
and keep all & singular the s^d. covenaunts
herein before agreed upon, that then it shall
and may be lawfull to and for the s^d. M^l.
Fraser and Elizth. hys Wife to *enter* into
and enjoy the same, but in case of non performance or non payment *of the same* that
then

then it shall be lawfulle to & for the s^d. *Willam* Shakespeare and John Hemynge again to have & enjoy the same."

I⊤ is here observable, that previous to this proviso for the performance of *all &* *singular covenaunts*, no covenant has been mentioned except that for the payment of rent, *half yearly*. If however the lessees keep this covenant, what is the boon granted to them ? Why truly to enter into the pre- misses and enjoy them : that is, these unfor- tunate people after they have paid half a year's rent on the 29th day of Sep. when their lease is to commence, and after they shall have regularly made several other half yearly payments, are, at the end I suppose of two or three years, to be quietly put in possession of the premisses. But " in case of non performance or non payment of the same," that is, in case they do not make several half yearly payments of rent before they get possession of the premisses, then the said *Willam* Shakspeare and John Hem- ynge are to re-enter *upon themselves*, and to be restored to that possession of which they never have been devested.

T⊞E

THE next clause is still more extraordinary. " — And the said W^m. Shakespeare and John Hemynge for themselves theyr H^s. Ex^s. Ad^s. & Assigns shall and will clearly *exonerate and discharge from tyme to tyme the s^d. M^l. Fraser and Eliz^{tb}. hys wyfe from the payment of such rent*, and well & sufficiently keep harmless the s^d. M^l. Fraser and Eliz^th. hys wife, theyr Ex^s. Ad^s. & Assigns & every of them, of & from all incumbres whatsoever by them the s^d. W^m. Shakespeare & In^o. Hemynge at any tyme before committed or done."—As in the former part of this demise the lessees were somewhat hardly dealt with, in being obliged to make several half yearly payments of rent before they should be permitted. to enter, it must be acknowledged that here ample compensation is made to them by an entire and total discharge and acquittance of all rent during the term.—The fabricator had heard that it was usual for the lessor to discharge, save and keep the lessees and the premises harmless from all former grants, leases, charges, and incumbrances whatsoever; and to make the matter sure, instead of covenanting to give the lessees

N N   from

from time to time proper acquittances, has made the lessors covenant wholly to exonerate and discharge them from the payment of any rent whatsoever.[166] Of this covenant the only precedent I have been able to find in our law-books, after a long search, is

[166] What was *meant* here, would in the time of James the First have been thus expressed :—" And the said W. S. & I. H. for themselves, &c. do covenant, that they, their executors, &c. shall from time to time, and at all times, well and sufficiently discharge, save & keep harmless, as well the s^d M. F. & E. his wife, their executors, &c. as also the said Messuages, & all other the premises by these presents mentioned to be demised, with all & singular their appurtenances, & every part & parcel thereof, of and from all & singular former grants, bargains, sales, leases, charges, & incumbrances whatsoever, had, made, granted, &c. And also shall save harmless the said M. F. &c. their executors, &c. & the said Messuages, &c. of and from all & all manner of quit-rents, annuities & rent-charges whatsoever, issuing or going out, or to be issuing or going out, of the same or any part thereof, *other than the said yearly rent of* 44*l.* *reserved by these presents, yearly to be paid for the said messuages & other the premises.* And that *upon every payment made of the said yearly rent,* or any part thereof, to the said W. S. or I. H. their executors or assigns, by the said M. F. & E. their executors, &c. according to the tenor and true meaning of these presents, *the said W. S. or I. H.* their executors or assigns, *shall and will subscribe to such a reasonable writing or acquittance* as the said M. F. and E. their executors or administrators shall reasonably require, *testifying and declaring the receipt of the said payment.*"

ı

one

one in the PUZZLED CLERK'S GUIDE, by
Mr. Serjeant Grimgribber, whose works,
though now superseded by the more refined
jurisprudence of modern times, were in
some request before the statute which directed all legal proceedings to be in English,
and in the early part of the present century
are cited with respect in Sir Richard Steele's
Reports.

IN addition to all this nonsensical jargon,
we find at the end of this lease,—" In
witnesse whereof the s.d Ptes to these Indres
interchangeablie have sett their hands &
seales the daye & yeare first above written :
Anno-Dom (1610)." Now even in so
small a matter as this, fiction has betrayed
itself ; for this was not the abbreviation of
the time, but either Anno Dn̄i., or A. Dn̄i.,
or An. Dn̄i.—At the back we find—" 14th
July 5 Jams.", for which in the ERRATA
we are desired to read—" 8 Jams.", which
is not a whit better than the other. It should
be as I have already observed,—8 Jac.

THROUGHOUT this deed, as in the conclusion of the contract with Lowin, we have

Willam

Willam Shakspeare, and for the reason already
assigned. But as in the former case the Scrivener would not keep his employer in countenance by writing his christian name in his
own absurd way, so here, to punish him for
his oscitancy or his perverseness, our poet
leaves him in the lurch, subscribing his name
to this deed, in plain and legible characters,
WILLIAM Shakspeare.

XIX. A DEED OF TRUST TO JOHN HEMYNGE.

WE are at length arrived at the last legal
instrument presented to us in this new
ANTHOLOGY, which is a Deed of Trust
pretended to have been made by our poet to
John *Hemynge*, (as he is here improperly
called,) on the 23d day of February 1611-12,
the consideration of which necessarily demands particular attention. All the absurdities and incongruities, which have been
already noticed, must now yield the palm
to superior absurdity and incongruity ; the
thickest Cimmerian darkness being bright
sunshine compared with the vapid nonsense
and impenetrable obscurity of this fabrication.

IT

IT sets out with informing us that Shakspeare, on the day above mentioned, had not yet retired to the country; an important piece of information, could we rely on our informer. In the deed of purchase and mortgage in the next year, March 10 and 11, 1612-13, (I am now speaking of genuine deeds,) he is described as of Stratford *upon*[167] Avon, from whence I am inclined to believe that he had then retired from the stage.

SOME years ago I conjectured that he had originally some slight knowledge of law, and particularly of the lower branches of conveyancing; and I have since found no reason to think that my conjecture was ill-founded. He was at the supposed time of making this deed living in intimacy with Mr. Francis Collins, an eminent attorney who practised both at Stratford and Warwick, and who was a witness to his Will, which, without doubt, Collins drew. I must also observe, that our poet had a cousin, who at this time had chambers in

[167] Not " *on* Avon," as we find it in this and several other of these deeds.

the

the Middle-Temple, Mr. Thomas Greene, a barrister, or solicitor in Chancery,[168] with whom he was connected by friendship as well as blood. Thus circumstanced, he is made to preface the deed before us with these words : " *Having founde muche wickedness amongste those of the lawe* and not liking to leave matters at theyre wills, I have herein named a trusty and tried friende who shall afterr mye dethe execute withe care myne orderrs herein given."

I SHALL not stay to observe on the modern expression, — " not liking to *leave matters* at theyre wills :" but the reason assigned for his making this deed, his "having founde muche wickedness amongste those of the law," is well worthy of notice. Had tradition informed us that, like Dekker, Jonson, and many other poets of the time,[169] he

[168] In one of his papers he mentions his having attended Sir Edw. Coke on law-business, in terms that seem to denote that he was a Solicitor ; but in the superscription of letters addressed to him, he is styled Thomas Greene, *Esq.* an addition not then given to solicitors, or attorneys at law.— He expressly calls our author—" my cousin Shakspeare."

[169] " Lent unto Thomas Downton the 30 of JaneCary 1598 to descarge Thomas Dickers from the areaste of my lord chamberlenes men, I saye lent—— iij[ll]. xs."

" Lent

he had been in any part of his life necessi-
tous and embarrassed, and that in consequence he had felt the strong gripe of the
law, that is, had the whole history of his
life and character been the reverse of what
it was, such a reflection might perhaps have
been plausibly ascribed to him : but that
the gentle, ingenuous, honest, wealthy, and
liberal Shakspeare should transmit to pos-

" Lent unto the Company the 4 of Febreary 1598 to
discharge Mr. Dicker out of the counter in the poultrey, the
some of fortie shillinges I say dd. [delivered] to Thomas
Downton—xxxxs."

In another place, as I remember, Mr. Henslowe redeems
Dekker out of the *Clinke* ; but I cannot at present find the
passage.

" Lent unto Bengemen Johnson player the 28 of July
1597 in Redey money the some of fower powndes to be
payd yt agayne when so ever ether I or any for me shall
demande yt, I saye——iiij^{li}.
" Witness E. Alleyn & John Synger."

" Lent Bengemyne Johnson the 5 of Janewary 1597
[1597-8] in Redy mony the some of——vs."

" Lent unto Thomas Downton the xvij of Janewary
1598 to lend unto harey chettell to paye his charges in the
Marshallsey, the some of——xxxs."

Henslowe's Register, MS.

Henry Chettle was author of above thirty plays, of which
the only one now extant (entirely written by him,) is THE
TRAGEDY OF HOFFMAN ; printed anonymously in 1631.

terity

terity such a malevolent and unfounded stigma on a most useful and honourable profession, with some of whose members he was at the same moment living in great amity, is utterly incredible.

But let us now hear his reasons for making this deed. He has already told us that he relies on a trusty friend to execute his orders. " But in case I shoulde att any tyme hereafterr make a Will as perr-chaunce I shall in manner of forme I have lefte some things nott herein given or dis-posedd of that maye serve to fylle upp said Will and therebye cause no hyndraunce in the Executyonn of thys mye deede of gifte. But sho^d. I nott chaunce make a will thenn I doe give all suche things afs^d. not herein ment^d. unto mye lovynge Daughterr and her heyres for everr.—Firste untoe mye deare Wife I doe orderr as folowithe thatt she bee payde withinne oune monthe afterre mye dethe the somme of oune hondrythe and fowre score Pounds fromm the moneys whyche be nowe *layinge* onn Accompte of the Globe *Theatre* in the hands of Master John Hemynge Also I doe give herr mye suyte of grey vellvett *edged* withe silverr tog^r. withe

mye

mye lyttelle Cedarr Trunke in wyche there bee three Ryngs oune lyttel payntyng of *myselfe* in a silverr Case & sevenn letters wrottenn to her before oure *marryage* these I doe beg herr toe keepe safe if everr she dydd love me.—To mye deare Daughterr who hathe alwaye demeaned *herrselfe* well I doe give as folowithe the somme of twentye Pounds and sevenne shyllyngs thys muste bee payde herr withinne two Months afterr mye dethe & for raysyng s^d. summe of 20^l. & sevenne shyllyngs I doe herebye orderr Masterr hemynge toe sell mye share of the two houses neare the Globe butt sho^d. that nott be enough thenne I doe herebye orderr him toe make it upp oute of the Moneys inn hys hands onne Accompte of the Theatre.—I doe allso give herr mye suyte of blacke silke & the Rynge whyche I doe alwaye weare givenne toe mee by hys *Grace* of Southampton thys I doe beg herr as she dothe love mee neverr toe parte fromm."

BEFORE we examine the different clauses of this nonsensical passage, allow me to give your Lordship a clew that may enable you to find your way out of this labyrinth of folly and imposture. As every thing

that

that relates to Shakspeare is interesting, we
are not to wonder that some observations
have been made on the last solemn act of
his life, his Will, which was executed on
the 25th of March 1616, a month before
he died. It has particularly been remarked
that at first he had taken no notice whatsoever of his wife, and when he did recollect or was reminded of her, he left her no
other memorial of his affection but his
" second-best bed with the furniture."[170]
From this and some other circumstances it
has been conjectured, not without probable
ground, that he was not very strongly attached to her. Another observation naturally arises on the perusal of his Will;
that he had a stronger affection for his eldest
daughter Susanna, who in the year 1607
was married to Dr. John Hall, an eminent
physician of Stratford, than for his second
daughter Judith, who not long before his
death married, I believe without his approbation, Mr. Thomas Queeny, who in the
researches which I made there some years

[170] It was long supposed that he had bequeathed her his
brown best bed; but by examining and collating the *original*
Will, I discovered that the donation (which at best denoted
no great kindness,) was still less valuable.

ago

ago to obtain materials for our poet's Life,
I found was a Vintner in that town. On
these observations, naturally suggested by
Shakspeare's Will, and stated in the edition
which I had the honour to present to the
publick, the Instrument before us was constructed ; [171] with a view at the same time
to cover and give some collateral strength
and authenticity, not only to the lock of hair,
love-letters, and pictures, already noticed,
but to all such trumpery of the same kind
as the credulity of the town at any future
period might digest.

PASSING over the orthography of this
deed, which is like that of all the rest, I
shall confine myself to the instrument itself.
What in plain English is the meaning of
the passage which I have transcribed ? Our
poet thinks it not improbable that he shall

[171] How then, I suppose it will be said, came it to pass,
that the fabricator has here made our poet mention his
wife with kindness, and bequeath her a considerable sum
of money ? Either on the principle adopted in many other
places, to surprize by novelty, or (which is more probable,)
because it had been suggested that Shakspeare, previous to
the making of his Will, had made some provision for his
wife.

make

make a Will, in which however he foresees
there may be some defects and omissions;
and therefore he gives certain things *not*
mentioned in this deed, (what they are
some Œdipus must inform us,) which
may supply the deficiencies of the last solemn act of his life. But if he should not
make a Will, then he gives all things
aforesaid (though nothing whatsoever has
been specified) unto his *lovynge daughterr*.
To this same " deare daughterr, who hathe
alwaye demeaned *herrselfe* well," he gives
the sum of twenty pounds and seven shillings, &c. This CODICIL to an unmade
Will surely surpasses any instance of Second Sight that ever has been recorded in
Scotland.

THERE is no maxim of law better established than that every gift should be *certain*; and, like many other rules of law,
it is adopted, because it is agreeable to
reason and common sense. A gift therefore " to his dear daughter who had always
demeaned herself well," would have been absolutely void, for these words denote that he
had more daughters than one; and this kind
of

of ambiguity being what Lord Verulam calls
patens,[172] or appearing to be ambiguous
upon the deed or instrument, cannot be
holpen by averment, or parol evidence to
shew which of his daughters he meant :
for that (says Bacon) " were to make all
deeds hollow and subject to averments, and
so in effect that to pass without deed,
which the law appoints shall not pass but
by deed."—For the sum given (twenty
pounds seven shillings) no probable reason
can be assigned, all gifts of this kind, or
legacies, being usually even sums. The
fabricator, however, of this instrument seeing that in Shakspeare's Will, and other
old Wills, legacies of twenty-six shillings
and eight pence, or thirteen pounds six
shillings and eight pence, &c. were bequeathed, supposed these were odd sums ;
whereas in fact, and in the contemplation
of the testator, they were as much even
sums as our modern five, ten, or twenty
pounds ; for the former sum (1l. 6s. 8d.)
was *two marks*, and the latter (13l. 6s. 8d.)
which is Shakspeare's bequest to his friend
Francis Collins, was exactly *twenty marks*.

[172] MAXIMS OF THE LAW. Reg. 23.

As

As therefore in the stage-contracts and the promissory note (given almost a century before it was known) the even sums of one pound one shilling, and five pounds five shillings, (*even*, so far as they correspond with the present current gold coin of the realm,) were *primo intuitu* suspicious, and when attended with other circumstances of imposture were more than suspicious ; so in the present deed the uneven sums of twenty pounds and seven shillings given to Shakspeare's dear daughter, thirty-seven shillings given to Master Shancke, and forty-nine shillings to Master Rice, are all equally objectionable, and manifest denotations of fiction.

THE sum of twenty pounds and seven shillings is ordered to be paid to his dear daughter two months after his death, (the regulation of a Will, instead of a deed of gift,[173]) and how does your Lordship think

[173] " If a gift does not take effect by delivery of immediate possession, it is then not properly a gift, but a contract, and this a man cannot be compelled to perform but upon good and sufficient consideration." 2 Blackst. Com. 441.

There being no consideration expressed here, the whole deed, were it even to be considered as a deed, would have been void : but it is a Will rather than a deed of gift.

it

it is to be raised ?—To raise this little sum,
Shakspeare's trusty friend, Heminges, is
not to put his hand into the chest of which
we shall hear more presently, but to sell
our author's moiety of his estate near THE
GLOBE BY BLACKFRIARS (for it seems
he had but a moiety of it, though in the
lease to Fraser and his wife the whole is
called his) ; and if the sale of this moiety
should not produce twenty pounds and
seven shillings, then the deficiency is to
be made good out of money in Heminges'
hands.

In the year 1612 an estate in houses was
commonly sold at the lowest at twelve years
purchase, and an estate in land at about
sixteen.[174] At twelve years' purchase Shakspeare's pretended moiety of this estate,
which consisted of both land and houses,
and was let for sixty-one years at 44l. per
annum, would have produced a sum of two
hundred and sixty-four pounds at the
least : and yet the owner, who we shall
presently find is a most excellent *counter-*

---

[174] Briefe, easie, and necessarie Tables for the valua-
tion of Leases, &c. 8vo. 1622.

caster,

caster, is here made to doubt whether it will supply about the thirteenth part of that sum.

As the " *Rynge* givenne by hys *Grace* of Southampton" was mentioned to give countenance and support to the correspondence between him and our poet, which had before been *brought forward*, so in the gift to his *dear* wife, " the sevenn letterrs wrotten to her before oure marryage," the " three Ryngs," " oune lyttell payntyng of *myselfe* in a silverr case," and the " lyttelle Cedarr Trunke," were all introduced in this last instrument, (for it was the *L'envoy* of all these fictions,) with a view to afford a friendly cover to the washed drawing, and the amorous effusions of our poet, with which the world had previously been gratified. Nothing therefore need be said of them. All the money bequeathed to her, (for so I must call it,) as well as the other sums afterwards mentioned, are to be drawn out of the fund now *layinge* [175] in Heminges'

[175] For this vulgarism the fabricator is answerable ; for though it is a very old one, it occurs, I think, no where in our author's plays.

I   hands

hands " onn accompte of the Globe Theatre :" so that we are to suppose that the
playhouse in Blackfriars produced nothing ;
whereas the fact is, that from about the
year 1605 *that* was the place of exhibition
during a great part of the year, and they
played at the Globe only for a short time in
the summer.

AFTER the detection of Chatterton, and
the demolition of the chest with six keys,
I did not expect to have heard again, for
some time at least, of such a repository for
ancient Manuscripts : from a similar recep-
tacle, however, the *unknown* gentleman is
hardy enough to draw all his *speciosa mira-
cula* ; for an OAKEN CHESTE at the Globe
playhouse, it seems, contained not only our
poet's theatrical, but his domestick wardrobe,
his love-letters to his wife, (for though he did
not, like one of Congreve's coxcombs, write
letters to himself, we find he kept the letters he had written to her, *among the play-
house stuff*, she, poor woman, all the while
remaining quietly at Stratford,) rings, pictures, caskets, and plays of all sorts, new
and old.

P P   IT

IT is irksome to me to dwell longer on this foolish deed; yet it still demands some further animadversion. When plays were sold to the theatre, which was the practice of our author's time, they became the property of the house, that is, of the Sharers who constituted the company; who though they did not purchase them in the first instance, (the money being paid by the proprietor of the building, at the appointment of four or five of them nominated for this purpose,) afterwards acquired the property of the copies by reimbursing the proprietor for this and all other expences defrayed by him.[175] Shakspeare therefore well knew that he had no title to any of his plays then in the hands of his associates; yet in this deed he distributes them about most liberally; that is, he very bountifully gives to individuals what already belonged to them all collectively. At that time no

---

[175] " Alsoe wee have paid him for plaie-books 200li. or thereabouts, and yet he denies to give us the copies of anye one of them."

From a paper drawn up by Joseph Taylor and other players, entitled " Articles of Grievance and Oppression against Mr. Hinchlowe," MS.

notion

notion of literary property was entertained,
unless where a particular licence to print
and vend certain books for a limited time
was granted by the Crown. In this deed,
however, all the provisions and regulations
relative to our author's plays printed and
in manuscript, are founded on the now
received idea of literary property to a certain extent vested in *authors* or their assigns
by the statute of Queen Anne.

THAT all might be of a piece, the various
donations to the several actors named, are
as absurd, capricious, and incongruous, as
those to his wife and daughter. To the
obscure Cowley, we are told, he gives his
Tempeste, his Mydsomerrs dreme, Mac-
bethe, Henry VIII. and his *altered* playe of
Titus Andronicus; and " *sho^d they bee
everre agayne Impryntedd,*" he desires it may
be done from these his " true writtenn
playes," and that all the profits of such
new imprinting may belong to Cowley.
The plain and direct meaning of the words
" *sho^d they bee everre agayne impryntedd*" is,
that at the time of making this pretended
deed, (23 Febr. 1611-12,) these five plays
had appeared in print; but the TEMPEST,

MAC-

MACBETH, and HENRY VIII. were not
printed till about ten years afterwards,
being first published by John Heminges,
here named, and Henry Condell, in 1623,
when for the first time they were entered in
the books of the Stationers' Company.[176]
This circumstance alone would defeat the
deed before us. In the History of the
Stage I ascertained that there was an old
play entitled TITUS ANDRONICUS, played
by the servants of Lord Sussex at the
theatre belonging to Philip Henslowe, in
January 1593-4. From this circumstance,
and Heminges' having admitted a play with
this title to stand among Shakspeare's
works, it is, I think, manifest that he made
some alterations and additions to that piece,
as I have shewn he did in the second and
third part of KING HENRY THE SIXTH.
Hence the mention in this deed of " my
altered play of Titus Andronicus." I state

[176] See the Register of the Stationers' Company,—" Nov.
8, 1623, Mr. Blount and Isaak Jaggard.—Mr. William
Shakespeares Comedyes and Tragedyes, soe many of the
said copies as are not formerly entered to other men : Viz.
The Tempest, - - Henry Eight, - - - Macbeth," &c. &c.
SHAKSP. 1790. Vol. I. P. I. p. 259.

this

this minute circumstance, because it, as well as many others that I have noticed, prove, that the greater part of these fabrications was made subsequent to November 1790, when that History was published.

In the year 1600 the play of Sir John Oldcastle was printed, and ascribed to Shakspeare, whose name appears at full length in the title-page. It was always considered as an imposture, but was never certainly known to be such till I produced an entry from an old theatrical Register of the precise sum paid to the four poets who were the authors of that piece.[177] We do not, however, find that on the publication of this play, the careless Shakspeare, who, as Pope most truly and happily described him,

" For gain, not glory, wing'd his roving flight,
" And grew immortal in his own despite,"

took any step to vindicate his reputation, on this head ; nor did he, as he might easily have done, mention in his Will that

[177] Anthony Mundy, Michael Drayton, R. Wilson, and R. Hathwaye.

several

several dramatick pieces had been fraudu-
lently ascribed to him. After his retirement
from the stage he did not think his works
worth collecting, at least he never did col-
lect or publish them ; nor did he even leave
a fair correct copy of them in manuscript to
his children. Such was the man who is
here represented as extremely anxious that
the future impressions of his plays may be
printed from his true copies.

IN the Essay on the Chronological Order
of his Plays, I had occasion to quote a
passage from Meres's WITS TREASURY,
in which Anthony Mundy, a dramatick
poet of the day, is spoken of as " *our best
plotter.*" Hence we have here a donation
of 5l. and the four following plays,—" mye
Moche adoe aboute noethynge, The Wives
of Windsor, Rycharde yᵉ 3ᵈ as allso mye
Coryolanus, to Masterr Lowinne, *oure beste
Actorr.*" Lowin, I have already shewn,
was in a very low state in the year 1604,
only eight years before the date of this
deed ; and instead of being considered as
the best actor in our author's life-time, he
undoubtedly did not rise into the first parts
till after the death of Shakspeare and Burbadge,

badge, and the retirement of Heminges and Condell. [178] All the writers of the time who have left us any memorials of the stage, concur in informing us that at this time not Lowin, but Burbadge, who is here passed over without any eulogy, was the principal actor of the Blackfriars and Globe Theatre. He was, we know from the testimony of Bishop Corbet, [179] and other documents, the original representative of Richard the Third; and therefore if the copy of that play had been in our poet's disposal, which it was not, to him both justice and gratitude might have directed it. Sir Richard Baker, who was born in 1568, and lived till 1644-5, and had therefore an opportunity of marking the progress of his reputation through the whole of his theatrical career, pronounces him to have been such an actor " as no age must look to see the like." In the very next year after the date of this deed, his reputation and his property placed him in so high a rank, that the King's Servants are called by

---

[178] See p. 251.

[179] See his ITER BOREALE, and an old comedy entitled THE RETURNE FROM PARNASSUS, 4to. 1606.

a very

a very intelligent and accurate writer of that time, " Bourbege his Companie ;"[180] and six years afterwards, when he died, he is styled by Camden " *alter Roscius.*"[181] Though our author, as I have already observed, is somewhat niggard of his praise to this eminent tragedian, he gives him from the OAKENN CHESTE not only the plays of CYMBELINE and OTHELLO, but a play which we have never seen, called the VIRGINN QUENE, his " *chosē* interrlude neverr yette impryntedd," which had been acted only three times before her namesake, " y[e] profytts fromm *prynting* same to bee whollye for s[d] Burbage."

HENRY Condell, who at his death was a man of good property, and who at the time when this deed is pretended to have been made must have been in easy circumstances, was, we find, indebted to Shakspeare in so small a sum as three pounds nine shillings, which he very kindly forgives him ; and

[180] Letter from Mr. Thomas Lorkin to Sir Thomas Puckering, Knight and Baronet, dated the last of June, 1613. MSS. Harl. 7002.

[181] R. JAC. ANNAL. sub ann. 1619.

with

with equal liberality our poet sends three pounds and a gold ring after his " good Kempe," who appears to have been then dead.[182]

THE next donation, or legacy, is somewhat unlucky, for it is " toe my pleasaunte and *wittye* Masterr Armynne," an actor who, I have shewn, usually performed the part of a Clown. Now if the fabricator of this deed had followed the eulogium with which I furnished him, and called him " honest *gamesome* Master Armin," he would have been safe. But, poor man, " he would be talking," and has stumbled on a word that bore no such meaning as was here intended to be affixed to it.[183]

THE gifts to Shanke and Rice,[184] two low

[182] SHAKSP. *ut: supr.* Vol. I. P. II. p. 197.

[183] See p. 206.

[184] The " greene *sloppd* suyte of velvette," which is given to Rice, is just as intelligible as if a man at this day were to bequeath to his servant his " *breeched suit* of blue cloth." *Slops* was the ancient term for large breeches. So, Falstaff: " What said Mr. Dombledon about the sattin for my short cloak and *slops* ?" The green velvet suit here mentioned had doubtless a pair of white sattin breeches sewed on each

Q Q   of

low players, are chiefly observable for the absurd sums allotted to them ; to one 37 shillings in money, and 18 shillings to buy a ring, and 39 shillings to another. No number of nobles or marks will make any of these sums.

Our author in the last place rewards his trusty friend John Hemynge (as he is here called) for *managing all his matters* at the Globe ; for he was such a driveller that he could do nothing for himself ; and as for the Blackfriars theatre, though he at this time derived almost his entire profits from it, he does not think it worth mentioning. As a " *recompence*" for all Heminges' good services, he is to have " ye somm of 1ol. & 20 shyllyngs to buye hymm a Golde Rynge," and the following plays out of the CHESTE: " Mye Gentlemenn of Verona *alterrd*,[185] mye Measure for Measure, Comedye

of the sleeves by way of ornament.—The fabricator seems to have thought if he could but introduce an ancient word, all would be well: whether it was sense or nonsense was no part of his consideration; or rather was quite beyond his *ken*.

[185] This word was added in consequence of the suggestion of Hanmer and Upton, that THE GENTLEMEN OF

medye of Errorrs, Merrchaunte of Venice,
togetherr with my newe Playe neverr yette
imprynted (he is still " at his old *lunes*")
called Kyng H^y vii."[186]

THERE still remains in the hands of
Heminges precisely the sum of 287l. 14s.
od. by which we learn how admirable an
arithmetician our poet was : this sum there-

OF VERONA was not entirely of the hand of Shakspeare ;
a notion for which, in my opinion, there is not the slightest
foundation.

[186] In a note on the Dissertation on the Three Parts of
K. Henry VI. I observed that several portions of the English History had been dramatized before the time of Shakspeare ; (EDWARD I. II. and III. HENRY IV. and V.
&c.) and that he was induced by the popularity of those
pieces to make some of the principal historical events of
preceding times the subject of various plays. Hence we
have here—" Kynge Henry VII. ;" in a former deed,
" Kynge Henrye thyrde of Englande ;" and another, which,
we are told, yet remains in the *oakenn cheste*, " Kynge Henrye Seconde of Englande."—But the device is somewhat
of the stalest ; for a tricking bookseller in 1653 entered at
the Stationers' Hall—" Henry I. and Henry II. by William Shakespeare and Robert Davenport ;" how honestly,
will appear from an entry in the Office-book of Sir Henry
Herbert, Master of the Revels to King James and King
Charles the First, MS. " For the Kings Company. The
Historye of Henry the First, written by Damport, [the
old pronunciation of Davenport,] the 10 of April, 1624.—
1l. os. od."

fore

fore and " the eyghte Playes thatt bee stylle inne s^d Cheste as allso mye otherr Playe neverr yett Impryntedd called Kynge Vor- tygerne" are appropriated to the use of the child of whom he and Heminges had " spokenne butt who muste not bee named here." This child, I presume, was Shak- speare's Godson, young Will. D'Avenant ; and I fear I am answerable for his having been thus again *brought forward* to publick notice, by having stated that there were good grounds for supposing him our poet's natural son ; a tradition first mentioned by Wood in a MS. now lost, and of which I have lately found a strong confirmation in the biographical papers of Mr. Aubrey at Oxford. [187] The poor lad, however, never derived any benefit from his supposed fa- ther's kindness ; for about six years after the date of this deed he became a chorister of Magdalen College, where nearly thirty pounds a year (the interest of 287l.) beside the profit of these eight plays, and above all the *copy-right* of that matchless piece

[187] Of the whole of Aubrey's biographical collections, deposited in the Ashmolean Museum, I made a transcript last summer, which will hereafter be laid before the publick.

" Kynge

" Kynge Vortygerne" would in those days
have supported him very well in a higher
rank. Of this last fiction also, I fear, I
have been (though very innocently) the
cause ; by mentioning that a play with
this title was acted in 1593 at the Rose
theatre, by the Earl of Pembroke's servants.

OUR poet concludes this important instrument by declaring that he trusts to his
" freynd John Hemynges *honorr*," (a phrase
which he foresaw would come into use
after his death,) " and allso onn hys promys
of beynge clouse of speeche inn thys laste
Matterr."—On the back we look in vain
for the name of a Scrivener among the
Witnesses ; [188] but, by way of compensation,
we have, as before, the year of the king's
reign in English—" 9 James."

IT will naturally be asked, how came it
to pass that none of the actors here men-

---

[188] I do not mean to say that *all* deeds were attested by
the Scriveners who drew them ; or that this deed is proved
by the circumstance here mentioned to be a forgery. It
was, however, the general practice.

tioned

tioned availed themselves of these valuable gifts on the death of our author, at which time they might very properly claim them, though no specifick time of delivering the plays, I think, is mentioned. Shakspeare without doubt, would notify to his friends his kind intentions towards them. Why did not Burbadge, and the rest, immediately after his death print the TEMPEST, MACBETH, OTHELLO, &c. which had been so long withheld by " the *grand possessors*," and for which doubtless the retired scholars of Oxford and Cambridge who had it not in their power to visit the metropolis, were exceedingly impatient? Why at least, did not Mrs. Shakspeare receive her own letters, the " rings and things" and all the other *bravery* here mentioned? The answer is " as ready as a barber's chair;" that faithless villain, John Heminges, never fulfilled the trust reposed in him. Why, however, did not some of the actors institute a suit against him, to enforce a specifick execution of this trust? To this question I know not what answer will be given. Why again, it may be said, did not this unprincipled Trustee destroy the deed, so as to

save

save himself at least from future infamy ? Or if he only suppressed it, and the parties interested knew nothing of the kindness intended to them, why did not Heminges in the fourteen years which he survived our poet, produce for his own benefit some of these virgin plays at the Globe or Blackfriars; and why were they not printed in the Collection of our author's works ? If again, they were unaccountably neglected, and made no use of whatsoever, why have they not all come down to us along with the deed that relates to them; and why have they not been *brought forward?* This last is, however, a very dangerous question ; for in good time I make no doubt we shall have them all.—But most unluckily for this fine hypothesis of the dishonesty of poor Heminges, a real deed has been discovered since I began this Inquiry, to which I have already alluded, and by which it appears that he did very honourably on the 10th of February 1617-18, fulfill the only trust (as far as we know) that Shakspeare ever reposed in him. This deed being important, both in this respect, and as having furnished us with the genuine autograph of

I   that

that Actor, I shall subjoin it by way of Appendix[189] to these sheets.

———

HAVING now gone through all this *far-rago* of papers and deeds, I should in due form proceed to the copy of "Kynge Leare" and a fragment of " Hamblette," which in fact form the most bulky part of the extraordinary volume lately presented to the publick. But three words on this subject will suffice. Had the fabricator of this piece been content to exhibit it as a play-house copy that by good fortune had escaped the ravages of time, it might, if genuine, have been a curiosity at least to the editors of Shakspeare's works : but he has gone a step further, and has ventured

[189] See the APPENDIX, N°. III.—Why John Heminges was made a trustee by our author, when he purchased his estate in Blackfriars, is not very clear. He did not execute the only part of the deed of conveyance now extant, though he is a party named in it ; and the estate would with equal certainty have descended to Shakspeare's daughters, or followed the directions of his Will, without the aid of Heminges.—These trustees seem to have succeeded the old feoffees to uses, of the former age.

to write in the first page—" Tragedye [not *The* Tragedye] of Kynge Leare isse *fromme* Masterre *Hollinneshedde* I have *inne* somme lyttle *deparretedde fromme hymme butte thatte* LIBBERTYE will *notte* I truste be blamedde bye mye gentle *Readerres*. — Wm Shakspeare."—In this case therefore—" AUT ERASMUS, AUT DIABOLUS,"—may be fairly applied: if it is not of Shakspeare's own hand, it is nothing.

SOME gentlemen, I find, have taken the trouble to collate several passages of this spurious piece with the most authentick copies. For my part, I have not collated nor ever shall collate a single line of it, excepting only the speech which I shall presently transcribe. Life is not long enough to be wasted in the examination of such trash, when almost a single glance is sufficient to shew that it is a plain and palpable forgery, written by the same hand which fabricated all the other deeds and papers that have been already examined. To prove this decisively, it is only necessary to quote a passage from it. Being possessed of the original quarto copy of this play, your Lordship knows that in consequence

R R   of

of being printed from a playhouse transcript, made by some ignorant person, it is the most corrupt of any of the quartos : and yet with all its faults, it is of great service in correcting in certain places the errors of the folio. I suppose it will be allowed that Shakspeare knew verse from prose, and sense from nonsense, and that therefore he could not have written with his own hand any play in which metrical speeches are written unmetrically, and the most ridiculous blunders occur in every page. Take as a specimen the following passage, which many months ago was mentioned to me as a standard by which all the rest of the piece might be truly estimated :

" *ALB.* Whats the Matterre Sir

LEARE. Marke mee Ile telle the life ande deathe
                                    [I amme
ashamd thou hast powerre toe shake mye Mann-
                                    [hoode
thusse thatte these hotte teares thatte breake fromme
mee perreforce shoud *make worse* blasts ande foggs
onne the *unnetennederre* woundynges of a Fatherres
usse playe thys parte agayne *Ile plucke ye oute*
ande caste you with the Waterres thatte you maye
temperre claye."

THUS

THUS *clearly* and *intelligibly* is this speech exhibited as written *by our poet's own hand*, instead of the following *stuff*, which the foolish player-editors have substituted in its room :

ALB. What's the matter, Sir ?

LEAR. I'll tell thee ;—Life and death ! I am
  asham'd   [*To* Goneril.
That thou hast power to shake my manhood thus :
That these hot tears, which breake from me per-
  force,
Should make *thee worth them.*—Blasts and fogs
  upon thee !
The *untented* woundings of a father's *curse*
Pierce every sense about thee !—*Old fond eyes,*
Beweep this cause again, I'll pluck you out,
And cast you with the waters that you *lose,*
To temper clay.

IT has been suggested[190] that the only archetype the fabricator of this piece had at first before him was the second folio. Whether this was the case, I shall never take the trouble to examine. Certainly, however, that spurious and adulterated copy of our author's plays was very " german to the

---

[190] LETTER to George Steevens, Esq. *ut supr.*

    matter,"

matter" in hand, and was very properly chosen for the basis of a new fiction. Afterwards he is supposed to have got one of the early quartos for his model ; but it is much more probable that those very rare editions were beyond his reach, and that he used the re-impression of them published in 1766. It is of no consequence how the forgery was effected. As the whole of this play is in the hand-writing *assigned* to Shakspeare in the MISCELLANEOUS PAPERS, and as it is manifest that it cannot be genuine, on the single ground which I have stated, (without embarrassing the question with the consideration of the absurd orthography used throughout,) it follows necessarily that it is an absolute forgery : for the stickler for its authenticity, or its value in any way, is precluded, for the reasons already given, from changing his ground, and saying that, though it is not of Shakspeare's own hand-writing, it is an old playhouse copy of this admirable tragedy.

THE speech of Kent in the last scene of this play having been thought by the commentators too short and bald, in vamping this

this piece, two lines which the poet has allotted to him have been beaten out and amplified into seven ; and though the verses which have been supplied are not better than any school-boy who had ever composed a line of poetry could write, for want of better arguments they have been quoted as teeming with energy and pathos.

THAT all might be consistent and of a piece from the first to the last, the lines throughout are numbered in the margin, a practice unexampled in our author's time ; and Shakspeare, who in none of his plays has ever mentioned what author he followed, is made here to tell his *readers* (still with a view to *the press*) where he found his story, and to apologize for the *liberty* he has taken in departing from the Historian ; a word not used in that sense till long after his death. The term of his age (here required) was *licence*.—That this piece might have two *ear-marks*, he subscribes his name to it, by way of prelude, I suppose, to a similar subscription to KYNGE VORTIGERNE.

I HAVE but little more to say on the subject of this play, but it is material,
being

being equally applicable to all the other manuscripts which have been examined. The editor has informed us that the paper on which it is written exhibits more than twenty different paper-marks. I have already taken notice how little of the true antiquarian form is found in this publication, by the purchasers' not having been gratified with a *fac-simile* of the paper-mark on each of these MSS. However what has been stated, will answer our purpose just as well.

THERE are two or three obvious ways of procuring old paper, proper for the execution of such a scheme as the present. In publick offices it is a rule to write every memorial, account, or whatever else is to be written, however short, on a whole sheet of paper. In consequence of this practice, in the State-Paper Office, and in many other publick offices where ancient documents are preserved, many superfluous half sheets are from time to time thrown away, when the papers that have become old are arranged and bound up in volumes ; the second leaf of the sheet being often mere lumber. I do not, however, believe

that

that the unknown country gentleman to whom we are indebted for these fabrications, could very easily gain access to our publick offices. The old Houshold-Books and Diaries of ancient families, many of which are but half filled, would also furnish an abundant supply of the same material. But this also was out of his reach. The true and natural paper-warehouse for such a schemer to repair to is, the shop of a bookseller, where every folio and quarto of the age of Elizabeth and James would supply a couple of *single* leaves of white-brown paper, of the hue required.— When these wonders were first announced, I immediately asked some of the *true believers*, whether they had ever seen this tragedy of LEAR, in its *integrity*, as Dr. Warburton would call it,—whole and entire; how was it sewed, what number of leaves did it contain; were the edges in their natural rough state, &c. &c. Not one, I found, had ever seen, I will not say the play, but even a single *sheet* of it. It was produced from time to time (probably as fast as the country gentleman could write it,) in single leaves, that is, in other words, it was written on such paper as the old

volumes

volumes that had been collected for this purpose would furnish : and because such a kind of paper is but of a bad texture, and would not well bear writing on both sides, these half sheets, cut down to the size of our old plays printed in small quarto, were presented to the admiring crowd written *on one side* only.—When I first received this account, I immediately took down from their shelf half a dozen old plays of Shakspeare's time, of which I am possessed, and shewed them to any friend who happened to talk with me upon this subject. They are precisely in the same state as when they first came into my hands, and are neither trimmed nor ornamented in any way, but stitched in covers and well embrowned with dust and age; but unluckily for these *half-covered half* or *quarter sheets* of Kynge Leare, my plays are all written on both sides : nor did I ever see a manuscript play of that age that did not in this respect correspond precisely with those now in my Library. Your Lordship, I remember, purchased a few years ago a curious volume containing no less than fifteen manuscript plays, (most of them nearly of the time of Shakspeare,) among which is

The

THE ELDER BROTHER of Fletcher; I
believe you will find every one of them
written on both sides.—What would an
author naturally do when he sat down to
write a play, at least such an author as
Shakspeare, who at the time LEAR was
produced was in the zenith of his reputation, and in affluent circumstances.
Would he not purchase a paper-book, or at
least a quire of paper, which would be sufficient for the longest piece he ever wrote,
and could then be procured for five pence?
But what would he do who sat down to
write a play for him near two centuries
after his death? He would pick up as well
as he could such scraps of old paper as he
could find, at various times, and in various
places; he would, as in the present case,
not be able to shew any of his pretended
originals except in the form of half or
quarter sheets, and these single leaves having been collected from various quarters
would exhibit more than twenty different
paper-marks. [191]

HAVING

[191] I have been lately informed, that a very honest and
intelligent bookbinder at Cambridge has for some years
past preserved, as a literary curiosity, all such fly-leaves (as
I think they are called,) as the old books put into his hands

HAVING now done with KYNGE LEARE, I may perhaps be expected to say a word on the far-famed tragedy of KYNGE VORR- TYGERNE, and all the KKYNGES and all the QQUEENES which have been announced from the same quarter. But any disqui- sition on this subject is, I conceive, wholly unnecessary ; the outworks being all demo- lished, the fort must surrender of course. If the tragedy of KYNGE LEARE and all the other Manuscripts which have been produced, in some of which this matchless play is mentioned, have been proved not to be genuine, VORRTYGERNE, which affects, like all the rest, to be of, and in the hand of Shakspeare, and is issued from the same repository, cannot but be a forgery also. If it had exhibited any other hand- writing but the *pretended* hand-writing of Shakspeare, it might have been supposed a genuine old play, though it could not boast of so high a parentage as his dramas; but the writer of it having " assumed the person of the noble father" of the stage,

to be re-bound have supplied ; a circumstance which would have saved our unknown gentleman a great deal of trouble, if he had been apprized of it in due time.

it

it can be no other than a modern fiction;
and whether it is a good or a bad fiction, I
shall leave to others to determine.

———

THE topicks which have been the subject of the foregoing pages have been
suggested by the various pieces lately presented to the publick in a folio volume;
but there are some particulars relative to
this matter, not noticed in any part of that
publication, which are well worthy of your
Lordship's attention.

SEVERAL months ago we were informed
by the believers in these fictions, that the
unknown gentleman to whom we are indebted for all these fooleries, was possessed
of a whole-length portrait of Shakspeare,
painted in oil colours; that he there appeared a most goodly personage, of no
ordinary stature; that he had been long
concealed from the vulgar ken by having
been consigned to a garret, and from his
owner's eye by his whole person being
entirely covered over with the leaves of old
black-letter books, (carefully pasted on,) of

some

some of which the titles were specified :
that Mr. *Ignoto* never thought of wash-
ing the poet's face till he was prompted
to it by the discovery of the other treasures which he has so liberally poured
forth ; but that this invaluable portrait
being at length perfectly cleaned and var-
nished, it would by the very first opportunity be conveyed to the Metropolis.
Week after week, however, has passed
away, and month succeeded to month,
without the amateur's being gratified with
this most curious sight. In the same repository also, we were told (about the same
time) two copies of the first folio edition of
his plays had been found, with the edges
of the leaves uncut, which had been the
actual copies that had belonged to Messrs.
Heminges and Condell, (the gift no doubt
of Mr. Isaack Jaggard, and the other publishers of the work,) and added such authenticity to all the rest of the discoveries,
as must flash conviction into the most in-
credulous, and strike all opponents dumb.
Happily however for them, neither picture
nor books have appeared, and those who
shook their heads on that occasion are yet
possessed of the gift of speech.—We must
however

however acknowledge that whenever these folios and this portrait (the latter of which I do not yet despair of seeing) shall be *brought forward*, they will add considerable support and credit to the manuscripts in question; for " who can receive it other" than that all these treasures originally belonged to the same person, and that this person must necessarily be either a descendant of Shakspeare, or some person intimately connected with him? Till however that day shall arrive, we may safely regulate our judgments by the old law maxim—*de non apparentibus et de non existentibus eadem est ratio.*

THERE is yet another very curious circumstance of which we have no notice in the editor's preface; an omission which I shall here endeavour to supply. While these rarities were on shew, among other extraordinary specimens of ancient lore was exhibited to several persons, as I have heard from themselves, a Letter from Shakspeare to his dear friend Richard Cowley, in which he gives an account of having passed the preceding evening with Ben Jonson at a tavern (no doubt his old haunt, THE DEVIL);

DEVIL); our poet adds, that Ben was very surly and dogged, and at length behaved with great rudeness to him, which, however, he says, he was inclined to overlook, as he attributed the ill-behaviour of his old antagonist to his understanding being *deranged* by liquor.[192] By some odd accident this very curious Letter has not been given to the world in the late Miscellany ; by which our author has been defrauded of that fair fame to which he is entitled, since in addition to all his other extraordinary endowments this paper ascertains that he had the gift of prophecy ; foreseeing not only that after his death the French would introduce the word *deranger* and *derangement* into their language, but that we should within these very few years adopt those words from that nation.[193]—
The

[192] Or " to the *derangement* of his understanding by liquor ;"—I am not sure which of these expressions was used.

[193] In our poet's time the French had not the words— *arranger, deranger,* nor *derangement.* In Cotgrave's Dict. in 1611, and its republication by Howel in 1650, we find only *ranger*—" to range, rank, order, arraie," &c. *Deranger* and *derangement* were introduced long afterwards.

The words—*deranged* and *derangement* have been introduced so recently in England, that there are those living who remember

The omission however of this Letter is the less to be regretted, as it is probably only withheld for a short time, and will hereafter appear with the various complimentary Sonnets which Shakspeare wrote to the Earl of Cumberland, Lord Essex, and many other noblemen, (in *imitation* of Spencer,) in the two folio volumes of his posthumous works with which the publick are at a future day to be gratified. [194]

ON reviewing what I have written, I find that I have yet a few observations to make on these papers, and that the very few arguments which have been or may be produced in favour of them yet remain to be answered.

IT has already been mentioned that Sir William D'Avenant was possessed of a

remember their being at first spoken with a French accent, as not being yet made denizens. Dr. Johnson has given neither of them a place in his Dictionary.

[194] The Letter in which Shakspeare speaks very highly of his play of VORRTYGERNE, and insists on a larger price for the *copy-right* of it than his bookseller was willing to give, will, it is hoped, appear at the same time, as it places our author in an entirely new light.

gracious

gracious Letter written by King James to
our poet with his own hand. Here therefore our fabricator had a fair ground to
work upon; and why it may be asked,
did he not adhere to this received tradition,
and produce this Letter of James, which
is known to have once existed, rather
than invent a fiction for which the world
was not so well prepared.—In speculating
concerning the motives of actions, we are
always liable to error; but it is not very
difficult in the present case to assign plausible reasons for the course that has been
taken. The fabricator of the Letter of
Elizabeth might not have been sufficiently
acquainted with the Scottish idiom, to have
ventured on devising an Epistle for our
British Solomon. This difficulty, however,
might perhaps in due time have been got
over. But there was another that never
could be surmounted: he could not be sure
that the Letter of James was not still extant
in some unexamined repository; and whenever it should be produced, detection would
necessarily follow. He abstained therefore
from this fabrication, for the very same reason which induced him to describe Lord
South-

Southampton's bounty to our poet in general terms, instead of naming a specifick sum.[195]

As I have once more had occasion to mention this Letter of King James, it naturally leads me to another inquiry. We will allow for a moment that the Epistle of our maiden Queen which has been so minutely examined, and the paper which accompanies it, are genuine. As our author was so extremely anxious that this mark of his gracious Mistresses favour to him should be preserved " withe alle care possyble" in his family, why was he not equally solicitous about the Letter of James ? and why were not these two royal epistles " feat and affectedly enswathed with sleided silk," and placed together in the " lyttelle cedarr trunke," or in any casket proper for their reception ? It does not fall to the lot of many men to receive letters from two crowned heads : and when it does, if either from the love of fame, or any other motive, the person thus honoured should have any solicitude about the transmission of such memorials to posterity, he would naturally place them *together*, and preserve them in the same

[195] See p. 169.

T T   cabinet.

cabinet. — We do not however find that
Shakspeare did so in the present instance :
but in due time, I make no doubt that
what I have now suggested as probable, will
be found to be the truth, and after a proper
search the Letter of King James will be
discovered in the same repository which
contained that of Elizabeth.[196]

THE various specimens of old language
which have been given in the preceding
pages, prove incontrovertibly that the orthography used in these spurious manuscripts
is the orthography of no time whatsoever :
but say the partisans of these fictions, though
we cannot produce any examples of the *ande*
and *forre* used here, and of such an extraordinary redundancy of consonants and vowels,
it does not therefore follow that these papers
are modern fabrications ; for that being an
age of no curiosity or consistency in this
respect, particular persons might have fallen

[196] It is not improbable also, that in some time after the
fac-similes of the genuine hand-writing of Queen Elizabeth
and Lord Southampton exhibited in this volume, shall have
reached the *unknown gentleman*, he may discover a new correspondence between those personages and our poet, " of a
better leer" than what we have now reviewed : but I here
before-hand enter my protest against this device.

into

into *unexampled* modes of capricious and irregular orthography. Be it so then : in the books and manuscripts of the time we certainly find great irregularity of orthography; the courtier spells in one way, the lawyer in another, the gentlewoman in a third, the artisan in a fourth. But unfortunately *here*, the Queen, the Nobleman, the Actor, the Scrivener, all spell exactly like each other, and like no other Queens, Noblemen, Actors, or Scriveners, that lived before or since their time. Can we have a stronger proof than this, that this miscellaneous collection was the composition of one and the same hand, or rather (on account of the *deeds*) of two hands acting in concert with each other?

But the following defence of the authenticity of these pieces is of a finer texture. It is easier, it is said, to give credit to all these papers with all their absurdities and incongruities of spelling and language, the total dissimilitude of the hand-writing to that of the persons in whose names they appear, and all the other denotations of fraud belonging to them, than to suppose that any person should devote a large portion of his life to

T T 2   such

such a scheme; that he should be such a
fool as to make use of orthography unknown
in any age, run his head against known
facts, and not endeavour to produce some
kind of resemblance to the hand-writing of
the persons whose genuine papers were
pretended to be shewn. This incongruity,
and wild deviation from ordinary practice,
is what no fabricator of such manuscripts
would have ever thought of, or hazarded;
and therefore this circumstance, instead of
weakening their credit, gives them the
strongest support, and proves their authenticity with irresistible force.

THIS reasoning is evidently formed on the
well-known thesis of your Lordship's old
acquaintance, Hume, respecting miracles,—
that if it be more miraculous that a certain
fact should have happened than that the
relater of it should deceive or be deceived,
it is incumbent on the serious inquirer, after
weighing probabilities, to decide according
to the superiority discovered, and to reject
what he calls THE GREATER MIRACLE.
In like manner, in the present case we are
told, it is easier to believe all these papers
to be genuine, than that such an extraordinary

dinary combination of folly and imposture should exist, as must have produced them on the supposition of their being spurious : this is the greater miracle of the two, and therefore we must acquiesce in their authenticity, be the objections to them what they may :—the arguments of their opponents only serve to support and authenticate them ; for the most ordinary forger might have imitated the hand-writing of Elizabeth and the rest with sufficient accuracy ; and when Holinshed and Shakspeare's own works lay before him, he never would have thought of departing so widely from verisimilitude by adopting an orthography and language unknown alike to them and the age in which they lived.

ONE knows not well how to answer this *crotchet*, for I will not call it argument. According to this doctrine, if the theatrical accompts, and the correspondence of our poet with his mistress and Lord Southampton, had been produced in Latin or Greek, they would be still less disputable, or rather indubitably authentick ; for what forger would have ever devised any thing so improbable ?

probable ?—In deeds the usual and orderly
parts are, the *premises*, which contain the
number and names of the parties ; the
habendum and *tenendum*, which determine
what estate or interest is granted, and the
tenure by which it is to be held ; the *red-
dendum*, or rent or services reserved ; the
clause of warranty, the covenants, and the
conclusion, which last mentions the execution and date of the deed. Supposing
therefore this mode of reasoning to be just,
if a deed should be constructed for the me-
ridian of that country where Ralegh, and
after him Shakspeare, tell us the heads of
the inhabitants grow beneath their shoulders, and the *habendum*, instead of being in
the middle, should be placed in the beginning of the instrument ; or if, in honour of
Abbé Sieyes, and to gratify the Convention
of Palace-yard, the bottom should be placed
at the top, and the names of the parties
and their hands and seals should change
places ; " by this kind of chase," I say, if
such a deed should be produced as executed
by Shakspeare, these or any other similar
fantastick absurdities ought to be considered
as the strongest marks of its authenticity ;
for if we will but assume that no fabricator
of

of a forged instrument would ever venture
to depart from verisimilitude, the more incongruous, untechnical, and absurd any deed
or paper is, the more likely it is to be
genuine. But did the partisans of these
fabrications never hear of cunning over-
reaching itself ? Might not all these incongruities and absurdities have been adopted
for the purpose of laying a foundation for
this very argument ? or lastly, might not
many of them have been the genuine offspring of " dull, unfeeling, barren ignorance," eager to effect a lucrative and
difficult imposture, but totally unfurnished
with the means of accomplishing it ?

REASONING such as this may be, and
sometimes is, used at the bar, because a
barrister must employ such topicks as his
cause will admit. An eminent lawyer in
Ireland, now dead, your Lordship remembers used a similar argument in a great
cause decided some years ago in your
House, and endeavoured to shew that a
certificate of marriage, which was the *cardo
causæ*, was the more authentick for its not
having a very fair appearance, " the blots and
alterations of letters in it being all owing
(as

(as he contended) to its being written with a split pen, the nib of which divided in making the strokes. Had it been forged, it would have been fabricated in such a manner as not to be liable to any suspicion or objection. All its little inaccuracies only tended to shew that it was not a writing framed to impose upon the world : and if these were purposely introduced, it was a deeper policy than that of the elder Brutus, who was said to have carried on treasonable designs under the countenance of an idiot."

To this argument the praise of ingenuity may be allowed ; but (without in the least impeaching the cause of the gentleman who produced it,) it will not bear any very critical investigation. Though the common practice, in cases of fabrication, is to follow the beaten path, and to aim at an identity of language, hand-writing, &c. yet this is not always the case ; either because ignorance sometimes may not know how to effect its purpose, or a subtle practiser, like great wits, may sometimes intentionally

" From vulgar bounds *with brave disorder* part,"

to give a grace and gloss to his scheme, beyond

yond the conception or reach of ordinary artists.——But in spite of all the gloss, and graces, and refinements, of art, truth and falshood can never be so confounded as not to be distinguishable from each other : and though the exact similitude of hand-writing is no certain proof of the authenticity of any paper, because the art of forgery is so well understood and practised, that even the Clerks of the Bank of England cannot sometimes distinguish their own hand-writing from its counterfeit, yet to the plain and common sense of mankind a great *dissimilitude* of hand-writing, and the use of words or stamps that were not known till many years after the date of the writings or deeds exhibited, are as ftrong proofs of forgery as can be produced.

I MAY add that " the whymsycalle conceyte" by which these manuscripts are attemped to be supported, stands on a false hypothesis ; namely, that it would have taken a large portion of life to have fabricated such various and numerous pieces, and that it is incredible so much folly and imposture as is acknowledged in the present case, should

u u   be

be found united in the same person or persons. In answer to the last observation, it
is only necessary to ask, who can ascertain
the boundaries of ignorance and imposture ?
With respect to the quantity of these fabrications, which has been much relied on,
and has struck a few persons as a proof of
authenticity, it may be proper to be more
particular.—In this, as in many other cases,
admiration arises only from not having sufficiently examined the subject. The whole
of what has been produced is, twelve short
papers, four deeds, and two plays, consisting,
we will say, of three thousand lines each ;
all of which, instead of employing a large
portion of life, might have been produced
in one year. We are not tied down to suppose that only one person was concerned. It
is much more probable that the composition
of all but the deeds was the work of one,
and that the Shakspearean rags (for I will
not call it *cloathing*) were sewn on by another. He, or she, (for we know not even
the sex of the author) who might be able
to " spin a thousand lines a day," might
know nothing of old hands ; and the adept
in the art of counterfeiting old hands might
not have the faculty of writing a line of
poetry.

poetry. The invention of the smaller pieces
and of the play, it is surely not unreasonable
to suppose, might have been effected in six
months ; and in six more not only these,
but the tragedy of LEAR, might have been
copied in the hand required.—It should be
recollected that no hand-writing but that of
Shakspeare has been exhibited, excepting
the miserable attempts at that of Elizabeth,
Lord Southampton, Heminges, Condell,
and Lowin ; all of which could not have
taken a month. Of Shakspeare's hand-
writing we have but eleven letters of the
ordinary alphabet, and three capital letters,
extant. Here therefore the artist had an
open field. There was no large quantity
of writing of the poet known to be any
where existing, to which an appeal could
be made, and which, from a peculiarity in
the manner of his forming certain letters, [197]
might lead to detection. He had nothing
therefore to do but to attain what he
thought [198] a general resemblance, and when
once

[197] Thus, for example, Lord Southampton appears to
have formed the letter *f* in a manner peculiar to himself.

[198] I say, what *he* thought ; for he will not find many
who will allow that it has even a general resemblance. It
is remarkable that he had not sagacity enough to reflect

that

once that was attained, I have no doubt
that he transcribed the printed pages of
LEAR, or the written pages of VORRTY-
GERNE, nearly as fast as he could have
transcribed them in his ordinary hand. The
present fabrication therefore differs from
all others in this respect, that the artificer
thought he might take a greater licence, and
consequently was enabled to proceed with
much more facility and despatch than in
ordinary cases.

How much may be done by assiduous
application, where a particular object is in
view, I can from my own experience furnish a strong instance. I transcribed the
poem of ROMEUS AND JULIET, which I
afterwards published, and which consists of
above three thousand long lines of fourteen
syllables each, in seven days : but to effect
it, I was obliged to work from morning till
night. A similar application in the present
instance would have effected this audacious

that the hand-writing of the youth of eighteen generally
differs much from that of the man at fifty. Hence, we
find our poet's name subscribed to the pretended Letter to his
mistress, which must be referred to 1582, evidently formed
on the signature to his Will in 1616, and undistinguish-
able from the other pretended signatures to the deeds, &c.

fabrication

fabrication in a much shorter time than I have allowed. But supposing all my calculations to be erroneous, why may not this forgery have been the work of three or four years?—In that time even its most zealous partisans must acknowledge it might have been all completed. [199]

THE usual spelling of the time might have been easily copied, but it was departed from for the reason already assigned,—to give a greater air of originality to the fabrication; and the mass of papers and deeds was hazarded, to subdue all suspicion by its magnitude. As for the correct imitation of hands, which it is contended might have been accomplished, that certainly was not so easy; because in several instances the fabricator had no archetype whatsoever. Queen Elizabeth's ordinary hand-writing he had no means of getting at. He might indeed have found it in the Museum; but *tracing* it there, as it is called, with the

---

[199] I think it extremely probable that the scheme was laid, and that books, &c. were collected five or six years ago, and the executive part effected in the year, or at most in the two years, which preceded January 1795.

proper

proper apparatus, might afterwards have induced suspicion, and endangered the whole
scheme. Lord Southampton's hand-writing
he certainly had no means of imitating at
all ; for that there was a Letter written by
him among the Harleian Manuscripts, was,
I have reason to believe, known to few
beside myself, there being no reference to
it in the Index to the Harleian Catalogue,
and it being unknown even to the judicious
and well-informed Librarians of that noble
collection. The other Letter of the same
nobleman in the Cotton Library was discovered only a few months ago, in consequence of a particular examination being
ordered to be made of the three volumes of
Royal and State Letters there reposited,
which are only generally mentioned in the
old catalogue. The hand-writing of Heminges, Lowin, and Condell, were all equally
unknown, and, like Southampton's, were
all supposed to be out of the reach of the
most curious inquirer. As to language and
phraseology, what was conceived to be the
phraseology of that time *was* imitated, according to the slender abilities of the fabricator of this fiction ;—how well we have
seen :

seen : very different abilities, and taste, and knowledge, would have been requisite to have produced any fiction that should not be assailable on that ground ; and I doubt much whether those who have travelled longest in the paths of antiquity would not be liable to stumble in such an attempt. Dr. Johnson, if I remember right, has somewhere observed, that the imitators of Spencer think they have performed their task, when they have adopted his stanza, and disfigured their verses by a due sprinkling of old spelling and old language ; but they forget that if any word is introduced unknown to Spencer's age, the poem can be no just imitation of that author.

In addition to the mass of papers produced, we are assailed by the whole Library of Shakspeare, consisting, according to some accounts, of eleven hundred volumes ; of which a very fair CATALOGUE is produced, and *some* of the pretended volumes have been displayed. How this circumstance can have made any impression on any one, (as I am told it has on two or three persons,) appears to me very extraordinary. Was it then a matter of such mighty

mighty achievement, (for the purpose of
forming this Catalogue,) to transcribe Mr.
Capell's List of the volumes of that age,
which he collected for the purpose of
illustrating Shakspeare's works, and to add
to it from any old Catalogues whatever
might be wanting?[200]—"But some of the
books themselves have been produced."—I
make no doubt of it. But are old books so
very difficult to be procured? And could not
two or three hundred have been picked up
on stalls, and elsewhere, in five or six years,
during which this scheme may have been in
contemplation? Within these few years
past the price of Holinshed's Chronicle has
doubled, in consequence of his having been
pointed out as the author whom Shakspeare
followed in his Historical Plays, and of our
poet's daily-increasing reputation: yet still
it is without much difficulty to be procured;
and I have seen no less than four copies of
it on sale within the last year. The same
observation may be made on many other
valuable books of that age, for which a high

[200] By turning over the pages of the late editions of Shakspeare, I make no doubt, the names of a thousand books
or tracts of his age, might be collected in a few days: and
names alone are wanting to make a *catalogue*.

price

price might very well occasionally have been given, where a great object was in view. But valuable or costly books were not always necessary; worthless books, when duly appropriated by writing our poet's name forty or fifty times in them, would do just as well. [201]—With respect to smaller tracts, a different process was to be pursued, for they could not be safely exhibited as Shakspeare's, while they remained in miscellaneous volumes. It is well known to the collectors of these rarities, that very often pieces extremely discordant, both in their subjects and dates, are strangely blended together under the same covering. Thus " The Golden Legend," printed by Wynken de Worde, or " the Gorgeous Gal-

[201] In the margins of several of these books, I have been told, are displayed remarks by Shakspeare, each of which is subscribed with his name; and very properly,—for how else should the inspector have known that these books came out of his Library?

This trick of our author is quite peculiar to himself. Few scribblers in books think of appropriating their marginal remarks by this kind of subscription to each of them; but his *known vanity*, and attention to his *literary property* and fame, were without doubt the cause of this practice.

lery

[338]

lerv of Gallant Inventions, [202] or Greene's
" Art of Connycatching," [203] or " A Fig for
Momus," [204] or " The Nest of Ninnies," [205]
or " The Art of Swimming," [206] (not by the
renowned William Henry Ireland of Blackfriars, but by Christopher Middleton,) or
" The Essayes of an Apprentice in Poetry,"
[207] or " The Arte of Legerdemaine," [208]
or " the Arbour of Amorous Devices," [209]
or some other of those delectable treatises
which the late editors of Shakspeare's
works have thought it necessary to read for
the illustration of their author, may happen
to be bound up in the same volume with
" A Plot for the good of Posterity," [210] or
" Tom of all Trades," [211] or " A Pacquet of
Wonders brought over in Charon's ferry-
boat," [212] or " Fair Warnings to a Careless
World," [213] or " The Counter-Scuffle," [214] or
" The Unloveliness of love-locks," [215] or
"Papers Complaint against the paper-spoylers
of these times," [216] which belong to a period

[202] 4to. 1578. [203] 4to. 1592. [204] 4to. 1595. [205] 4to.
1609. [206] 4to. 1595. [207] By King James. Edinb. 4to.
1584. [208] By Samuel Rowland, 4to. 1612. [209] 4to. 1580.
[210] By Francis Cheynell, 4to. 1646. [211] 4to. 1631.
[212] 4to. 1641. [213] 4to. 1662. [214] 4to. 1628. [215] 4to.
1648. [216] By A. H. 4to. 1624.

6   subsequent

subsequent to Shakspeare's death. No such volume therefore could be safely exhibited as his. What then is to be done? The process is extremely simple. The *unknown* gentleman from whose store-house all these rarities have issued, has nothing to do but to cut out such tracts as are dated prior to 1616; and after each of them has been separately cloathed with morocco or vellum, or any other covering that fancy may direct, and the name of William Shakspeare has been written in the upper, lower, and side margin of twenty or thirty pages, it becomes a most valuable relick, miraculously preserved for near two hundred years, and now first displayed to the gazing world, an undoubted and invaluable original. The prying Antiquary without doubt may occasion a little embarrassment by regretting the loss of the original cover, which, beside its comely ancient simplicity, he may suppose a mark of authenticity; but he is only one of many, and on all others it will pass very well.——In two months two hundred such volumes might be procured. Let us then hear no more of Shakspeare's Library.

BUT

BUT still, it is said, the deeds at least
must be ancient ; for the parchment, writing,
and seals, have all the appearance of antiquity. Is then " the state of these *good
believers* so gracious" that they have never
heard that the whole writing of ancient
deeds may be discharged by the essential
salt of lemons, or marine or nitrous acid ?
The contents of these deeds being proved to
be forged, it necessarily follows, if the
parchments be really old, that the original
writing has been discharged by one or other
of these processes, and new writing substituted in its place. But the parchments
themselves may be as modern as the writing ; for the process by which parchment
acquires the air of antiquity is not very
tedious or difficult. [217] Supposing the parchment

[217] As probably the greater part of my readers are wholly
unacquainted with the art and mystery of *making old deeds*,
the following extract from a cause of much celebrity in
the last century, which contains some curious information
on this subject, may not be unacceptable to them. I mean
the case of Mossam, v. Dame Theodosia Ivy, reported in
the STATE TRIALS, vol. vii. p. 571. The property
in contest was a large district in the parish of Shadwell,
(about seven acres,) on which between three and four hundred houses had been built, and the question was, whether
these

ment to be old, which however I do not
believe to have been the case, some of the
seals

these seven acres were part of the inheritance of the Dean
of St. Paul's, to whom a Mr. Neale was lessee, and then
lessor of the plaintiff, or part of Wapping Marsh, that had
been drained by one Vanderdelf, and afterwards was sold
to a person of the name of Stepkins, under whom Lady
Ivy claimed. The deeds on which her title principally de-
pended, were two leases, one alleged to have been made
on the 13th of November, and the other on the 22d of December in the second and third years of Philip and Mary,
[Nov. and Dec. 1555,] who were styled in these deeds
King and Queen of England, *Spain*, France, the two Si-
cilies, &c. Dukes of *Burgundy*, *Millain*, and Brabant, &c.
—The King and Queen not having assumed the title of
King and Queen of Spain till some months afterwards,
(before which time they were styled *Princes* of Spain,) and
Millain being always in their true style put *before* Burgundy,
these deeds were thus ascertained to be forged.—In the
course of this trial several facts were ascertained, that may
throw some light on the question before us.

*　　*　　*　　*

" *Sir John Trevor*. My Lord, we would gladly know
where they had this Lease, that so it may appear whence it
came ; for we know they have an excellent art at finding
out of deeds.

Mr. Att. Gen. Mr. Knowles, do you know any thing of
that deed ? When did you first see it ?

Mr. Williams. And where had you it ?

Knowles. My lord, I had it in a garret, in a kind of a
nook, about six feet long, and three feet and an half wide,
in my own house, in the garret among other writings.

[Mr.

seals have been newly *tempered*, like Shallow, *between the finger and the thumb* ; for
great

[Mr. Sutton *sworn and examined*.]

Mr. Sol. Gen. [*After a few questions had been asked,*] Pray, my lord, give me leave to ask him [*Knowles*] a question, which I hope may clear all this matter, for it is plain the man is mistaken.

Lord Ch. J. Mistaken! Yes, I assure you very grossly. Ask him what questions you will, but if he should swear as long as Sir John Falstaff fought, I would never believe **a** word he says.

[Knowles *was then examined again*.]

* * * *

Mr. Att. Gen. [*After a long examination.*] We must lay aside the testimony of this man.

Lord Ch. J. Ay, so you had need.

Mr. Att. Gen. We shall desire your lordship to consider all the use we make of this deed is, to prove that the mill was removed to another place.

Lord Ch. J. I do not know what it proves ; but if you had kept your witness, Knowles, in the mill, I think you had done better than brought him hither.

* * * *

Mr. Att. Gen. They go about to blemish our deeds by the folly of our witnesses, which we cannot help. We however leave the deeds to the Jury, and let them see *if those seals and other things look like counterfeits.*

* * * *

Mr. Bradbury. My lord, we have had a violent suspicion that these deeds were forged ; but we suspect now no longer, for we have detected it ; and will shew as palpable self-evident forgery on the face of these deeds as ever was.

[Part of the deeds of the 13th of Nov. and 22d of Dec.

2 and

great indeed must be his credulity who
believes Shakspeare's pretended seal with
the

2 and 3 of Philip and Mary, was then read ; as were the
titles of the acts of the parliament which began Oct. 22,
and ended 9th of Dec. 2 and 3 of Philip and Mary, and
several of the fines levied in the following Hilary and Easter
Term, in which the true style of the King and Queen was
found. In Trinity term the style was changed.

Mr. Bradbury. I cannot see how these deeds can be
truly made at that time, when they stand single, and *none*
like them can be shewn, except they come from the same forge
that these do. I cannot believe that the Miller alone, or
he that drew his leases for him, *could so long before prophecy*
what manner of style should hereafter be used.

    *   *   *   *

Mr. Williams. Pray, swear that lady.—[*Mrs. Duffet*
sworn.] Mrs. Duffet,—Will you acquaint my Lord and the
Jury what you know has been done by my Lady Ivy, or
by her direction, in making and altering of deeds ?

Mrs. Duffet. My lord, I did see Mr. Duffet forge and
counterfeit several deeds for my Lady Ivy.

Lord Ch. J. Was my Lady Ivy by, when the writing
was made ?

Mrs. Duffet. She was by, giving him order how to make
it, and what ink he should use, to make it look old ; and
they forced me to make the ink, and *to fetch saffron to*
put in it, to make it look old.

Mr. Serj. Stringer. Pray, what did they do to the deeds
they made, to make them look like ancient true deeds ?

Mrs. Duffet. For the making of the outsides look old
and dirty, they used to rub them on windows that were
very dusty, and wear them in their pockets to crease them,
for some weeks together, according as they intended to
make

the impression of a boar's head, in honour of Falstaff's tavern, or that of Lowin, shadowed out after the head of one of our Saxon Monarchs, or some similar original, to be genuine. The former of these seals furnishes one of those instances to which I have already alluded, where cunning over-reaches itself; for this doubtless was

make use of them.—When they had been rubbed upon the window to make them look dirty, and they were to pass for deeds of a great many years standing, it was used to lay them in a balcony, or any open place, for the rain to come upon them and wet them, and then the next sun-shiny day they were exposed to the sun, or a fire made, to dry them hastily, that they might be shrivelled.

Mr. Dolbens. What do you know of counterfeiting any seals?

Mrs. Duffet. Mr. Duffet once had the impression of a seal in his hand, with which he said he was going to one Mr. Dryden to have it counterfeited: but I do not remember what the seal was.

Mr. Williams. When the deeds were written, how did he use to put the names to them?

Mrs. Duffet. I have seen my Lady herself write some great letters of the names first upon paper, which Mr. Duffet could not so well hit; and he has writ the rest."—

Verdict for the plaintiff; and a motion was made by his counsel that the several deeds produced by the defendant, that were detected of forgery, might be left in court, that an Information might be brought against Lady Ivy for forging and publishing them; which information was accordingly fyled in Trinity Term, 1684.

thought

thought a most happy device, while in fact
it is a manifest denotation of fraud.

LET me ask, before I conclude, what
would have been the process, if any person
had really discovered a coffer, or old cabinet, filled with original manuscripts of
Shakspeare? Would he not immediately
have perused them *all* most eagerly, and
after having made an exact list of the
whole, would he not then proclaim his good
fortune to the world, and invite all his
friends to see and examine them, to whom
he would naturally relate in what manner
he had made the discovery, how long they
had been in his possession, and from whom
they were derived? And could not all this,
excepting the invitation to friends, have
been done in a week, as well as in three or
four months? I am myself at this moment
surrounded with not less than a hundred
deeds, letters, and miscellaneous papers,
directly or indirectly relating to Shakspeare;
and though they are not in the most exact
order, in consequence of my having frequent occasion to consult them, I would
undertake to arrange and make a list of
them all in two days, without omitting a

Y Y   single

single article.—In the present case, on the other hand, that there might be no one circumstance or ground of suspicion wanting, we find that no such complete list was made by the unknown gentleman, or ever produced : he fed the publick precisely in proportion to their credulity, issuing out his papers and deeds by *driblets* in the course of four or five months, during which it is manifest that some of those produced in the latter part of that period were devised and fabricated, in order to cover and give a kind of sanction to those which had been previously transmitted from that dark and unknown repository where they were originally framed.

THERE is yet another difficulty, which not only never has been, but never can be got over. Allowing for a moment that not one of the decisive proofs of forgery which have been produced, are valid, from what quarter could such a mass of heterogeneous papers and deeds be derived? Lady Barnard, Shakspeare's granddaughter, or her executor, might have her grandmother's love-letters, the rings and lock of hair of her grandfather, and the

coun-

counterparts of any leases he had made; but how should she have a deed of trust made by her ancestor to John Heminges, and *suppressed by him*, or a deed made by Shakspeare to his beloved friend Mr. William Henry Ireland, &c.? On the other hand, among the papers of Mr. Heminges might have been found this suppressed deed and stage-contracts, and leases made jointly by him and Shakspeare; but how should he or his representatives become possessed of letters written by the poet to his mistress, the lock of hair which he presented to her, the valuable ring given to him by Lord Southampton, or the gracious epiſtle with which Queen Elizabeth honoured him? Whatever quarter is fixed upon, will be found equally objectionable; and accordingly, after frequently shifting the ground, this point has been given up in despair, and we are not furniſhed with even a plausible conjecture upon the subject.

IMPOSTURES of this kind are no novelties in the History of Letters. Muretus, about the time Shakspeare was born, deceived Joseph Scaliger by some verses

of

of an ancient dramatick poet named Trabeas,
which, he said, he had recently discovered.[218]
In 1693, Francis Nodot, a Frenchman,
published at Paris what he called a complete copy of Petronius, from a MS.
which he pretended to have found at Bel-
grade five years before: but it is now
well known to have been a forgery.[219]
The fable of Psalmanazar will be long
remembered for the great ingenuity and
deep contrition of that learned impostor.[220]

At

[218] Scaliger revenged himself by the well-known epigram:

Qui rigidæ flammas vitaverat ante Tholosæ,
Muretus, fumos vendidit ille mihi.

[219] The following Hendecasyllables, which were written on that occasion, are sufficiently applicable to the author
of the present clumsy imposture:

Salve, nec latio libelle naso,
Nec lingua facili, nec elegante,
Nec sane nimis Attici saporis,
Proles patris imaginosa Galli.
Tu te ludere credis et jocari
Romano sale, Gratiis Latinis?
Tun' fucum facere auribus Batavis?
O inscitia ruris inficeti,
O vecordia putidi cerebri.

[220] There are many now living who remember the deep
contrition of Psalmanazar, whose real name is yet unknown.
In his last Will he thus penitently expresses himself, relative

At Venice in the present century (1738) an entire Manuscript of Catullus was fabricated, which the forger said he had discovered at Rome, and which happily supplied all the defects found either in preceding manuscripts or the printed editions of that author.[221]—The fabrications of

tive to this imposture : "But the principal manuscript I thought myself bound to leave behind is a faithful narrative of my education and the sallies of my wretched youthful years, and the various ways by which I was in some measure unavoidably led into the base and shameful imposture of passing upon the world for a native of Formosa, and a convert to Christianity, and backing it with a fictitious account of that island and of my own travels, conversion, &c. all or most of it hatched in my own brain, without regard to truth and honesty.—If the obscurity I have lived in during such a series of years should make it needless to revive a thing in all likelihood so long since forgot, I cannot but wish that so much of it was published in some weekly paper, as might inform the world, especially those who have still by them the fabulous account of the island of Formosa, &c. that I have long since owned both in conversation and in print, that it was no other than a mere forgery of my own devising, a scandalous imposition on the publick, and such as I think myself bound to beg God and the world pardon for writing, and have been long since, as I am to this day and shall be as long as I live, heartily sorry for and ashamed of."

[221] The fabricator of this spurious MS. was G. F. Corradini.—" Corradinum mendacii manifestum tenemus, ipsemet

of Lauder, and of the poems of Offian
and Rowley, are yet fresh in the memory
of every one ; and some time before
either Ossian or Chatterton was heard of,
William Rufus Chetwood, an obscure bookseller, distinguished himself by the fruit-
fulness of his inventions, which, like those
now before us, related to Shakspeare : he
did not, however, aspire to the dignity of
forging manuscripts, contenting himfelf
with inventing the titles of editions of our
author's plays, never seen by any one
except himself.[222] But none of these im-
postors

semet namque codicem Romanam sibi confinxit, quin
de hac ludificatione ridebat interdum, fabulando." Maf-
feius in Append. ad Museum Veronense, p. ccv.

By following this copy, the elegant edition of Catullus
printed by Coustelier at Paris, in 1743, is of no value.

[222] William Rufus Chetwood had been Prompter to
Drury-Lane Theatre for twenty years, and was also a
Bookseller. Having been obliged to leave London, he removed to Dublin, and died in the Marshalsea there about
the year 1760. While he was in confinement, a book
entitled THE BRITISH THEATRE was published in
Dublin, (12mo. 1750) compiled, as the editor says, from
Chetwood's papers, in which, in order to give them an
additional value, he inserted the titles of several fictitious
editions of Shakspeare's plays which, he said, were printed
in small quarto in the author's life-time:

" An

postors were daring enough to produce any pretended original manuscript, as written by

"An excellente conceyted Tragedie of *Romeo and Juliette, with the Wranglyngs of the two famous houses of* Mountague and Capulette, 1593."—" The *Tempeste*,wythe the Enchantments of the banished Lorde Prospero, 1595." " A most pleasaunte Comedie called *A Midsummer Night's Dreame, with the Freakes of the Fayries,* 1595."—" The true Chronicle of *Kynge Henrie the 8th*, wythe the costlie coronatione of Queene Anne Bulleyne, after his divorce from Queene Catharine ; the cunninge of Cardinal Wolsey wythe his disgrace and deathe ; wythe the birthe and *christianing* of our gracious Princess, Elizabethe, 1597, 1598, *(with alterations)* 1605."—" A wittie and pleasaunte Comedie called *the Taminge of the Shrewe*, 1598, 1601, 1607, 1608. *There are great alterations in the two last editions.*"—" *Hamlet, Prince of Denmarke* his Tragedie, wythe his just revenge on the adulterous Kynge Claudius, and the poisoning of the Queen Gertrude, 1599, 1605, 1609."—" *The Twoe Gentlemen of Verona*, a pleasaunte Comedie, 1600, 1613, 1614."—" The true Tragedie of *Timon of Athens*, wythe the dogged veine of Apemantus, 1604."—" The excellente Tragedie of *Cymbeline*, wythe the warres of the Romans wythe the Brittaines, 1606."— " A *Winter Nighte Tale*, an excellent Comedie, 1606."— " *Caius Martius Coriolanus*, his lamentable Tragedie, 1606," &c. &c.

His invention seems to have reached its utmost height in the two following paragraphs, which doubtlefs he thought master-pieces :

" *Measure for Measure.* This play is without a date, but by an Advertisement at the end, viz. *Where may be boughte at his shopp printed last year* (1600) *the Twoe Gentlemen*

by the author himself : all these fictions
therefore, however reprehensible, were,
for obvious reasons, harmless and innocent
compared with the present fabrication,
whether it be considered with a view to
society, or to the character and history of
the incomparable poet whose handwriting
has been counterfeited.

BUT to draw to a conclusion.—In the
course of this inquiry it has been shewn
that the artificer or artificers of this clumsy
and daring fraud, whatever other qualifica-
tions they may possess, know nothing of
the history of Shakspeare, nothing of the

---

tlemen of Verona by W. Shakespeare, GENTLEMAN, we may
venture to date this play in 1601."

" The Whole Contentione betweene the two famouse houses
of Lancastre and Yorke, &c. in two parts.—These two plays
are printed without a date, but we are assured they must be
acted about this time ; for at the end of Romeo and Juliet,
printed for Andrew Wise in 1597, is the following Advertisement. At the Shopp of Andrew Wise Mr. William
Shakespeare his Henrie the 6th, in two parts, may be boughte.—
The 3d part is printed in 1600 ; but we make no doubt
that it was printed before that date, though the edition is
not in our possession."

Romeo and Juliet was printed in 1597, not for Andrew
Wise, but John Danter, and at the end of the play there is
no advertisement whatsoever.

I   history

history of the Stage, or the history of the
English Language. It has been proved,
that there is no external evidence whatsoever that can give any credibility to the
manuscripts which have been now examined, or even entitle them to a serious consideration. That the manner in which they
have been produced, near two centuries
after the death of their pretended author, is
fraught with the strongest circumstances of
suspicion. That the orthography of all the
papers and deeds is not only not the orthography of that time, but the orthography of
no period whatsoever. That the language
is not the language of that age, but is in
various instances the language of a century
afterwards. That the dates, where there
are dates, either express or implied, and
almost all the facts mentioned, are repugnant to truth, and are refuted by indisputable documents. That the theatrical contracts
are wholly inconsistent with the usages of
the theatres in the age of Shakspeare; and
that the law of the legal instruments is as
false as the spelling and phraseology are
absurd and senseless. And lastly, that the
hand-writing of all the miscellaneous pa-

z z pers,

pers, and the signatures of all the deeds,
wherever genuine autographs have been obtained, are wholly dissimilar to the hand-
writing of the persons by whom they are
said to have been written and executed; and
where autographs have not been found, to
the general mode of writing in that age.
If any additional proof of forgery is wanting, I confess I am at a loss to conceive of
what nature it should be.

I HAVE now done; and I trust I have
vindicated Shakspeare from all this " im-
puted trash," and rescued him from the
hands of a bungling impostor, by proving
all these Manuscripts to be the true and
genuine offspring of consummate ignorance
and unparalleled audacity. [223]

WHILE

[223] It has often been a subject of regret among the
friends of that great and good man, the late Dr. Johnson,
that his valuable life was not protracted a few years longer;
that he did not live to see the attempts which have been
made in a neighbouring kingdom to obliterate from men's
minds the belief of a future state, and every principle which
tends to enforce a conformation of human actions to the
Divine laws; with all the wild and pernicious theories of
government which have been propagated by the republican
zealots of the present day, both in this country and France,
alike

WHILE I was employed in this investigation, I sometimes fancied that I was
pleading

alike subversive of those establishments which he so justly
revered, and of the peace and happiness of mankind. On
such a subject how would he have kindled, and with what
strength of argument, and energy, and eloquence, would
he have treated it!—Though he would not have displayed
equal ardour on a subject comparatively of so little importance as the present fabrication, yet even here, he who in
opposing the fictions of Ossian and Chatterton was as
strenuous as any of their most determined assailants, would
not have been an indifferent spectator: and as his sagacity
and discernment would have immediately seen through the
whole of the fraud, he would not have been slow to express
his indignation at it.——Strongly impressed with this
notion, while I have been employed in the present work,
I have sometimes imagined that I beheld him looking
down from the abodes of the blessed, animating me to proceed in the cause of Shakspeare and of truth, and exclaim-
ing in his firm and sonorous tone,

—— *cape saxa manu, cape robora, pastor.*

The warm part he took on the detection of Lauder, naturally brought this excellent man to my mind. It is well
known that he wrote the greater part of that impostor's
penitentiary Letter to Dr. Douglas, (the present Lord
Bishop of Salisbury,) which Lauder afterwards was base
enough to retract. As I trust, that the now unknown contriver of the present imposture will hereafter be discovered,
and hope that he will have a due sense of the heinousness
of his offence against society and the cause of letters, the

Z Z 2   following

pleading the cause of our great dramatick
poet before the ever-blooming God of me-
lody

following formulary of recantation and contrition, written
for Lauder by Dr. Johnson, may very properly *(mutatis
mutandis)* be recommended to him :

" I publickly, and without the least dissimulation, sub-
terfuge, or concealment, acknowledge the truth of the
charge which you have advanced. On the sincerity and
punctuality of this confession, I am willing to depend for
all the future regard of mankind; and cannot but indulge
some hopes that they whom my offence hath alienated from
me, may by this instance of ingenuity and repentance be
propitiated and reconciled.—Whatever may be the event,
I shall at least have done all that can be done in reparation
of my former injuries to *Shakspeare*, to truth, and to mankind; and entreat that those who shall still continue im-
placable will examine their own hearts, whether they have
not committed equal crimes without equal proofs of sorrow,
or equal acts of atonement.—For the violation of truth I
offer no excuse, because I well know that nothing can excuse it. Nor will I aggravate my crime by disingenuous
palliations. I confess it, I repent it, and resolve that my
first offence shall be my last. More I cannot perform,
and more therefore cannot be required of me."—MILTON
no Plagiary, or a Detection of the Forgeries contained in
Lauder's *Essay on the imitation of the Moderns in the* PA-
RADISE LOST, &c. By the Rev. John Douglas, A. M.
2d edit. 1756, p. 84.

Lauder published his recantation in 1751, in a Letter
to the Rev. Mr. Douglas, drawn up for him by Dr. Johnson,

lody and song. Possessed with this idea, and
having after a very restless night closed my
eyes at an early hour of the morning, I
imagined myself transported to Parnassus,
where Apollo and his nine female assessors
were trying this question, and were pleased
to call on me to deliver my sentiments, as
Counsel for Shakspeare, before they should
proceed further in the cause. The various
poets of all times and countries were amus-
ing themselves with their lyres on this celebrated hill, which was richly stored with a
profusion of bay trees, and ivy, interspersed
with a great variety of aromatick shrubs,
which perfumed the air with the most de-
lightful fragrance. I immediately knew our
author by his strong resemblance to the
only authentick portrait of him, which belonged to the late Duke of Chandos, and of
which I have three copies by eminent mas-
ters. He appeared to be a very handsome
man, above the middle size, and extremely
well made. The upper part of his head

son, to which however he added a contradictory postscript
of his own. He afterwards went to Barbadoes, where
he died in great poverty about the year 1770.

was

was almost entirely denuded of hair ; his
eyes were uncommonly vivid, and his
countenance was strongly marked by that
frankness of air, and gentle benignity,
which all his contemporaries have attributed to him. At the top of the hill he
had found out a pleasant even lawn, where
he was playing at bowls with Spencer, Sir
John Suckling, little John Hales, and two
other friends ; wholly inattentive to what
was going forward in the Court, though
Apollo was seated but a few paces from
him. He had been hunting at an early hour
of the morning (as I learned from his conversation) in the adjoining plains of Phocis,
with Diana (who was then on a visit to her
brother) and a bevy of her nymphs, who
were now spectators of the game in which
he was engaged. Recollecting the numerous proofs which his writings (corrobo-
rated by the testimony of his contemporaries)
exhibit, of the tenderness of his heart and
his passionate admiration of the fairer part
of the creation, whose innumerable graces
add a zest to all the pleasures, and sooth
and alleviate all the cares of life, I was not
surprised to hear him tell one of his female
associates

associates in the chase, that his sport that day had far exceeded any amusement of the same kind he had ever partaken of in his sublunary state. His old and surly antagonist, Ben Jonson, was seated on an empty cask, looking on the game, in which from the great corpulency and unwieldiness of his frame he was unable to join. Being now unfurnished with his beloved sack, he was obliged to betake himself to the pure stream of the Castalian spring, of which an immense flaggon stood near him ; and he appeared to have taken such large potations of it, that he was become perfectly bloated and dropsical.

WHEN I had urged the principal topicks which have been enlarged upon in the present Inquiry, and the Counsel of the other side had done pleading, Apollo proceeded to pronounce sentence. He began with observing, that this was one of the most important causes that had ever been argued in that court ; not only as it concerned the history and reputation of the greatest poet that the world had seen since the days of Homer, but also involved in it the history of language, and of that species of poetical composition

6

over which two of his assessors on the
bench particularly presided. That the rights
of authors were as sacred as any other, and
that the Statute in this case made and provided had very wisely guarded their literary
property from every kind of invasion, by
securing to them for a certain period an ex-
clusive privilege of printing and publishing
their works, for their own benefit. That
the present, however, was entirely a new
case, no mention being made in the Act
of the injury which might be done to the
reputation of poets, long after their death,
by attributing to them miserable trash
printed from pretended ancient manuscripts,
made in some obscure corner *for the nonce*,
and thus debasing and adulterating their genuine performances, which had been admired
for ages, by the most impure and base
alloy : that this offence, though not within
the letter, was clearly within the spirit and
equity of the statute, and was a still greater
injury than that expressly provided against,
inasmuch as that only affected the property
of an author, whereas this robbed him of
that good name and reputation which to all
men of sensibility is dearer than life itself.

He

He added, that to remove all doubts in future, he thought it highly necessary that the Act on this subject should be explained and amended, and he hoped a select committee of poets would draw up a bill for that purpose. Without however waiting for such an explanatory act, he thought himself fully justified on the ground before stated, in pronouncing the sentence of the law in the present case, in which the whole court were unanimous. He therefore ordered in the first place that a continual *hue and cry* should be made for one year after the original contriver and fabricator of those Miscellaneous Papers which had been recently published in a folio volume, and attributed to the illustrious Shakspeare and others; that a perpetual injunction should issue to prevent the further sale of them, and that the whole impression now remaining in the hands of the Editor should immediately be delivered up to the Usher of the Court; and when a proper fire had been made of the most baleful and noxious weeds, that all the Copies should be burned by Dr. Farmer, Mr. Steevens,

3 A   and

and myself, assisted by Mr. Tyrwhitt, [214]
who I perceived was honoured with a seat
on the bench, and whose polite demeanour
and thoughtful aspect displayed all that
urbanity and intelligence for which he was
distinguished in life : (for in this calenture
of the brain, your Lordship cannot but
have observed that the imagination often
unites the most discordant circumstances,
and without any difficulty brings together
the future and the past, the living and the
dead.)—He should not, however, (the
God of Verse added,) content himself with
vindicating the reputation of this his favourite son ; but, as his Court involved a
criminal as well as a civil jurisdiction,
should proceed to give sentence on those
persons who had been arraigned at the
bar, for giving a certain degree of counte-

---

[214] It is not, I believe, generally known, that the very
learned editor of Chaucer was himself a poet. While he
was yet at college, (1749,) he published a poem entitled
" An Epistle to Florio at Oxford," which I have never
met with, but I have been informed by a very good judge
that it abounds with poetical merit. He also published at
Oxford, " Translations in Verse. Mr. Pope's *Messiah*,
Mr. Philips's *Splendid Shilling*, in Latin ; the Eighth
Isthmian of Pindar in English." 4to. 1752.

I

nance

nance and support to this audacious fiction. As their offence was not of a very heinous kind, he should treat them with lenity ; and the punishment, being wholly discretionary in the court, should be proportioned to the various degrees of guilt in the offenders. With respect to the multitude of persons of each sex and of all ages and denominations, who had flocked during the preceding year to see these spurious papers, and expressed the highest admiration of them, (they were so brown and so yellow, so vastly old, and so vastly curious !) the Ringleaders, who were then in custody, should be dismissed with only a gentle reproof, and an admonition never again to pronounce judgment on matters with which they were not conversant, without taking the advice of Counsel learned in the laws —— of Parnassus :—— but on a small group of hardened offenders, who were placed at the bar by themselves, and did not appear to me to be more than seven or eight, [225] he thought himself bound

to

---

[225] In this group I did not see my friend, the learned and ingenious Author of the " Essay on the writings and

genius

to inflict a much more severe punishment.
That if these gentlemen had modestly and
ingenuously said that they had too hastily
given a judgment on a matter which they
did not understand,—that they knew nothing
of old hand-writing, and nothing of old
language, (which he conceived they might
have done without any impeachment of
their understandings,) he should have had
great tenderness for them. But inasmuch
as they had pertinaciously adhered to error
after it had been made as manifest as his
own Sun at noon-day, and clung to an opi-

genius of Pope," who, though he has passed his seventieth
year, retains all the ardour and vivacity of youth ; nor a
very respectable clergyman well known to the learned
world, and eminently distinguished for his love and knowledge of the fine arts, his literature, and suavity of manners ; nor another very worthy friend, who presides at one
of our revenue-boards, with great credit to himself and advantage to the publick ; a scholar, a man of excellent taste,
and much various knowledge ; all of whom, though at first,
and on a cursory view, they were dazzled by the quantity
and specious appearance of this mass of imposture, always
expressed themselves with great moderation and reserve on
the subject, and never gave a decided opinion on hand-
writing and phraseology to which the course of their studies
had not led them to pay any particular attention.

nion

nion because they had once given it, which they were unable to maintain and unwilling to retract, he thought they ought to be made a publick example. That in every sentence he pronounced he kept in mind the rule of a great judge of their own nation, "always remembering when he found himself swayed to pity, that there was ALSO A PITY DUE TO THE COUNTRY ;" and that he wished the tribunals of that nation, (which on account of the eminent poets it had produced was extremely dear to him,) whether consisting of *one*, or of *one dozen*, would always keep that just rule before their eyes. That the pity to the country, in the present instance, was, by the punishment of these offenders, (who, though not so guilty as the undiscovered principal, yet, as accessories after the fact, had a considerable degree of guilt,) to maintain and establish truth and honesty, the best supporters of all human dealings, and to prevent the propagation of error, and the success of forgery and imposture.—The pains and penalties however of that Court extending only to that kind

of

of chastisement which men of wit best
know how to inflict, he ordered that Butler,
Dryden, Swift, and Pope, should forthwith
compose four copies of verses on the subject, either ballad, epigram, or satire, as
their several fancies might direct ; and that,
after he had affixed his sign-manual to them,
they should be conveyed by Mercury to
England, and inserted for one month in
the Poets' Corner of all the loyal Morning
and Evening Newspapers of London, to the
end that each of these credulous partisans
of folly and imposture should remain

 " Sacred to ridicule his whole life long,
 " And the sad burthen of some merry song."

ON this mild and just sentence being pronounced, all the poetick tribe who were within hearing gave a loud shout of applause,
which drew Shakspeare and his companions
from their game, and awakened me from
my dream.

FAREWELL, my dear Lord ! You are,
I know, too well convinced of my unalter-
able esteem and attachment, to need any
publick

publick assurances on that head ; and therefore I shall only add in the usual style of papers intended for the publick view, that I have the honour to be, &c.

EDMOND MALONE.

QUEEN-ANNE-STREET, EAST,
March 19, 1796.

APPENDIX.

APPENDIX,

NUMBER I.

ORIGIN AND HISTORY OF PROMISSORY NOTES AND PAPER-CREDIT.

THE inquiry into the authenticity of the note of hand, said to have been given by Shakspeare to John Heminges in the year 1589,[1] is naturally

[1] It has been already printed in p. 133; but in order that the arguments of my ingenious and learned friend may appear to the best advantage, and be fully understood, I shall give it a place here also:

" *One moneth from the date* hereof I doe *promyse to pay* " to my good and Worthye Freynd John *Hemynge* the fume " of *five Pounds and five shillings* of English Monye as a " recompense for hys great trouble in settling and doinge " much for me at the *Globe Theatre* as also for hys trouble " in *going downe* for me to *statford*. *Witness my Hand* " Wm Shakspere.

" Sepember the Nynth 1589."

In the multitude of objections to this spurious Promissory Note, I forgot to take notice of the phrase *going down* to Stratford, for that is the place meant, " save, as Fluellen says, the phrase is a little variations." The pre-eminence of the Capital over the Country was then without doubt as fully acknowledged as it is at present : but though the inferiority

3 B   of

naturally conne&ted with the history of personal securities and paper-credit in England. The in-

of every other part of the kingdom is now marked by our constantly ufing the phrases of " going *down* to the Country," and " coming *up* to London," there is no ground for suppos- ing that this was the language of Shakspeare's age. I have never met with it in any of the familiar letters of the time, where, if the phrafe had then been in ufe, it would un- doubtedly have been found.

" The *Globe theatre*," which I alfo omitted to notice, is equally objectionable. When they spoke of the playhouses of that time, they said the Globe, the Rofe, or the Curtain, not the Globe theatre, &c. So in the Contract between Henslowe, Alleyn, and Streete, for building the Fortune play-houfe, —"and with such like steares, &c. as are made and contrived in and to the late erected play-house on the Bancke, in the faid parish of St. Saviours, called *the Globe*."

So also in a stage-contract, which will appear in a subse- quent page, (Appendix, No IV.)"—used or to be used or exercised within the play-house of the said P. H. and E. A. commonly called THE FORTUNE." Again, in a Memo- randum by Edward Alleyn (Shakspeare's PLAYS and POEMS Vol. I. Part II. p. 43): " What THE FORTUNE [not the Fortune theatre] cost me, Nov. 1599."

Again, in Randolph's MUSES LOOKING-GLASS, 1632:
——That the GLOBE
" Hath been confumed; the PHOENIX burnt to ashes,
" The FORTUNE whipt for a blind whore; BLACKFRYERS
" He wonders how it scaped demolishing."

See also the title-page to OTHELLO, 4to. 1622: " The tragedy of OTHELLO, as it was played at THE GLOBE on the Bankside, and at the private house in the Black-friers."

If Heminges had thought it necessary to add any word after " the Globe," it would have been the plain English word, *play-houfe*, not *theatre*.

I   strument

strument is very properly entitled a *note of hand*. In all its leading characteristicks it clofely corresponds with the *promissory notes*, which under the familiar name of *notes of hand*, are current at this day. It begins with the time of future payment ; contains merely a " promise to pay," without any antecedent acknowledgement of a debt; and is authenticated by the signature only, without a seal. A question therefore arises whether any such instrument is known to have been in use at that period, and what were the instruments, most nearly resembling a *promissory* note, which were then in use; and the result will be still more satisfactory, if the time can be positively ascertained, when such instruments as this ascribed to Shakspeare, first came into circulation, and were established by law.

ENOUGH has been already done, in all probability, to satisfy every candid inquirer of the fabrication in the present instance. But the subject altogether is curious, and may not be uninteresting in a country which has carried its commerce to such an unexampled height, by the aid, in a great degree, of thefe very promissory notes. One considerable source of information has hitherto escaped the search of professed writers on Commerce. They have occasionally drawn some materials, though not all they might, from the statute-book, but they have neglected the Reports of proceedings in Westminster-Hall, and Law-treat-

ises

ises on the nature and forms of instruments. The
study of these authorities, in black-letter and
barbarous French, interlarded with as barbarous
Latin and obfolete English, all three full of abbre-
viations, is not very inviting ; but there are few
diggers and delvers after antient customs and manners in the mines of antiquity who would not find
enough to reward their labour, if they sometimes
followed the vein by that leader.

THE personal securities used in the time of
Shakspeare, and for centuries before, were either
Obligations, now commonly called Bonds, with a
penalty and condition ; or *Bills*, sometimes denominated *bills of debt* or *bills obligatory*. The latter
are chiefly to the present purpose. They were
single bonds without any penalty or condition ; but
they were equally *deeds*, requiring to be *signed
sealed* and *delivered*. [2] In one of the oldest cases,
where a bill was ruled to be invalid, [3] one of the
grounds appears to have been that it had no claufe
expressing the sealing, though it seems to have
been actually sealed. It would be idle to mul-
tiply authorities to prove that there was always a
seal to these bills. One more may be sufficient, [4]
from the time of Shakspeare. The case arose on
a bill dated only three years before the pretended

[2] Cowell, in v. *Bill*, & Co. Lit. 272.

[3] Year book, 40. E. III. p. 2.

[4] Talbot and Godbolt. Yelv. 137 & 147. 6 Jac.

note

note of hand ; and it is a memorable instance, where an unfortunate retainer of the Law, the clerk of a learned Serjeant, burned his fingers with his own sealing-wax. The poor man, (as lawyers do not always succeed the best in their own affairs) drew a bill, binding himself by mistake, instead of his master. He acknowledged the receipt of 40l. for his master's use, to be paid the Michaelmas following ; but forgetting to express by whom it was to be paid, was held to be responsible himself, as he had sealed the bill.

THE use of the seal indeed was so familiar at this period, that it was even applied on other occasions, where, with rules of evidence lefs favourable, no person now would expect it to be affixed. We learn from an act of Parliament passed in 1610, [5] that Shop-books and other accompt-books between persons who were in a course of dealing with each other, were received in evidence, even for the party by whom they were kept. Much more then, and according to the strictest rules of evidence would they be binding against the party who made any particular entry in them, such as were probably those acknowledgements of debt in the text, extracted from the old theatrical Register of Dulwich : yet it was a common practice with Merchants and Tradesmen in London at the latter end of Queen Elizabeth's reign, to have

[5] 7 Jac. c. 12.

regular

regular *bills of debt* or *obligations* inserted in their books by their debtors, signed, sealed, and delivered. [6]

ONE of the names of the single bill, that of *a bill of debt*, by which it most frequently passed about the time of Shakspeare, points to an express acknowledgement of a debt as an essential part of the instrument. Accordingly West who compiled his SYMBOLEOGRAPHY the very year after the supposed *note of hand* in question, defines a bill or obligation to be " *a deed, whereby the Obligor* " *doth knowledge himself to owe* unto the Obligee a " certaine summe of money or other thing. " In which (continues he) besides the parties' " names, are to be confidered the summe or thing " due, and the time, place, and manner of paiment " or delivery thereof." All his precedents, of which there are many, some more some less formal, have of course all the parts required by himself, as well as the clause of *sealing*. One of his precedents of a bill for a thing lent has probably been very seldom copied, at least in our times. It may be well however to preserve the memory of it, as it may fhortly be of utility to some harmless people of antiquated prejudices, if the anti-crusaders of modern philosophy fhould succeed in making the thing as scarce in this country, as it was

[6] Fox and Wright, 40 Eliz. Cro. Eliz. 613.

in

in times of ancient ignorance. It is an acknowledgement of having received, and an engagement
to re·deliver——a Bible.

It is true that a *bill obligatory* might be con-
ftituted by any words of power to create an obligation to pay, without any acknowledgement of
owing. And it was early so ruled. But of the
real bills, actually put in issue, very few indeed,
if any, will be found before the 17th Century,
that are without some direct admission of the debt.

All bills that have been preserved to us at
full length in reports from the Year-books down-
wards, have some phrase or word of introduction.
The more methodical and technical begin with
" *Know all men by these presents*", " *Be it known*",
or *This bill witnesseth*", or something to that effect,
whether in Latin or English: the looser and less
regular are ushered in with the word " *Memorandum*" or some abbreviation of it. This word is to be
found at the head of the oldest instrument of the
kind on record in the reign of Edward the III^d;
and it stood unmoved in the time of Charles the I^ft.
The Touch-Stone of Common Assurances was
published in 1641. It goes under the name of
Shephard, but is believed to have been the production of Mr. Justice Doderidge, who was raised to the
bench in the life·time of Shakspeare; and that book
has no less than fourteen or fifteen of the shorter
and more simple forms, [7] to every one of which

[7] Tit. Obligation. p. 68.

without

without exception the word " *Memorandum*" is prefixed.

THE *obligatory* or promissory part of the ancient bill was generally expressed by the words, " *to be paid*," a translation of the Latin word " *Sol—vendum*." It is observable that when the phrase " *I promise to pay*" first crept into a bill of debt, about a century before our Poet, an objection was taken to it by Mr. Serjeant Vavasour.[8] " Here are no " words of obligation (said he); a promise does not " constitute an obligation." The Court, it is true, over-ruled the objection; the new phraseology however, was not adopted, but the accustomed form still continued to prevail.

ANOTHER circumstance in which the old *bills of debt* differed from our modern *notes of hand* was in the grammatical structure of the sentence. The term fixed for future payment always followed, and never preceded the obligatory words of the bill. This is invariable in all the inftances to be found down to the period now in question, of 1589. The concluding claufe too was always full : not " *witness my hand*," but " in witnesse whereof I have hereunto set my hand and seale" or to that effect; as will be found in every one of West's precedents, and wherever else the form of a bill is set forth at length. Neither was the date ever

[8] Year-book. 22 E. IV. 22.

placed

placed by itself in a corner, but embodied in the bill.

BUT as examples best illustrate, it may be proper to add two or three precedents of different kinds. They will be found to correspond generally in their form with the entries taken from Henslowe's Register.

The first shall be the bill where the phrase " I " promise to pay" originally appeared. It ran thus : " *Md.* that I Master Jo. Hately have re- " ceived of W. K. twenty pound, the which " twenty pound I the said Maister Jo. Hately " promise to pay to K. In witness whereof I set to " my seale,[9]" &c. &c.

The following is very few years prior in date to the pretended *note of hand*: [10] " *Me.* That I owe to A. B. twenty pound to " be paid in watchets.—In witness whereof," &c.

It has been hinted above that some benefit might occasionally be reaped by Antiquaries, if they were somewhat better Lawyers; and it is but justice to say here in return, that Lawyers would some-times not be the worse for being better Anti-quaries. The modern Abridgers, Viner, Bacon,[11]

[9] Year-Book, 22 E. IV. 22.
[10] Hil. 26 Eliz. And. 117.
[11] Tit. Obligation.

3 c   and

and others, for *watchets*" (that is, watchet-lights,
a sort of taper,) have substituted " *watches*." An
Antiquary who should take their word without
going back to the genuine black-letter, would
think he had made a rare discovery.

The next specimen is still nearer to the date of
1589, and must be presumed of good authority.
It is the bill of Mr. Serjeant Gaudy's Clerk, who
probably followed the most approved form in
popular use. He did not suffer for departing from
sound precedents, but rather for adhering to them
too closely. He was fined for wanting judgement
to vary them as circumstances required. The
words are, " *Memor.* that I have received of Ed-
" ward Talbot to the use of my Master, Master
" Serjeant Gaudy, the sum of forty pound to be
" paid at Michaelmas following. In witness where-
" of," &c.

THIS bill is described to have been dated in
the 28th of Elizabeth. It probably ran like the
following, which is dated in the 32d of the same
reign, or 1590, and is the only English precedent
in West, for payment of a debt at a future day
certain :

" BEE it knowne unto all men by these presents
" that I, T. K. of D. in the county of S. yeoman,
" do owe unto T. S. of the said towne and county,
" gentleman, 100 l. of good and lawfull English
money,

" money, to be paid to the said I. S. his heires,
" executors or administrators, upon the feast of
" Easterday next comming after the date hereof:
" for which paiment wel and truly to be made,
" I bind me and mine heires firmly by these pre-
" sents. In witnesse whereof I have hereunto
" put my hand and seale. Dated the first day of
" Januarie, in the two and thirtieth year of our
" Soveraign Lady El." &c.

But it may be asked, whatever were the forms
alone recognized by the common law, were there
no instruments, like this in Shakspeare's name,
then used by merchants and others in their confi-
dential transactions ?—It will be found, on the contrary, that the want of them was a theme of complaint for more than half a century after his
death.

Malines wrote his book called *Lex Mercatoria,*
or Law-Merchant, in 1622, about six years after
the death of our great dramatick poet. This writer allots two whole chapters, the xii[th] and xiii[th]
as well as half of the xi[th] to the subject of *bills of
debt* or *bills obligatory,* as employed in buying and
selling by the merchants-adventurers of Amsterdam, Middleburgh, and Hamburgh. He tells
us, that " in the East Countries," (that is, in the
countries about the Baltick,) " and sometimes in
" the Low-Countries, they will put a *seale,*" but

that

that sealing is not necessary." The use and transfer of these bills in commerce he declares to be
" a laudable custome *not practised in England*,"
but which he thinks " might with great facility
" neverthelesse be established, and would be very
" beneficiall to the King and the Commonwealth
" in generall." He is very full in explaining
the nature and all the circumstances of one of these
bills obligatory, as of a thing almost unknown; and
he inserts the form, which is a foreign form, but
which, except in being made payable to the
bearer, and having no seal or mention of a seal,
resembles in general substance the precedents of
West. If any thing, it is more full:

" I A.B. Merchant of Amſterdam, doe acknow-
" ledge by these presents to be truly indebted
" to the honeſt C. D. English merchant dwelling
" at Middleborough, in the summe of five hundred
" pounds currant money, for merchandize, which
" is for commodities received of him to my
" contentment, which summe of five hundred
" pound as aforesaid I do promise to pay unto
" the said C. D. (or the bringer hereof) within
" six months next after the date of these presents :
" in witnesse whereof I have subscribed the same
" at Amsterdam the 10th of July 1622, *Stilo*
" *novo*. A. B."

ONE of this author's remarks plainly shews, that he, like West, thought the acknowledgment of the debt to be of the essence of the bill. "The " Civil-Law, and the Law-Merchant, (says he) " doe require, that *the bill fhall declare for what* " the debt *groweth*, either for merchandise or " monie, or any other lawfull consideration."

UNDER the Protectorate of Cromwell, in the year 1651, John Marius, a Notary Public, wrote a work entituled " Advice concerning Bills " of Exchange;" and in 1655 printed a second edition much enlarged. This he gives as " the " crop of four and twenty years experience in " his employment in the art of a Notary Pub- " like, which (he tells us) he yet practised at " the Royal Exchange in London both for *In-* " *land* and outland instruments." The work is a folio of forty close pages; but though it has so much on *inland* as well as outland bills of ex- change and letters of credit, and contains short directions for merchants' book-keeping, there is not a fingle syllable upon *bills of debt*, or *bills obligatory*. We learn too that even the validity of *inland* bills of exchange under the Law- merchant was then controverted by foreign wri- ters, and was clearly not acknowledged by the Common Law of England.

JUST

JUST before the Restoration in 1660 a book called " Amphithalami" was published by Abraham Liset, which amongst other things contains, " Instructions for a merchant." What this writer says upon *bills of debt* or *bills obligatory* is extracted and abridged from Malines. He continues the same complaint that " this laudable " custom was not practised in England," and the same instances to enforce its adoption in this country : It is to be inferred therefore, that no alteration with regard to these bills had taken place from the time of Malines.

SOON after the Restoration, the rigour of the Common Law gave way by degrees to the less formal instruments of the Law-Merchant founded on the Civil Law. Bills of exchange were the first mercantile instruments thus favoured, and with respect to them the custom of merchants was allowed to be pleaded. This had been done before with regard to *foreign* bills of exchange; but now these bills extended to all money-transactions between all men residing at a distance from each other, and at laft every person by drawing a bill of exchange was considered by the law as having become a merchant in that particular act. The various stages of their progress are thus shortly, but satisfactorily, related by Chief Juftice Treby of the Common Pleas, in the year 1696.[12]

[12] Bromwich and Loyd, 8 W. III. 2 Lutw. 1585.

7

" Bills

" Bills of exchange (says he) at first extended
" only to merchant strangers trading with English
" merchants, and afterwards to *inland* bills between
" merchants trading the one with the other here
" in England, and afterwards to all traders and
" negociators, and OF LATE *to all persons traf-*
" *ficking or not.*"

WHEN *inland bills of exchange* had gained a foot-
ing in Weftminfter-Hall, and were judged to be
good between all traders and negociators, it
seemed an easy step to establish also in some form
or other, the transferrable *bill of debt* or *bill obli-*
gatory used by merchants abroad, and so much
and long recommended for introduction here.
The origin of the new *promissory note* is distinctly
attributed to the Goldsmiths; and such a note
in our books of reports after the Revolution is
often called by its familiar name of a *Goldsmith's*
note. The period of time to which an authority,
that will hereafter be quoted at length, refers
the beginning of these notes, is about the year
1673.

IT is well known that previous to the year
1640 the mint was the usual place of depofit
for the running cash of merchants. The seizure
of the money there by Charles the I^t. in 1640,
deftroyed for ever the credit of the Mint. The
frequent elopement of clerks with all the money
in

in their hands to one army or the other, when the Civil War broke out, prevented the merchants from leaving cash in the charge of cashiers at home, and thus about the year 1645 the Goldsmiths became the general bankers. [13] The situation of the country, first from the real and necessary distresses of the Parliament and Protector, and afterwards from the profusion of Charles II. gave the new bankers great opportunities of making emoluments, and of tempting all men of property by the allowance of a small interest to deposit money in their hands. Thus their trade grew and flourished till the year 1667, when, an alarm taking place in consequence of the Dutch sailing up the Thames and burning some ships at Chatham, a run was made on the Goldsmiths, and their credit was shaken. They seem however to have been recovering from that blow, when Charles II. in 1671-2, took the violent measure of shutting up the Exchequer, and impounding there between thirteen and fourteen hundred thousand pounds of their principal money, beside the current interest due upon it.

PREVIOUS to this period, their prosperity was so encreasing, and money came so fast into their hands, that they were perpetually employed in

[13] Anderson's HIST. of COMMERCE, under the years 1645, 1665, and 1672: on the authority of a curious pamphlet printed in 1676.

devising

devising new modes of disposing it to advantage without being under the necessity of having recourse to their own paper-credit to support their trade. But the shutting of the Exchequer threw the whole commerce of the city into confusion, and made extraordinary expedients necessary to sustain every part of the system. It is just about this time that we find the Goldsmiths to have first issued their *promissory notes*.

THIS date of their first introduction seems indeed to be very nearly ascertained from contemporary evidence. A little anonymous work of considerable merit was published in 1680, under the title of " The Interests of Princes and States." It is said in the prefatory Advertisement to have been written some years before, and on that ground an apology is made for any thing which from subsequent changes might not apply at the time of publication. The internal evidence in truth dates it between the years 1668 and 1672. Now it clearly shows *promissory notes* not to have been in circulation when it was written : for in a list of measures which the author proposes for the interests of this kingdom, he reckons as the fifth, that " the transferring of *bills of debt* should be " made good in law : it being, as he says, a " great advantage to traders (especially young men " of small stocks) to be able to supply them- " selves with money, *by the sale of their own bills* " *of debt.*"

3 D   ON

ON the other hand, that the introduction of these notes had taken place between the writing and publishing of that passage we learn from a case of the year 1680 [14] (the earliest Law Report in which they are mentioned); and there they appear in a way which plainly shews them at once to have been common among merchants, and yet not received into general use in the new form with a signature only. The action was brought on a *note* by which one Hentley promised to pay to the bearer thereof on the delivery of the note, 100l. But *the note was sealed* according to the old practice, and was argued as a scroll which had become a *perfect deed* by the delivery of it to the plaintiff, who was then the bearer. This was a moment of public ferment, and the Chief Justice, Sir Francis Pemberton, had not many days filled his situation, to which he was promoted on the removal of Sir William Scroggs, in consequence of his impeachment by Parliament. He may therefore have been desirous, circumstanced as he was, of doing what would be popular. He inclined to the doctrine of the Plaintiff's Counsel, and observed, that *when a merchant promises to pay to the bearer of a note, any who brings the note shall be paid*; but Mr. Justice Jones said, that *it was the custom of merchants* which made that good. The decision was adjourned, and the sequel has not been reported.

[14] Shelden and Hentley, E. 33. Car. II. 2 Show. 160. 161.

THE

THE success which attended the adoption of *promissory notes*, one of the projects urged in vain during the usurpation, seems to have suggested the notion of reducing others also, connected with that, into practice. [15] Accordingly in 1683 the scheme of a general bank, supported by a numerous association of subscribers, (a scheme which had been proposed in different shapes under Cromwell) was revived by Dr. Chamberlain and Mr. Robert Murray, [16] who had lately established the Penny Post. Though this scheme of a Bank did not take effect, yet as it probably gave the hint of the Bank of England, erected by other more fortunate projectors about eleven years after, it may not be unentertaining to insert here a curious account of the plan from the unpublished papers of Aubrey the antiquary, with which I have been furnished by Mr. Malone :

" THE Penny Post was set up on our Lady-
" day, (being Friday) A° Dñi. 1680; a most
" ingenious and useful project; invented by Mr.
" Robert Murray first, and then Mr. Dockwra
" joined with him. The Duke of York seized
" on it in 1682. Mr. Murray was formerly clerk
" to the general commissioners for the revenue
" of Ireland, and afterwards clerk to the com-
" missioners of the grand Excise of England;
" and was the first that invented and introduced

[15] Anderson's History, 1651.   [16] Ibid. 1683.

" into

" into this city the Club of Commerce, consist-
" ing of one of each trade ; whereof there were
" after very many elected and are still continued in
" this city. And he also contrived and set up
" the office or BANK OF CREDIT at Devonshire
" House in Bishopgate Street without, where
" men depositing their goods and merchandize,
" were furnished with bills of current credit, at
" two thirds or three fourths of the value of the
" said goods according to the intrinsick value of
" money; whereby the deficiency of coin might
" be fully supplied : and for rendering the same
" current, a certain number of traders, *viz.* ten
" or twenty of each trade (whereof there be five
" hundred and ten several traders within the city,)
" were to be assembled or formed into such a
" society or company of traders, as might
" among them complete the whole body of com-
" merce ; whereby any possessed of the said cur-
" rent credit might be furnished among them-
" selves with any kind of goods and merchandize
" as effectually as for money elsewhere". [17]

BUT the great epoch in the history of paper-
credit, is the formation of the Bank of England
in 1694, and there we have on the authority of

[17] From a paper entitled *Nouvelles*. MS. Aubrey. in Mus.
Ashmol.

Mr. Aubrey adds, that " Robert Murray was a citizen
of London, a Millener, [Andersocn alls him an upholsterer,]
of the company of Clothworkers ; his father a Scotchman,
his mother English ; born in the Strand, Dec. 12, 1633."

Parliament some material evidence applying to our immediate object. There is a clause in the act of Incorporation which plainly indicates the true birth and parentage of promissory notes, as derived from the bills of debt, or bills obligatory, of former times. It is exprefsly provided " that all *bills* " *obligatory, under the seal* of that corporation, might " be assignable *toties quoties* ; and that fuch as- " signments should absolutely vest the property " in the assignees." [18] This latter provision was necessary to obviate one strong objection originally made, as we learn from Malines, to the transfer of *bills obligatory*, or *bills of debt* : " that " by the Common Law debts were *chofes in action*, " whereof no property could passe by assignement " or alienation." The original *bank notes* were actually *fealed bills*, [19] and bore an interest of two pence by the day for every hundred pounds.

THE establishment of the Bank of England gave a new fpring to the minds of projectors, and among other plans soon after published, was one for promoting the circulation of notes of hand and letters of credit. This plan did not take effect ; but the circulation gained ground. Soon afterwards this fort of Paper-credit had the fanction of the State. In 1696 Exchequer-bills were first issued.

IN the mean time, however, the Common Law

---

[18] 5 and 6 of W. and M. c. 20.
[19] Anderson's History, 1694.

had

had made a powerful stand against these notes of the Goldsmiths; especially against the legal operation which their inventors and patrons endeavoured to give them. It was attempted to assimilate them to bills of exchange, and to bring actions upon them in the same manner under the custom of merchants. Indeed, the mere signature of an acceptor to a bill of exchange being allowed to raise an obligation of payment to the holder over of the bill, it was not unnatural to conclude that a signature to a direct promise of payment in another form would be admitted as equally binding, and capable of being pleaded in the same way. And it may perhaps have been to avoid an apparent distinction on the face of the instrument, that the first part of the old form recommended by Malines for a bill obligatory (the acknowledgement of the debt) was omitted, and the subsequent promise to pay alone retained. The change in the local arrangement of the date, which was now taken out of the body of the note, and placed separately in a more conspicuous part, generally at the top, was probably made that it might more readily present itself to the eye for the calculation of the discount. At the same time the old formal clause of attestation was cut down to " Witness my hand."

A CASE arose upon one of these bills so early as the second year of William and Mary.[20] It

[20] Horton v. Coggs, 2 W. & M. 3 Lev. 299.

was

was an action brought in the Court of Common
Pleas against Coggs, a Goldsmith. A Jury found
a verdict against him on his promissory note; but
upon a motion in arrest of judgement it was ruled
that the custom pleaded of being bound to pay
the bearer, was too general. It was said too (as
we learn from Chief Justice Holt in a subsequent
case)[21] that such notes were not bills of exchange.

IT would be to no purpose to mention every
case which followed; but it may be right cursorily
to notice, that in the earliest the defendants appear to have been actual Goldsmiths. The Court
of Common Pleas seemed at one time inclined to
favour these notes as a great convenience to
trade; but the Court of King's Bench was strenuous in opposing them. It was in the first year
of Queen Anne that the doctrine was there settled
on various points in different cases.

THE first of these (and an important testimony
it is on the present inquiry) was a suit instituted
against a person of the name of Martin, on his
promissory note payable to I. S. *or Order*;[22] and
one of the counts was upon the custom of merchants, as for a bill of exchange. It was argued
that though it never had been endorsed, yet by

[21] Clerke & Martin.
[22] Clerke & Martin, 1 Anne, 2 Ld Raym. 757.

being

being made payable to order, instead of the bearer, the note was brought within the principle of a bill of exchange. But Chief Justice Holt was against it " *with all his might,*"as the Reporter says. He said " that the note could not be a bill " of exchange : that *the maintaining of these actions* " *upon such notes were innovations upon the rules of the* " *Common Law ; and that it amounted to the setting up* " *a new sort of specialty, unknown to the Common Law,* " *and invented in Lombard Street,* which attempted " in these matters of bills of exchange to give " laws to Westminster-Hall."

THE custom of merchants was there laid gene-rally. In another case [23] which followed immediately after, the special custom of London was pleaded. But the Court held this also to be a void custom, since it bound a man to pay money without a consideration. In the same year one of these notes having been established in the Common Pleas on an action which went in one count of the declaration upon the custom of Merchants, the judgement was reversed by a writ of Error in the King's Bench. [24]

STILL the merchants persisted, and the next year, 1703, a new point was tried. A *promissory note* payable to *order,* was put in suit by an *En-*

[23] Clerke & Martin,   1 Anne, 2 Lᵈ Raym. p . 759.
[24] Cutting & Williams, 1 Anne,1 Salk. 25.

dorsee against the Drawer. [25]   And there the whole
history of these instruments as well as of *inland*
bills of exchange appears fully from the best evidence.   Chief Justice Holt said, that he remembered when actions upon *inland* bills of exchange
first began.   The action was against the acceptor,
and a particular custom between London and
Bristol was laid.   Since that time these actions
had become frequent, as the trade of the nation
encreased.   " But *the notes in question* (added he)
" *are only an invention of the Goldsmiths in Lombard*
" *Street, who had a mind to make a law to bind all that*
" *dealt with them.* And sure to allow such a note to
" carry any lien with it, were to turn a piece of
" paper, which is in law but evidence of a parol
" contract, into a specialty : and besides it would
" impower one to assign that to another which he
" could not have himself ; for since he to whom
" this note was made could not have this action,
" how can his assignee have it ? These notes are
" not in the nature of bills of exchange ; for the
" reason of the custom in bills of exchange is for
" the expedition of trade, and its safety, and like-
" wise it hinders the exportation of money out of
" the realm."

JUDGEMENT however being for the present
postponed, on another day Chief Justice Holt
declared, " that he had desired to speak with

[25] Buller & Crips. 6 Mod. 29.

" *two*

" *two of the most famous merchants in London* to be
" informed of the mighty ill consequences that it
" was pretended would ensue by obstructing this
" course ; and that they had told him, it was very
" frequent with them to make such notes, and
" that they looked upon them as bills of ex-
" change, and that THEY HAD BEEN USED FOR A
" MATTER OF THIRTY YEARS ; and that not only
" *notes* but *bonds* for money were transferred fre-
" quently, and indorsed as bills of exchange :"—
that is, obligations, and *bills obligatory under seal,*
(which were one sort of bonds) were not even
then, in the beginning of the present century,
wholly driven out of use by the new promissory
notes of Lombard-Street.

THE Chief Justice was as firm in the conscien-
tious discharge of his duty against the Law-merchant, as on another memorable occasion he had
been against the Law of Parliament. The merchants were foiled in all their attempts. Nothing
therefore remained, but that resource, which Malines tells us was the wish of many good Lawyers
as well as Merchants in his days,—" an act of
" Parliament to establish this course in England."
Accordingly such a law passed soon afterwards, [26]
making all promissory notes recoverable by
action " in the same manner as inland bills of
" exchange drawn according to the custom of

[26] 3 & 4 Ann. c. 9.

" mer-

" merchants." In consequence, *bills obligatory* under the seal of the Bank of England, and under the seals of individuals, disappeared together; all men substituted *notes of hand*, which, though in rather more accurate spelling and terser phraseology, ran in effect like this ascribed to Shakspeare above a century before; and " I promise to pay" universally succeeded to " Memorandum that I owe." But the time of future payment continued to keep its station for many years in the body of the note.[27] It seems a very modern innovation indeed to place it in the beginning of the sentence.

On looking back there is much in this little historical outline to arrest and occupy a contemplative mind. What was recommended in vain as a publick benefit to the Grandfather (for to King James was the work of Malines dedicated) was at last the lucky consequence of an arbitrary act, to which the Grandson was driven by his prodigality : and the system of PAPER-CREDIT, which thus had its origin in the bad faith of the last Protestant King of the House of Stuart, when after the Revolution it had acquired strength,

[27] Smith *v.* Jarvis & Baily, 2 Ld Raym. 1484. Trin. 13 Geo. I. & 1 Geo. II. Burchell & Slocock, ibid. 1545. Mich. 2 Geo. II.—Youth's Introduction to Trade and Business, 1737. tit. Promissory Notes.—Cooke *v.* Colchan, 2 Str. 1217. 18 Geo. II.

solidity,

solidity, and body, from the establishment of the
Bank of England, became a main prop and pillar
of the settlement by which the immediate heirs of
the House of Stuart were excluded for ever from
the throne. But these are only sports of chance,
that amuse rather than instruct. What is most
worthy of attention and admiration is the excellent spirit of our Law. It accommodates itself,
though slowly and with becoming deliberation, to
the general law of Europe, where our intercourse
with foreign countries demands it : we have seen
it do so in regard to bills of exchange : and having
once admitted a principle, it gradually expands
itself to embrace the subject in its natural and just
extent. Yet at the same time it resists innovations, however specious, which hold forth only
internal convenience as their end, and leaves them
to the wisdom of the Legislature ; where, if they
are of approved utility, they will seldom meet
other than a favourable reception.

THE circulation of promissory notes however
was not opposed by Westminster-Hall alone.
Many of the mercantile interest, and even Sir
Josiah Child among the rest originally declared
against " the innovated practice of bankers, and
the new invention of cashiering ;" [28] to which all
of his name have not continued his animosity.
Nor did even the first proof of the benefits derived

[28] See his Discourses on Trade.

from

from this system preclude all invective against it.
Our great ethick Poet, in his Moral Essay " on
the Use of Riches," breaks into the most animated
satire upon this topick, while he too affords one
more testimony to the recent introduction of that
which he apostrophizes :

" Blest Paper-Credit ! *last* and best supply,
" That lends corruption lighter wings to fly !
" Gold, imp'd by thee, can compass hardest things,
" Can pocket States, can fetch or carry Kings ;
" A single leaf shall waft an Army o'er,
" Or ship off Senates to some distant shore ;
" A leaf, like Sibyl's, scatter to and fro
" Our fates and fortunes, as the wind shall blow :
" Pregnant with thousands flits the scrap unseen,
" And silent sells a King, or buys a Queen."

IF it were fair to attribute to this cause, as Pope
himself does in his notes, all the striking events of
a whole age, full as splendid a panegyrick might
be made on the other side, if equal abilities could
be found for the task. But without the glittering
visions of poetry we have witnessed and still witness the most happy effects in the publick prosperity. The whole real and imaginary opulence
of the nation is brought to bear effectively on
commerce, like the capital of one firm. Even
vices,

vices, the most selfish, are made to co-operate for
the good of the Common-wealth. Avarice itself
becomes liberal in parsimony and accumulation,
and while by trusting the custody of its hoards to
the banker, it escapes half the torments which
are its immediate and natural punishment in the
eternal order of things, it furnishes funds for the
advances of the manufacturer, the adventures of
the merchant, and the vast operations of the
Statesman to maintain or extend the happiness,
power, and glory, of his country. We do not now
require to read, for we behold in every thing
around us, the praise which Malines bestows on
the system of paper-credit; a praise no less just
than eloquent, according to the fashion of his age.
" It is," says he, " as money paid by assignation,
" whereby very great matters are compassed in
" the trade of merchandise; the commodities are
" sooner vented in all places; the custome and
" impositions of Princes do increase; the poore
" mechanicall people are set on worke; men are
" better assured in their payments; the counter-
" feiting of bils, and differences are prevented;
" the more commodities there are sold, the less
" ready money is transported, and life is infused
" into traffick and trade for the generall good.
" And herein we see and may observe that things
" which be indeed, and things which are not in-
" deed, but taken to be indeed, may produce all
" one effect; and every man is enabled with his

I   " own

" own meanes and credit, to augment com-
" merce." Perhaps the pre-eminence of England among the States of Europe at this hour,
compared with her subordinate rank then, even
after the glorious reign of Elizabeth, is more
to be attributed to the force of her public credit
under this system, which gives her the direction
of the great military powers on the Continent,
than to the native strength of her own arms.

AND who is the mighty benefactor of his country, to whom we are indebted for all this ? The
evidence here collected to shew the origin and
history of promissory notes seems to be full and
weighty. But the whole is fallacy and error, if
the note of hand attributed to Shakspeare be authentick. Writers on the Law-merchant, Com-
pilers of Precedents in Common Law, sad Report-
ers of Westminster-Hall, famous Merchants of
London, Lombard-street and Threadneedle-street,
private Banks of Goldsmiths and the Bank of
England, Judges and Juries, Year-books and Acts
of Parliament, every thing must vanish before a
ragged scrap of dirty paper, discovered we know
not where, and produced we are never to know
by whom. " All shall yield to the Mulberry-
tree," in a genuine box of which wood this precious relick no doubt must have been preserved.
Shakspeare, though it was never suspected by his
Commentator Pope when he wrote the passage
quoted

quoted above, nor by his other Commentator
Warburton, when in explaining that passage of
Pope, he considered paper-credit as an invention
since the time of William the Third,—Yes,
Shakspeare himself not only modelled the language of our Stage, but formed the style of Lombard-Street. His daring imagination, which
burst indignant from the trammels of Criticism,
was not to be cramped and confined by the fetters
of legal forms. In the prophetick spirit of a true
Poet he gave unsealed notes of hand to his
" Worthye Freyndes," which in the next century
but one were to become good securities in Law;
and he hit on a happy concinnity in the arrangement of their contents, which was not generally
attained by the slower talents of modern money-
changers till our own days, after these instruments
had been in circulation for more than half a century. No wonder then that the Merchants and
Lawyers too of his time, when compared to him in
their own way should all deserve to be set *onne
bys Table offe loggerre heades*. It is but a small
compensation to him for the loss of fame which
he has suffered from the long oblivion of this
most astonishing effort of his wonderful genius,
that some new and extraordinary honours should
be paid to his memory. The least which the
Goldsmiths' Company can do is, to erect a statue
to him over the front-door of the Bank in brown
papier maché. The countenance should be faithfully

fully copied from the "*whymsycalle conceyte*" of his own pencil, or the coloured drawing of him in the character of Bassanio. His " *Jerrekyne*," instead of " abundant ornaments of gold and silver," might be damasked over with all the water-marks of all the paper-makers in his day; and with his finger he might point to a scroll, not inscribed with the absurd rant of " Cloud-capt Towers and gorgeous Palaces," which like many of the finest speeches in Lear we are in future to consider as the bungling interpolation of the theatre, but displaying his own note of hand to Heminges, in capitals of gold. For the execution of this laudable design, a subscription should be immediately opened to receive contributions of true ancient paper. Our noble families may spare without inconvenience the half-filled household-books, which remain disgraceful memorials of the paltry œconomy practised by their ancestors; the publick offices may give the clippings and trimmings of dusty State papers; and private Libraries can supply, without missing them, many superfluous blank-leaves from venerable folios and quartos. As an example, I here offer, in the name of old Malines, eight brown half-sheets from the copy of his work which now happens to lie before me; and I trust, all black-letter Collectors in the kingdom will hasten to participate in this great act of national justice.

NUMB.

NUMB. II.

<small>CONVEYANCE FROM WALKER TO SHAKSPEARE.</small>

THIS INDENTURE MADE the tenthe day of
Marche, in the yeare of our Lord God according to the computacōn of the church of England
one thousand six hundrede and twelve, and in the
yeares of the reigne of our sovereigne Lord
James by the grace of God king of England,
Scotland ffraunce and Ireland, defender of the
faith, &c. that is to saie, of England, ffraunce
and Ireland the tenth, and of Scotland the six and
fortith : Betweene Henry Walker Citizein and
Minftrel of London of thone partie, and William
Shakespeare of Stratforde Upon Avon in the countie of Warwick gentleman, William Johnfon citizein and Vintner of London, John Jackfon and
John Hemyng of London gentlemen, on thother
ptie ; WITNESSETH, that the said Henry Walker
for and in consideracōn of the some of one hundred and fortie pounds of lawful money of England to him in hand before thensealing hereof by
the said William Shakespeare well and trulie paid,
whereof and wherewᵗʰ hee the said Henry Walker doth acknowledge himselfe fully satisfied and
contented, and thereof and of every part or parcell
thereof doth cleerlie acquite and discharge the saide
William Shakespeare, his heires, executors, admīstrators, and assignes, and every of them, by
theis pñts hath bargayned and soulde, and by theis
pñts doth fullie cleerlie and absolutlie bargayne
and

and sell vnto the said William Shakespeare, William Johnson, John Jackson, and John Hemyng, their heires and assignes for ever, All that dwelling houſe or Tenement wth thappurtenäncs situate and being w^{t}hin the Precinct Circuit and Compasse of the late black fryers London, sometymes in the tenure of James Gardyner Esqui^{re}, and since that in the tenure of John ffortescue gent, and now or late being in the tenure or occupacōn of one William Ireland or of his assignee or assignes; abutting vpon a streete leading downe to Puddle Wharffe on the east part, right against the kings Maiesties Wardrobe; part of wch said Tenement is erected over a great gate leading to a Capitall Mesuage wch sometyme was in the tenure of William Blackwell Esqui^{re} deceased, and since that in the tenure or occupacōn of the right Honorable Henry now Earl of Northumberland. And also all that plott of ground on the west side of the same Tenement wch was lately inclosed wth boords on two sides thereof by Anne Bacon, widowe, soe farre and in such sorte as the same was inclosed by the said Anne Bacon, and not otherwise; and being on the thirde side inclosed wth an olde Brick wall; Which said plott of ground was sometyme parcell and taken out of a great voide peece of ground lately vsed for a garden; and also the soyle where-vppon the said Tenement standeth, and also the said Brick wall and boords wch doe inclose the said plott of ground : With free entrie, accesse, ingresse, egresse, and regresse, in by and through the said

3 F 2   greate

greate gate and yarde there vnto the vsual dore of
the said Tenement; And also all and singuler
cello's, sollers, romes, lights, easiaments, profitts,
comodities, and hereditaments whatsoever, to
the said dwelling house or Tenement belonging or
in any wise app'teyning; And the reversion and
reversions whatsoever of all and singuler the premisses, and of every parcell thereof; And also all
rents, and yearlie profitts whatsoever reserved
and from hensforth to growe due and paiable vpon
whatsoever lease, dimise or graunt, leases dimises
or graunts, made of the premisses or of any parcell
thereof, And also all the state, right, title, interest,
propertie, vse, possession, clayme, and demaunde
whatsoever wch hee the said Henry Walker now hath,
or of right may, might, should, or ought to have, of
in or to the premisses or any parcell thereof; And
also all and every the deeds, evidencs, charters,
escripts, miniments, & writings whatsoever w^{ch}
hee the said Henry Walker now hath, or any
other person or persons to his vse have or hath,
or which hee may lawfullie come by w^{t}hout suite
in the lawe, which touch or concerne the premisses onlie, or onlie any part or parcell thereof,
Together wth the true coppies of all such deeds,
evidencs, and writings as concerne the premisses
(amounge other things) to bee written and taken
out at the onlie costs and charg^s of the said William Shakespeare his heires or assignes. WHICH
SAID dwelling house or Tenement, and other the
premisses above by theis prnts mencōned to bee

6   bargayned

bargayned and soulde the saide Henry Walker
late purchased and had to him his heires and assignes for ever of Mathie Bacon of Graies Inne
in the Countie of Midd͞ gentleman, by Indenture
bearing date the fifteenth day of October in the
yeare of our Lord god one thousand six hundred
and fower, and in the yeares of the reigne of our
said Sovereigne Lord king James of his realmes
of England ffraunce and Ireland the second, and
of Scotland the eight and thirtith : To HAVE AND
TO HOLDE the said dwelling house or Tenement,
shopps, cello͛s, sollers, plott of ground and all
and singuler other the premisses above by theis
p͞ntes menc͞oned to bee bargayned and soulde and
every part and parcell thereof wth thappurtenãnts,
vnto the said William Shakespeare, William
Johnson, John Jackson, and John Hemyng, their
heires and assignes for ever : To thonlie & proper
vse and behoofe of the said William Shakespeare,
William Johnson, John Jackson, and John
Hemyng, their heires and assignes for ever. AND
THE SAID Henry Walker for himselfe, his heires,
executo͛s, administrato͛s, and assignes, and for
every of them, doth Covenãnt, promise and graunt
to and wth the said William Shakespeare his heires
and assignes by theis p͞ntes in forme following,
that is to saie, That hee the said Henry Walker
his heires executo͛s administrato͛s or assignes
shall and will cleerlie acquite, exonerate, and
discharge or otherwise from tyme to tyme and at
all tymes hereafter well and sufficientlie save and
keepe.

keepe harmles the said William Shakespeare his
heires and assignes and every of them of for and
concernyng the bargayne and sale of the premisses, and the said bargayned premisses and every
part and parcell thereof wth thappurtenincs of and
from all and almanner of former bargaynes, sales,
guifts, graunts, leases, statuts, Recognizauncs,
Joynters, dowers, intailes, lymittacon and lymit-
tacōns of vse and vses, extents and judgments,
execucōns, Annuities, and of and from all and
every other charg^s titles and incumbrancs whatsoever, wittinglie and wilfullie had, made comitted,
suffered, or donne by him the said Henrye Walker, or any other under his authoritie or right,
before thensealing and deliverye of theis pnts;
Except the rents and services to the Cheefe Lord
or Lords of the fee or fees of the premisses from
hensforth, for or in respecte of his or their seig-
niorie or seigniories onlie to be due and donne.
AND FURTHER the saide Henry Walker for him-
selfe his heires executo^{rs} and administrato^{rs} and for
every of them, doth covenānt, promisse and
graunt to and wth the said William Shakespeare,
his heires and assignes, by theis pntes in forme
following; that is to saie, That for and notwth-
standing any acte or thing donne by him the said
Henry Walker to the Contrary, hee the said William Shakespeare his heires and assignes shall
or lawfullie maye peaceablie & quietlie have,
holde, occupie and enioye the said dwelling
house or Tenement, Cello^{rs} Sollers and all and
singuler other the premisses above by theis pntes
                                                    menconed

mencōned to bee bargayned and soulde and every
part and parcell thereof wch thappurtenãnces, and
the rents yssues and profitts thereof and of every
part and parcell thereof to his and their owne vse
receave perceave take and enioye fromhensforth
forever w'hout the lett troble eviccōn or interrupcōn of the said Henry Walker his heires
executo's or administrato's or any of them, or
of or by any other person or persons wch have or
may before the date hereof pretende to have any
lawfull estate, righte, title, vse, or interest, in
or to the premisses or any parcell thereof, by from
or under him the said Henry Walker. AND ALSO
that hee the said Henry Walker and his heires
and all and every other person and persons and
their heires which have or that shall lawfullie and
rightfullie have or clayme to have any lawfull
and rightfull estate, right, title, or intereſt, in
or to the premisses or any parcell thereof, by from
or vnder the said Henry Walker, shall and will
from tyme to tyme & at all tymes fromhensforth for and during the space of three yeares now
next ensuing at or vpon the reasonable request
and costs and charg^s in the lawe of the said William Shakespeare his heires and assignes doe make
knowledge and suffer to bee donne made and
knowledge all and every such further lawfull and
reasonable acte and acts, thing and things, devise
and devises in the law whatsoever, for the conveying of the premises, bee it by deed or deeds inrolled or not inrolled, inrolment of theis pnts, fyne,

feoffament,

feoffament, recoverye, release, confirmacōn, or otherwise, wth warrantie of the said Henry Walker and his heires against him the said Henry Walker and his heires onlie, or otherwise w'hout warrantie, or by all any or as many of the wayes meanes and devises aforesaid, as by the said William Shakespeare his heires or assignes or his or their Councell learned in the lawe shalbee reasonablie devised or advised, for the further, better, and more perfect assurance suertie suermaking and conveying of all and singuler the premisses and every parcell thereof wth thappurtenācs vnto the said William Shakespeare his heires and assignes forever to th'use and in forme aforesaid, AND FURTHER THAT all and every fyne and fynes to be levyed, recoveryes to be suffered, estats, and assurancs at any tyme or tymes hereafter to bee had made executed or passed by or betweene the said parties of the premisses or of any parcell thereof, shalbee, and shalbee esteemed, adiudged, deemed, and taken to bee, to th' onlie and proper vse and behoofe of the said William Shakespeare, his heires, and assignes forever; and to none other vse, intent or purpose. IN WITNESSE whereof the said parties to theis Jndentures Jnterchaungablie have sett their seales. Yeoven the day and yeares first above written.

William
Shaksper̄

Wm Johnson   Jo: Jackson.

Sealed

Sealed and delivered by the said William Shakespeare, William Johnson, and John Jackson, in the
pñce of Will: Atkinson

> Ed : Ouery
> Robert Andrewes Scr.
> Henry Lawrence servant to the same Scr.

NUMB. III.

DECLARATION OF TRUST BY JOHN HEMINGES AND OTHERS.

THIS INDENTURE made the tenth day of ffe-
bruary in the yeres of the reigne of our sovereigne Lord James, by the grace of God kinge
of England Scotland ffraunce and Ireland, defender of the faith, &c. That is to say, of England,
ffraunce, and Ireland, the fifteenth, and of Scotland the one and fiftith; Between John Jackson
and John Hemynge of London, gentlemen, and
William Johnson, Citizen and Vintnier of London, of thone part, and John Greene of Clements
Inn in the County of Midd. gent. and Matthew
Morryes of Stretford vpon Avon in the County
of Warwick gent. of thother part; WITNESSETH,
that the said John Jackson, Iohn Hemynge, and
William Johnson, as well for and in performance
of the confidence and trust in them reposed by

3 G   William

William Shakespeare, deceased, late of Stretford
aforesaid, gent., and to thend and intent that the
lands tenem[ts] and hereditam[ts] hereafter in theis pnts
mencōned and expressed, may be conveyed and assured according to the true intent and meaning of
the last will and testam[t] of the said William
Shakespeare, and for the some of ffyve shillings of
lawfull money of England to them payd, for and
on behalf of Susanna Hall, one of the daughters
of the said William Shakespeare and now wife of
Iohn Hall of Stretford aforesaid gent. before then-
sealling and deliuery of theis pnts, Have aliened
bargained sold and confirmed, and by theis pnts
doe and every of them doth fully cleerely and
absolutely alien bargaine sell and confirme vnto
the said Iohn Greene and Matthew Morry,
their heires and assignes for ever, All that dwelling house or tenem[t] with thapp[r]tuñts scituat and
being within the precinct, circuite, and compase
of the late Black-frieres, London, sometymes in
the tenure of James Gardyner Esquier, and since
that in the tenure of Iohn ffortescue gent, and,
now [29] or late being in the tenure or occupacōn
of one William Ireland or of his Assignee or Assignes, abutting vpon a street leadinge downe to

---

[29] These words are merely copied from Walker's Conveyance to Shakspeare in March 1612-13. From a subsequent
part of this deed it appears that John Robinson was
now the tenant in possession, under a lease made to him by
Shakspeare for a term of years.

Puddle

Puddle Wharfe, on the east part, right against
the kings Ma^{ts} warderobe, part of which tenem^{t}
is erected over a great gate leading to a capitall
messuage which sometymes was in the tenure of
William Blackwell Esquier deceased, and since
that in the tenure or occupacōn of the right Hono^{rble}
Henry Earle of Northumberland, And also all
that plot of ground on the west side of the said
tenem^{t}, which was lately inclosed with boords on
twoe sides thereof by Anne Bacon widdow, soe
farr and in such sort as the same was inclosed by
the said Anne Bacon, and not otherwise; and
being on the third side inclosed with an ould Brick
wall; Which said plot of ground was sometymes
parcell and taken out of a great peece of voyd
ground lately vsed for a garden; And also the
soyle wherevpon the said tenem^{t} standeth; And
also the said Brickwall and boords which doe inclose the said plot of ground; with free entry,
access, ingres, egres, and regres, in by and through
the said great gate and yarde there vnto the vsuall
dore of the said tenem^{t}; And also all and singuler
cellers sollars roomes lights easem^{ts} profitts
comodyties and hereditam^{ts} whatsoeuer to the
said dwelling house or tenem^{t} belonging or in any
wise apperteyning, And the revercōn and rever-
cōns whatsoever of all and singuler the premisses
and of every parcell thereof; And also all rents
and yerely profitts whatsoeuer reserued and from
henceforth to grow due and payable vpon what-

soeuer

soeuer lease demisse or graunt, leases demises
or graunts, made of the premisses or any parcell thereof; And also all thestate, right, title,
interest, property, vse, clayme, and demaund
whatsoeuer, which they the said John Jackson,
John Hemynge, and William Johnson, now have
or any of them hath or of right may, might,
shoold, or ought to have in the premises : To
HAUE AND TO HOLDE the said dwelling howse or
tenem', lights, cellers, sollers, plot of ground,
and all and singuler other the premisses aboue
by theis pñts mencōned to be bargained and sold,
and every part and parcell thereof, with thapp'-
tñts, vnto the said John Green and Mathew
Morrys their heires and assignes foreuer ; To the
vse and behoofes hereafter in theis pñts declared
mencōned expressed and lymitted, and to none
other vse, behoofe, intent, or purpose : That is
to say, to the vse and behoofe of the aforesaid
Susanna Hall for and during the terme of her
naturall life, and after her deceas to the vse and
behoofe of the first sonne of her body lawfully
yssueing, and of the heires males of the body
of the said first sonne lawfully yssueing ; And for
the want of such heires to the vse and behoofe
of the second sonne of the body of the said Susanna lawfully yssueing, and of the heires males of
the body of the said second sonne lawfully yssueing;
and for want of such heires to the vse of the third
sonne of the body of the said Susanna lawfully
yssueing and of the heires males of the body of the
said

said third son lawfully yssueing; And for want of
such heires to the vse and behoofe of the fowerth,
fiveth, sixt, and seaventh sonnes of the body of the
said Susanna lawfully yssueing, and of the severall
heirs males of the severall bodyes of the said
fowerth, fiveth, sixt, and seaventh sonnes, lawfully yssueing, in such manner as it is before lymitted to be and remeyne to the first, second, and third
sonnes of the body of the said Susanna lawfully
yssueing, and to their heires males as aforesaid;
And for default of such heires to the vse and
behoofe of Elizabeth hall daughter of the said
Susanna Hall and of the heires males of her body
lawfully yssueing; and for default of such heires
to the vse and behoofe of Judyth Quiney now
wife of Thomas Quiney of Stretford aforesaid
Vintner, one other of the daughters of the said
William Shakespeare and of the heires males of
the body of the said Judyth lawfully yssueing;
And for default of such yssue to the vse and
behoofe of the right heires of the said William
Shakespeare forever. AND THE SAID John
Jackson for himself, his heires, executors, admīstrators and assignes, and for every of them,
doth coveñnt, promise, and graunt, to and with
the said John Green and Mathew Morrys and
either of them, their or either of their heires and
assignes, by theis pñts, That he the said John
Jackson, his heires, executors, admīstrs or assignes, shall and will from tyme to tyme and at all
tymes hereafter within convenient tyme after every
reasonable

reasonable request to him or them made, well and
sufficiently save and keepe harmeles the said
bargained premisses and every part and parcell
thereof, of and from all and all manner of former
bargaines, sales, guifts, graunts, leases, statuts,
recognizauncs, joynctures, dowers, intayles, vses,
extents, iudgem^{ts} execucōns, annewyties, and of
and from all other charges, titles, and incom-
brauncs whatsoeuer, wittingly and willingly had,
made, comitted, or done by him the said John
Jackson alone, or joynctly with any other person
or persons whatsoeuer; Except the rente and
servics to the Cheiffe Lord or Lords of the fee
or fees of the premisses from henceforth to be
due and of right accustomed to be done, And
Except one lease and demise of the premisses
with thapp'tnncs heretofore made by the said
William Shakespeare, together with them the
said John Jackson, John Hemynge, and William
Johnson, vnto one John Robinson, now Tennant
of the said premisses, for the terme of certen yeres
yet to come and unexpired; As by the same
wherevnto relacōn be had at large doth appeare.
AND THE SAID John Hemynge for him self, his
heires, executors, admistrators, and assignes, and
for every of them, doth covennt, promise, and
graunt, to and with the said John Greene and
Mathew Morrys, and either of them their and
either of their heires and assignes, by theis prēts,
That he the said John Hemynge, his heires, executors,

cutors, admistrators, or assignes, shall and will
from tyme to tyme and at all tymes hereafter,
within convenient tyme after every reasonable request, well and sufficiently save and keepe harmeles the said bargained premisses and every part
and parcell thereof of and from all and all manner
of former bargaines, sales, guifts, graunts, leases,
statuts, recognizauncs, ioynctures, dowers, intayles, vses, extents, judgem[ts] execucons, Annewyties, and of and from all other charges, titles,
and incombraunces whatsoever, wittingly and willingly had, made, comitted, or done by him the
said John Hemynge alone, or ioynctly with any
other person or persons whatsoeuer ; Except the
rentes and service to the Chieffe Lord or Lords
of the fee or fees of the premisses from henceforth
to be due and of right accustomed to be done,
And except one lease and demise of the premisses
with thapp[r]tnants heretofore made by the said
William Shakspeare together with them the said
John Jackson, John Hemyng and William Johnson vnto one John Robinson, now Tennant of the
said premisses, for the terme of certen yeres yet
to come and vnexpired, As by the same wherevnto relacon be had at large doth appeare. AND
THE SAID William Johnson for him self, his heires,
executors, admist[ors] and assignes, and for every
of them, doth covenant promise, and graunt, to
and with the said John Green and Mathew Morryes, and either of them, their and either of their

6   heires

heires and assignes, by theis p̄nts, That he the said William Johnson, his heires, executors, ad-m̄istrs, or assignes, shall and will from tyme to tyme and at all tymes hereafter within convenient tyme after every reasonable request, well and sufficiently saue and keepe harmeles the said bargained premisses and every part and parcell thereof of and from all and all manner of former bargaines, sales, guifts, graunts, leases, statuts, recognizauncs, ioynctures, dowers, intayles, vses, extents, iudgements, execucōns, Annewyties, and of and from all other charges, titles, and incom-brauncs whatsoeuer, wittingly and willingly had made comitted or done by him the said William Johnson alone, or ioyntly with any other person or persons whatsoeuer ; Except the rents and ser-vice to the Cheiff Lord or Lords of the fee or fees of the premisses from henceforth to be due and of right accustomed to be done, And except one lease and demise of the premisses with thapp'tnncs heretofore made by the said Wil-liam Shakespeare together with them the said John Jackson John Hemynge and William Johnson vnto one John Robinson, now Tennant of the said premisses, for the terme of certen yeres yet to come and unexpired, As by the same wherevnto relation be had at large doth appeare. In witnes whereof the parties aforesaid to theis pnte Indentures have interchaungeably sett their

hands

hands and sealls. Yeoven the day and yeres first aboue written 1617.

Jo : Jackson   John Heminges   Wm Johnson

Sealed & delyvered by the
within named

John Jackson in the p$\overline{\text{n}}$ce of
Roc : Swale
    John Prise

        Sealed & delyvered by the w'thinamed

        Willm Johnson in the p'sence of

            Nickolas Harysone
            John Prise

Sealed and delyvered by the w'thinamed
John Hemynges in the p'nce of
        Matt^{y} Benson
        John Prise

Memorand. that the xith day of ffebruarye in the yeres within written John Robinson tenant of the p'mysses w'thinmenc$\overline{\text{o}}$ed did geve and delyver vnto John Greene w'thinnamed to the vse of Susanna Hall w'thinnamed five pence of lawfull money of England in name of Attorñment in the p'sence of
            Matt : Benson
            John Prise
    by me Richarde Tylor

NUMB. IV.

AGREEMENT BETWEEN PHILIP HENSLOWE AND
EDWARD ALLEYN, AND THOMAS DOWNTON,
PLAYER.

THIS INDENTURE made the   day
of   1608, And in the yeres of the
roigne of our sov'aigne Lord James, by the Grace
of God kinge of Englande, ffraunce, and Ireland,

30 Thomas Downton, whose name in Henslowe's
Register is sometimes written *Doughton*, and sometimes
Dowten, was originally a HIRELING in his theatre, as ap-
pears by the following entries :

" Mdom that the 6 of october 1597 Thomas Dowten
came & bownd hime sealfe unto me in xxxx^{li} in a somep-
sett by the Receving of iijd of me before witnes. the covenant is this, that he shold from the daie above written untell sraftid next come ij yeares to pleye in my howse & in
no other abowt. London publickley, yf he do with owt my
consent to forfet unto me this some of money above written. Wittnes to this
" E. Alleyn Robarte Shawe W^m borne John Synger
Dicke Jonnes."

" Thomas Downton the 25 of Jeneway 1599 [1599-
1600] did hire as his covenante servant   for ij
yeres to begyne at Shrofte tewsday next & he to geve hime
viijs. a weeke *as long as they playe*, & after they lye stylle
one fortnyght then to give hime halfe wages, Witnes P. H,
& Edward Browne & Charles Massey." Henslowe's Register, MS.

defender

defender of the faith, &c. the Sixt, and of Scotland the twoe and ffortith, Betweene Phillipp
Henslowe and Edward Alleyn, of the p'ishe of
St. Saviours in Southwark, in the county of Surry,
Esquiors, on th'one p'tye, and Thomas Downton
of the p'ishe of St. Gyles without Criplegate,
London, gentleman, on th'other p'tye, Witnesseth, That the said Phillipp Henslowe and
Edward Alleyn, for and in consideracōn of the
some of *Twenty and seaven pounds and Ten shillings*
of lawfull mony of England to them in hand att
or before thensealinge hereof by the saide Thomas
Downton paid, whereof and wherew'h they the
saide Phillipp Henslowe and Edward Alleyn doe
acknowledge them selves well and truly contented,
satisfied and paide, by theis p'sents haue demised,
leased, and to farme letten, and by theis p'sents
doe demise, lease, and to farme lett, vnto the saide
Thomas Downton *one-eight parte of a ffowerth part*
of all such clere gaynes in mony as shall hereafter du-
ringe the terme herevnder demised arrise, growe,
accrew, or become due, or properly belong vnto the
saide Phillipp Henslowe *and* Edward Alleyn, or
either of them, their or either of their executors
or assignes, *for or by reason of any stage-playinge, or*
other exercise comoditie or vse whatsoeuer vsed or to
be vsed or exercised, w'hin the play-howse of the
saide Phillipp Henslow *and* Edward Alleyn, *comon-*
ly called THE FORTUNE, situate and beinge betweene Whitcrosse streete and Goldinge lane, in the

3 H 2   p'ishe

p'ishe of St Gyles w^thout Criple gate London in
the County of Midd : *And the saide eighte parte of
a ffowerth p'te of all the saide clere gaynes properly
belonginge to the saide* Philipp Henslowe *and* Edward
Alleyn, *to be paid by the saide* Philipp Henslowe
and Edward Alleyn *or one of them, their or one of
their executors or assignes, vnto the saide* Thomas
Downton *or his assignes, eu'y day that any play or
other exercise shall be acted or exercised in the play
howse aforesaide upon the sharinge of the monyes gathered and gotten at eu'y of the same playes and exercises, as heretofore hath byn vsed and accustomed :*
To HAVE AND TO HOULDE and receave the saide
eight parte of a ffowerth p'te of the saide clere
gaynes to be gotten by playinge or by any other
exercise whatsoeu', and to be paide in manner and
forme aforesaide vnto the saide Thomas Downton,
his executors and assignes, from the feast of
St. Michaell tharchaungell last past before the
date hereof vnto thend and terme of Thirteene
Yeres from thence next ensuinge and fully to be
compleate and ended, in as full large ample and
beneficiall manner and forme, to all intents, con-
struccōns, and purposes, as they the saide Phillipp
Henslowe and Edward Alleyn, or either of them,
or the executors or assignes of them or either of
them, might, should, or ought to haue had, held,
enioyed, received, and taken the same as aforesaide, if this p'sent Indenture had never beene had
nor made : YIELDINGE and payinge therefore
yerely

yerely duringe the saide terme, vnto the saide
Phillipp Henslowe and Edward Alleyn, their
heires, executors or assignes, att the saide playe
howse called the FORTUNE, *ten shillings* of lawfull
mony of England, att fower feasts or termes of
the yere, (that is to say) att the feasts of the birth
of our Lord God, Thannciacōn of our lady, the
Natiuity of St. John Baptist, and St. Michaell
Th'archaungell, or wᵗhin ffowerteene dayes next
ensuinge eu'y of the same feast dayes, by euen por-
cōns : AND THE SAIDE Thomas Downton for
him, his executors, and adm'strators, doth cove-
n'nte and graunte to and wᵗh the saide Philipp
Henslowe and Edward Alleyn, and either of
them, their and either of their heires, executors,
and assignes, by theis p'sents, in manner and forme
followinge, that is to say, that he the saide Thomas
Downton, his executors, administrators or assignes,
shall att his or their owne p'per costs and charges
*beare, pay, and discharge one equall eight p'te of a
ffowerth p'te of all such necessary and needfull charges
as shalbe bestowed or layed forth in the newe build-
inge or repairinge of the saide play howse, duringe the
saide terme of thirteene yeres w'thout fraud or covyn :*
AND THAT *he the saide Thomas Downton shall not
att any tyme hereafter duringe the saide terme giue
over the facultye or qualitye of playinge, but shall in
his owne p'son exercise the same to the best and most
benefitt he can w'hin the play howse aforesaide, duringe
the tyme aforesaide, vnles he shal become vnhable by*
reason

reason of sicknes or any other infirmitye, or vnles it be w'h the consent of the saide Phillipp Henslowe and Edward Alleyn, *or either of them, their executors or assignes :* AND that he the saide Thomas Downton *shall not att any tyme hereafter during the saide terme of Thirteene yeres play or exercise the facultye of stage playing in any* Coūmon *play-house now erected, or hereafter to be erected w'thin the saide Cittye of London or Twoe myles Compasse thereof, other then in the saide play-house called the* FORTUNE *w'thout the speciall licence will consent & agreement of the saide* Phillipp Henslowe *and* Edward Alleyn *or one of them, their or one of their heires executors or assignes, first therefore had and obteyned in wrytinge vnder their hands and seales.* And that he the saide Thomas Downton shall not att any tyme hereafter duringe the saide terme, giue, graunte, bargaine, sell or otherwise doe away or dep'te wth the saide Eight p'te of a fowerth p'te of the saide clere gaynes before demised, nor any p'cell thereof, to any p'son or p'sons whatsoeu^r w'hout the like consent, licence, will, and agreement of them the saide Philipp Henslowe and Edward Alleyn or either of them, their or either of their heires, executors, admīstrators, or assignes, first therefore had and obteyned in wryting vnder their hands and seales for the same as aforesaide. AND THE SAID Philipp Henslowe and Edward Alleyn for them and either of them their and either of their heires executors & adm strators doe Co-

ven'nte

ven'nte and graunte to and w'h the saide Thomas
Downton his executors & assignes, by theis
p'sents, That he the saide Thomas Downton, his
executors and assignes (Payinge the saide yerely
rent of Ten shillings in forme aforesaide and
p'forming all other Coven'nts, graunts, articles and
agreements abovesaide on his and their p'ts to be
p'formed) shall or may duringe the saide terme of
Thirteene yeres, haue, hold, receave, and enjoy,
the saide Eighte p'te of a ffowerth p'te of all the
saide clere gaynes to be gotten by playing or any
other exercise as aforesaide in manner and forme
aforesaide, accordinge to the true intent and
meaninge of theis p'sents, w'hout the lett, trouble,
molestacōn, deniall, or interrupcōn of the saide
Philipp Henslowe and Edward Alleyn, or either
of them, their or either of their heires or assignes,
or of any other p'son or p'sons by their either or
any of their meanes, right, tytle, interest, or
p'curemente. PROUIDED alwaies, That if it shall
happen the saide yerely rent of Ten shillings or
any p'cell thereof to be behinde and vnpaide in
p'te or in all by the saide space of ffowerteene dayes
next over or after any feast day of paymente
thereof abovesaide, in w'ch the same ought to be
paide (being lawfully demaunded att the place
aforesaide) Or if the saide Thomas Downton, his
executors, administrators, or assignes, or any of
them, doe infrindge or breake any of the coven'nts
graunts articles or agreements abouesaide on his

6   or

or their p'tes to be p'formed, contrary to the te-
nore & true meaninge of theis p'sents, That then
and from thenceforth this p'sent Lease, Demise,
and graunte, & eu'y coven'nte, graunt, & article
herein conteyned, on the p'te & behalfe of the
said Philipp and Edward or either of them, their
or either of their heires excuto[rs] or Ass[ns] from
henceforth to be p'formed, shalbe vtterly void
frustrate & of none effect, to all intents con-
struccōns and purposes, Any thinge herein conteyned to the contrary thereof in any wise not
w[t]hstandinge. In Witnes whereof the said p'tyes
to theis p'sent Indentures sunderly haue sett their
hands and Seales. Yeoven the day & yeres first
abouewritten. [31]

[31] This deed was not executed.

THE END.

Pag. 103. l. 15. for *from*, r. *to*.
105. l. 21. for *circular*, r. *oval*.
278. l. 13. [*In part of the impression,*] for *choosing*,
r. *liking*.

The following PROSPECTUS, *which was published
last year, is added here only for the sake of the notices
subjoined to it, which by being more widely circulated
may perhaps be the means of illustrating the history of
the life of* Shakspeare, *by drawing from some hitherto
unexplored Repository papers of a very different com-
plexion from the miserable trash we have now been
examining.*

PROPOSALS for an Edition of SHAKSPEARE, in
Quarto, decorated with Engravings, having been
some time ago issued out by Mr. MALONE, and
the Bookseller who undertook the said Work
having relinquished it on account of the present
Season being unfavourable to such expensive
Undertakings, Mr. MALONE thinks it proper to
give this publick Notice, that the Proposals
above-mentioned are to be considered as a Nul-
lity.—Reverting, however, to his original idea,
(from which he was very reluctantly induced to
depart,) that of giving a new and splendid Edition
of the PLAYS and POEMS of this Author WITHOUT
ENGRAVINGS, he intends to present the Publick
with a SECOND EDITION of his former Work,

IN TWENTY VOLUMES, ROYAL OCTAVO,

On a larger Paper and Type,

BOTH FOR THE TEXT AND COMMENTARIES,

than have ever been employed in any Edition of
Shakspeare with Notes : which will be issued out
either in two deliveries, or the whole together, as
may suit the convenience of the Editor.

3 I

The first Volume will be appropriated to an
entirely
NEW LIFE OF SHAKSPEARE,
(COMPILED FROM ORIGINAL AND AUTHEN-
TICK DOCUMENTS,)

Which is now nearly ready for the Press;

The Second and Third to Mr. MALONE's
HISTORY OF THE STAGE CONSIDERABLY
ENLARGED,

and his other DISSERTATIONS illustrative of this
Poet's Works; together with the Prefaces of
former Editors, to which some new Elucidations
will be added. The twentieth Volume will com-
prize Shakspeare's POEMS, and the remaining
sixteen his PLAYS; (which will be arranged in
the Order in which they are supposed by Mr.
Malone to have been written;) with the Editor's
Commentaries, as well as those of his Predecessors, and several new Annotations. To the Plays
it is not proposed to annex any Engravings; but
the Life of Shakspeare will be ornamented with a
Delineation of his Bust at Stratford; (of the Head
of which Mr. Malone is possessed of a FAC-
SIMILE;) the engraved Portraits of Sir Thomas
Lucy and Mr. John Combe, from Drawings made
on purpose for this Work in 1793, by Mr. Syl-
vester Harding; and also with an Engraving of
Shakspeare, not from any FACTITIOUS or FICTI-
TIOUS Representation of that Poet, but from a
Drawing, of the same size with the original, made
in 1786 by Mr. Humphry, from the ONLY authentick Portrait now known, that which was
formerly in the Possession of Sir William D'Avenant, and now belongs to the Heir of the late
Duke of Chandos.

I

✱ Though Mr. Malone has already obtained several very curious and original Materials for the LIFE OF SHAKSPEARE, he will be extremely obliged by any further Communications on that Subject. He has always thought that much Information might be procured, illustrative of the History of this extraordinary Man, if Persons possessed of ancient Papers would take the trouble to examine them, or permit others to peruse them ; and he has already pointed out the sources from which such Information may probably be derived. Shakspeare's Grand-daughter, Lady Barnard, (the only Child of Susanna Hall,) died in January, 1669-70; and by her last Will appointed her kinsman Mr. EDWARD BAGLEY, Citizen of London, her Executor, and Residuary Legatee. This Person, (who, it is believed, was not related to Shakspeare, but kinsman either to Sir John Barnard of Abington near Northampton, or to the Family of Hall or Nash,) must have become possessed of all her Coffers and Cabinets, in which undoubtedly were several of her Grandfather's Papers. When and where Mr. Bagley died, is uncertain, no Will of his having been discovered in the Prerogative Office, though search has been made there for fifty years subsequent to 1670, to ascertain those Facts, as well as the Name of the Person to whom his Effects descended. But if any Person be now living who derives any Property from the said Mr. Bagley, he is requested to examine all such Papers as have descended to him, with the View already mentioned.

On the Death of Sir John Barnard in 1674, Administration of his Effects having been granted to his Daughters (by a former Wife) and their Husbands, and they being entitled under Lady

Barnard's Will to keep Possession of the NEW-PLACE (Shakspeare's House in Stratford) for six Months after the Death of Sir John, some of the Poet's Papers might have fallen into their hands. They were, Elizabeth, married to Henry Gilbert of Locko in the County of Derby, Esq. Mary, married to Thomas Higgs of Colesborne, Esq. and Eleanor, the Wife of Samuel Cotton, Esq.

SHAKSPEARE having purchased some Property from Ralph Hubaud, Esq. (Brother of Sir John Hubaud, of Ipsley in Warwickshire, Knt.) some Instrument executed by the Poet, on that Occasion, may perhaps be found among the Title-Deeds of that Gentleman's Estates, in whatever Hands they may now be :—And if any descendant of Mr. John Heminges be now living, he probably has among the Deeds and Papers of his Ancestor, Mr. Heminges' Accompt-Books and theatrical Contracts, which would throw much Light on the History of the Stage at the period when Shakspeare lived. Mr. John Heminges died in October 1630, leaving at least one Son, William, who died about the Year 1650 ; and four married Daughters ; Alice, the Wife of John Atkins ; Rebecca, married to Captain William Smith ; Margaret, married to Thomas Sheppard ; and another Daughter, the wife of a person of the Name of Merefield ; from which Families also some Information may possibly be derived.

EIGHTEENTH CENTURY SHAKESPEARE

During the one hundred and seven years covered by this series, the reputation of William Shakespeare as poet and dramatist rose from a controversial and highly qualified acceptance by post-Restoration critics and "improvers" to the almost idolatrous admiration of the early Romantics and their immediate precursors. Imposing its own standards and interpretations upon Shakespeare, the Eighteenth Century scrutinized his work in various lights. Certain qualities of the plays were isolated and discussed by a parade of learned, cantankerous, and above all self-assured commentators.

Thirty-five of the most important and representative books and pamphlets are here presented in twenty-six volumes; many of the works, through the very fact of their limited circulation have become extremely scarce, and when obtainable, expensive and fragile. The series will be useful not only for the student of Shakespeare's reputation in the period, but for all those interested in eighteenth century taste, taste-making, scholarship, and theatre. Within the series we may follow the arguments and counter-arguments as they appeared to contemporary playgoers and readers, and the shifting critical emphases characteristic of the whole era.

In an effort to provide responsible texts of these works, strict editorial principles have been established and followed. All relevant editions have been compared, the best selected, and the reasons for the choice given. Furthermore, at least one other copy, frequently three or more, have been collated with the copy actually reproduced, and the collations recorded. In cases where variants or cancels exist, every attempt has been made to provide both earlier and later or indifferently varying texts, as appendices. Each volume is preceded by a short preface discussing the text, the publication history, and, when necessary, critical and biographical considerations not readily available.

1. 1692 **Thomas Rymer**
A Short View of Tragedy (1693)
xvi, 184p.   75s.

2. 1693 **John Dennis**
The Impartial Critick: or, some observations upon a late
book, entitled, A Short View of Tragedy, written by
Mr. Rymer, and dedicated to the Right Honourable Charles
Earl of Dorset, etc. (1693)
xvi, 52p.
   1712 **John Dennis**
An Essay on the Genius and Writings of Shakespear: with
some Letters of Criticism to the Spectator (1712)
xxii, 68p.   70s.

3. 1694 **Charles Gildon [ed.]**
Miscellaneous Letters and Essays, on Several Subjects. Philo-
sophical, Moral, Historical, Critical, Amorous, etc. in Prose
and Verse (1694)
xvi, 132p.   55s.

4. 1710 **Charles Gildon**
The Life of Mr. Thomas Betterton, the late Eminent Tragedian. Wherein The Action and Utterance of the Stage, Bar,
and Pulpit, are distinctly consider'd ... To which is added,
The Amorous Widow, or the Wanton Wife ... Written by
Mr. Betterton. Now first printed from the Original Copy
(1710)
xvi, 176, 87p.   84s.

5. 1726 **Lewis Theobald**
Shakespeare restored: or, A Specimen of the Many Errors,
As well Committed, as Unamended, by Mr. Pope in his Late
Edition of this Poet (1726)
xiii, 194p. 4°   £5 5s.

6. 1747 **William Guthrie**
An Essay upon English Tragedy with Remarks upon the
Abbe de Blanc's Observations on the English Stage (?1747)
34p.
   1749 **John Holt**
An Attempte to Rescue that Aunciente, English Poet, and

Play-wrighte, Maister Williaume Shakespere, from the Maney
Errours, faulsely charged on him, by Certaine New-fangled
Wittes and to let him speak for Himself, as right well he
wotteth, when Freede from the many Careless Mistakeings, of
the Heedless first Imprinters, of his Workes (1749)
94p.   55s.

7. 1748 **Thomas Edwards**
         The Canons of Criticism and Glossary. Being a Supplement
         to Mr. Warburton's Edition of Shakespear. Collected from
         the Notes in that celebrated Work, and proper to be bound
         up with it. To which are added, The Trial of the Letter *Υ*
         alias Y; and Sonnets (Seventh Edition, with Additions 1765)
         368p.   £5 5s.

8. 1748 **Peter Whalley**
         An Enquiry into the Learning of Shakespeare (1748)
         84p.
   1767 **Richard Farmer**
         As Essay on the Learning of Shakespeare . . . the Second
         Edition, with Large Additions (1767)
         viii, 96p.   70s.

9. 1752 **William Dodd**
         The Beauties of Shakespeare: Regularly selected from each
         Play, With a General Index, Digesting them under Proper
         Heads. Illustrated with Explanatory Notes and Similar
         Passages from Ancient and Modern Authors (1752)
         2v., xxiv, 264; iv, 258p.   £10 10s.

10. 1753 **Charlotte Ramsay Lennox**
          Shakespear Illustrated . . . with Critical Remarks (1753-4)
          3v., xiv, 292; iv, 276; iv, 312p.   £15

11. 1765 **William Kenrick**
          A Review of Doctor Johnson's New Edition of Shakespeare:
          In which the Ignorance, or Inattention of That Editor is
          exposed, and the Poet Defended from the Persecution of his
          Commentators (1765)
          xvi, 136p.
    1766 **Thomas Tyrwhitt**
          Observations and Conjectures upon some Passages of

Shakespeare (1766)
ii, 56p.   75s.

12. 1769   **Elizabeth Montagu**
            An Essay on the Writings and Genius of Shakespear, com-
            pared with the Greek and French dramatic Poets. With some
            remarks upon the misrepresentations of Mons. de Voltaire
            (1769)
            iv, 288p.   90s.

13. 1774   **William Richardson**
     1784   Essays on Shakespeare's Dramatic Characters: With an
     1789   Illustration of Shakespeare's Representation of National
            Character, in that of Fluellen (sixth edition 1812)
            xii, 448p.   £6 6s.

14. 1775   **Elizabeth Griffith**
            The Morality of Shakespeare's Drama Illustrated (1775)
            xvi, 528p.   £9 9s.

15. 1777   **Maurice Morgann**
            An Essay on the Dramatic Character of Sir John Falstaff
            (1777)
            xii, 186p.   63s.

16. 1783   **Joseph Ritson**
            Remarks Critical and Illustrative of the last Edition of
            Shakespeare [by George Steevens, 1778], (1783)
            viii, 240p.
     1788   **Joseph Ritson**
            The Quip Modest; A few Words by way of Supplement to
            Remarks, Critical and Illustrative on the Text and Notes of
            the Last Edition of Shakespeare: occasioned by a Republi-
            cation of that Edition (1788, first issue)
            viii, 32p.
            With the preface (revised) to the second issue of *The Quip
            Modest* (1788)
            viii p.   84s.

17. 1785   **Thomas Whately**
            Remarks on some of the Characters of Shakespere, Edited

by Richard Whately (Third edition 1839)
128p.   55s.

18. 1785 **John Monck Mason**
     1797 Comments on the Several Editions of Shakespeare's Plays,
     1798 Extended to those of Malone and Steevens (1807)
           xvi, 608p.   £9 9s.

19. 1786 **John Philip Kemble**
           Macbeth and King Richard the Third: An Essay, in answer to
           Remarks on some of the Characters of Shakespeare [by
           Thomas Whately] (1817)
           xii, 172p.   63s.

20. 1792 **Joseph Ritson**
           Cursory Criticisms on the Edition of Shakespeare published
           by Edmond Malone (1792)
           x, 104p.
           Edmond Malone
           A Letter to the Rev. Richard Farmer, D.D. Master of
           Emanuel College, Cambridge; Relative to the Edition of
           Shakespeare, published in 1790. And Some Late Criticisms
           on that work (1792)
           ii, 40p.   60s.

21. 1796 **William Henry Ireland**
           An Authentic Account of the Shakespeare Manuscripts (1796)
           ii, 44p.
     1799 **William Henry Ireland**
           Vortigern, An Historical Tragedy, In five Acts; Represented
           at the Theatre Royal, Drury Lane. And Henry the Second,
           An Historical Drama. Supposed to be written by the Author
           of Vortigern (1799)
           8o, iv, 79p.   75s.

22. 1796 **Edmond Malone**
           An Inquiry into the Authenticity of Certain Miscellaneous
           Papers and Legal Instruments, published Dec. 24, 1795. And
           Attributed to Shakespeare, Queen Elizabeth, and Henry
           Earl of Southampton (1796)
           vii, 424p.   £7

23. 1796 **Thomas Caldecott**
Mr. Ireland's Vindication of his Conduct, Respecting the Publication of the Supposed Shakespeare Manuscripts (1796) iv, 48p.

1800 **George Hardinge**
Chalmeriana: or a Collection of Papers . . . occasioned by reading a late Apology for the Believers in the Shakespeare papers, by George Chalmers etc. (1800)
viii, 94p.   60s.

24. 1798 **Samuel Ireland**
An Investigation of Mr. Malone's Claim to the Character of Scholar, or Critic, Being an Examination of his Inquiry into the Authenticity of the Shakespeare Manuscripts, etc. (1797)
vi, 156p.   63s.

25. 1797 **George Chalmers**
An Apology for the Believers in the Shakespeare-Papers which were exhibited in Norfolk Street (1797)
iv, 628p.   £9 9s.

26. 1799 **George Chalmers**
A Supplemental Apology for the Believers in the Shakespeare-Papers: Being a Reply to Mr. Malone's Answer, which was early announced, but never published: with a Dedication to George Steevens, and a Postscript (1799)
viii, 656 p.   £9 9s.
